THE HIGHER CRITICISM

OF

THE HEXATEUCH

THE HIGHER CRITICISM

OF

THE HEXATEUCH

BY

CHARLES AUGUSTUS BRIGGS, D.D.
EDWARD ROBINSON PROFESSOR OF BIBLICAL THEOLOGY IN THE
UNION THEOLOGICAL SEMINARY, NEW YORK

WIPF & STOCK · Eugene, Oregon

Wipf and Stock Publishers
199 W 8th Ave, Suite 3
Eugene, OR 97401

The Higher Criticism of the Hexateuch
By Briggs, Charles A.
ISBN 13: 978-1-60608-036-8
Publication date 12/11/2008
Previously published by Charles Scribner's Sons, 1893

TO

FRANCIS BROWN D.D.

DAVENPORT PROFESSOR OF HEBREW AND THE COGNATE LANGUAGES
IN THE UNION THEOLOGICAL SEMINARY NEW YORK
PUPIL COLLEAGUE SUCCESSOR AND
TRUE YOKE-FELLOW

This Book

IS DEDICATED IN TRUST AND LOVE

PREFACE.

TEN years ago the author undertook to write a little book upon the Higher Criticism of the Hexateuch, and at that time he advanced some distance in its preparation. But on reflection he turned aside from it, with the opinion that the times were not yet ripe for it. He accordingly prepared the volumes entitled *Biblical Study*, in 1883, and *Messianic Prophecy*, in 1886. He has written a number of papers upon the Hexateuch in several different periodicals, and has ever kept in mind the ultimate accomplishment of his original plan. But it was his desire to wait until the completion of the new Hebrew Lexicon in order to use all the wealth of its fresh study of Hebrew words in the documents of the Hexateuch. It was also his desire to wait until he had completed his preparatory studies in the Higher Criticism of the Psalter, and in the Biblical Theology of the Old Testament. These studies are not in that state of forwardness which was anticipated before the publication of the present book. And yet they have gone so far as to produce a considerable amount of fresh evidence which now appears for the first time in this volume.

The circumstances in which the author is now placed make it necessary for him to define his position on the

Hexateuch. For this reason he presents to the public the result of his studies so far as they have gone. The only reason for any further delay in publication would be to make the evidence for his conclusions more comprehensive, more exhaustive, and entirely complete. But he is assured that the evidence is already so varied and comprehensive that there can be no reasonable doubt as to the answers which must be given to the chief questions which arise in the Higher Criticism of the Hexateuch.

The author has been engaged for many years in the study of this subject, since first he began original work upon it, in the University of Berlin, in 1866, under the instruction of Hengstenberg. He has advanced steadily and slowly, by constant revision and rectification of his opinions, until he has attained the results stated in this volume. He is glad that he is able to say that these results correspond in the main with the opinions which have been formed independently by leading Biblical scholars in all parts of the world.

The book has been written for the general public, rather than for Hebrew students. Accordingly the text has been made as free from technical matters as possible, and a large amount of material has been put in the Appendix, which thus becomes a volume by itself.

It is evident that these questions of the Higher Criticism can no longer be confined to theological schools and professional circles. The people desire to consider them and to know the answers to them. It is the earnest desire of the author to contribute to the removal of traditional prejudices, to the readjustment of opinions in accordance with facts, and to a better understanding and higher appreciation of the most ancient documents of our Holy Religion.

CONTENTS.

I.

The Problem, p. 1.

(1) The Lines of Inquiry, p. 2; (2) The Lines of Evidence, p. 4.

II.

The Testimony of Holy Scripture, p. 6.

(1) The Testimony of the Hexateuch, p. 6; (2) The Testimony of the Prophets, p. 13; (3) The Law Book of Josiah, p. 15; (4) The Testimony of the exilic and post-exilic Literature, p. 20; (5) The Testimony of the New Testament, p. 25.

III.

The Traditional Theories, p. 31.

(1) The Rabbinical Theory, p. 31; (2) The Views of the Fathers, p. 33; (3) The Position of the Reformers, p. 34.

IV.

The Rise of Criticism, p. 36.

(1) Carlstadt, Masius, and Hobbes, p. 36; (2) Objections of Peyrerius and Spinoza to Mosaic Authorship, p. 36; (3) Richard Simon's Historical Criticism, p. 40; (4) The Scholastic Resistance, p. 42; (5) Witsius, Vitringa, and other mediating divines, p. 43.

V.

THE DOCUMENTARY HYPOTHESIS, p. 46.

(1) Jean Astruc, p. 46; (2) The Evidence from the Divine Names, p. 48; (3) Eichhorn and his School, p. 49; (4) Marsh and Horne defend the traditional opinion, p. 54; (5) Geddes, Vater, and their Fragmentary Hypothesis, p. 57; (6) Taylor and Edward Robinson, p. 58.

VI.

THE SUPPLEMENTARY HYPOTHESIS, p. 60.

(1) De Wette and his School, p. 60; (2) Hengstenberg and his followers, p. 61; (3) Hupfeld, Knobel, and Ewald, p. 63; (4) Noeldeke and Schrader, p. 65; (5) Samuel Davidson, Perowne, and Stanley, p. 66; (6) Delitzsch, Kurtz, and Kleinert, p. 67.

VII.

THE ANALYSIS OF THE HEXATEUCH, p. 69.

(1) The Argument from Language, p. 69; (2) Differences of Style, p. 74; (3) Parallel Narratives, p. 75.

VIII.

THE DATE OF DEUTERONOMY, p. 81.

(1) Argument for the Composition of Deuteronomy shortly before the reform of Josiah, as stated by Riehm, p. 81; (2) As enlarged by Driver, p. 83; (3) The supposed Obstacles to this Theory tested, p. 85; (4) The old Mosaic Code and its recodification in Deuteronomy, p. 89.

IX.

THE DEVELOPMENT HYPOTHESIS, p. 90.

(1) Edward Reuss and his school, p. 90; (2) Colenso, Kuenen, and Kalisch, p. 92; (3) Wellhausen's analysis and its consequences, p. 94; (4) The newly discovered facts, p. 96; (5) The new theory, p. 96.

X.

THE DEVELOPMENT OF THE CODES, p. 99.

(1) The differences in point of view, p. 100; (2) The Judaic code and its parallels, p. 101; (3) The Ephraimitic code and its parallels, p. 101; (4) The code of Deuteronomy and the code of Holiness, p. 101; (5) The altars, p. 101; (6) The sacred tent, p. 103; (7) The priesthood, p. 104; (8) The sacrifices, p. 104; (9) The purifications, p. 106; (10) The feasts, p. 106; (11) The order of the codes, p. 107; (12) The arguments against the post-exilic composition of the Priest-code, p. 108.

XI.

THE WITNESS OF THE HISTORY, p. 110.

(1) Discrepancy between the codes and the history, p. 110; (2) The witness of the Literature to the non-observance of the Law, p. 118; (3) The religious development of Israel, p. 124; (4) The historians and the codes, p. 126; (5) Ezekiel and the codes, p. 126.

XII.

THE MORE RECENT DISCUSSIONS, p. 129.

(1) The case of W. Robertson Smith, p. 129; (2) The discussion in the *Presbyterian Review*, p. 130; (3) Dillmann, Baudissin, and Delitzsch, p. 131; (4) Cornill and Driver, p. 134; (5) The objection that the analysis makes the Hexateuch patchwork, answered from Tatian and St. Paul, p. 137; (6) The objection that the critics differ answered by proof of their concord, p. 142.

XIII.

THE ARGUMENT FROM BIBLICAL THEOLOGY, p. 146.

(1) Mode of divine revelation, p. 146; (2) Theophanies, p. 146; (3) Miracles, p. 147; (4) The covenants, p. 149; (5) Prophecy, p. 150; (6) The divine Spirit, p. 150; (7) The divine attributes, p. 151; (8) The doctrine of sin, p. 153; (9) The doctrine of divine judgment, p. 154; (10) The doctrine of redemption, p. 154.

XIV.

THE RESULT OF THE ARGUMENT, p. 156.

(1) The four documents and the five codes, p. 156; (2) Driver's statement, p. 157; (3) The final summary, p. 160.

APPENDIX.

I. THE TWO NARRATIVES OF THE REVELATION OF THE DIVINE NAME YAHWEH, p. 165.

II. THE CHARACTERISTIC WORDS AND PHRASES OF D, H, AND P ACCORDING TO CANON DRIVER, p. 168.

III. THE GENESIS OF THE TEN WORDS, p. 181.

IV. THE TWO NARRATIVES OF THE PESTILENCE IN EGYPT, p. 188.

V. THE DECALOGUE OF J AND ITS PARALLELS IN THE OTHER CODES, p. 189.

VI. THE GREATER BOOK OF THE COVENANT AND ITS PARALLELS IN THE LATER CODES, p. 211.

VII. VARIATIONS OF D AND H, p. 233.

VIII. THE SEVERAL REPRESENTATIONS OF THE THEOPHANY, p. 236.

INDEXES, p. 239.

I.

THE PROBLEM.

The Higher Criticism of the Hexateuch is a phrase which conveys little if any meaning to the general public. It is however a technical phrase with a definite meaning which, so soon as it is explained, becomes plain and evident and serves to fix the attention upon the problem in hand much better than any paraphrase could do.

The Hexateuch is composed of the Pentateuch and the book of Joshua. The Pentateuch comprehends the five books which in the Hebrew Canon constitute the Law, embracing Genesis, Exodus, Leviticus, Numbers, and Deuteronomy. Modern criticism has shown that the book of Joshua originally was an essential member of the group and therefore criticism has to deal with the Hexateuch.

The Higher Criticism is named Higher to distinguish it from the Lower Criticism. The Lower Criticism deals with the Text of the Scriptures. It searches all the versions and manuscripts and citations in order to ascertain the genuine original Text as it came from the hands of its authors and editors. It has to do with letters, words, and sentences, as such, without regard to their literary form or meaning. The Higher Criticism builds on the Lower Criticism as its foundation. It takes the Text of Scripture from the hands of Lower Criticism and studies it as literature. This distinction between the Higher and the Lower Criticism was not made by Biblical scholars, but by classical scholars in their studies of the great monuments of Greek and Roman literature. So soon as Biblical scholars began to study the Holy Scripture with scientific methods, they adopted this terminology with its distinctive meanings.

The Higher Criticism has four different lines of inquiry.

(1). *Integrity.* Is the writing the product of one mind as an organic whole, or composed of several pieces of the same author; or is it a collection of writings by different authors? Has it retained its original integrity or has it been interpolated? May the interpolations be discriminated from the original? The Pentateuch is ascribed by the prevalent tradition to Moses, and the book of Joshua to Joshua. The Higher Criticism of the Hexateuch traces this tradition to its sources, examines the references to the Hexateuch in other writings, and then searches the Hexateuch itself, in order to learn whether this tradition corresponds with the facts of the case or not. It finds that the tradition has no sound historical basis, that the references to the Hexateuch in other writings and the testimony of the Hexateuch itself tell a different story, and show conclusively that the Hexateuch embraces Mosaic originals, several different codes and historical documents and the handiwork of a number of editors at different epochs in the history of Israel, and that the unity of the Hexateuch is the result of a final redaction of all the earlier elements.

(2). *Authenticity.* Is the author's name given in connection with the writing? Is it anonymous? Can it be pseudonymous? Is it a compilation? The Higher

Criticism of the Hexateuch finds that the Hexateuch is anonymous and that it is a compilation.

(3). *Literary Form.* Is the writing poetry or prose? Is the prose historic, didactic, rhetorical, or statistical? Is the poetry lyric, dramatic, epic, pastoral, or composite? What is the style of the author and what are his distinctive characteristics in form, method, and color? The Higher Criticism of the Hexateuch finds four great historical narratives, of different styles and methods of historical composition. It finds a large number of ancient poems embedded in the narratives, so many indeed as to make a collection nearly as large as the Psalter, if they were gathered together in a separate book. It finds several law codes, differing in method of codification and style as well as in bulk and contents.

(4). *Credibility.* Is the writing reliable? Do its statements accord with the truth, or are they colored and warped by prejudice, superstition, or reliance upon insufficient or unworthy testimony? What character does the author bear as to prudence, good judgment, fairness, integrity, and critical sagacity? The Higher Criticism of the Hexateuch vindicates its credibility. It strengthens the historical credibility (1) by showing that we have four parallel narratives instead of the single narrative of the traditional theory; and (2) by tracing these narratives to their sources in the more ancient documents buried in them. It traces the development of the original Mosaic legislation in its successive stages of codification in accordance with the historical development of the kingdom of God. It finds minor discrepancies and inaccuracies such as are familiar to students of the Gospels; but these increase the historic credibility of the writings, as they show that the writers and compilers were true to their sources of information even when they could not harmonize them in all respects.

The Higher Criticism has several lines of evidence upon which it relies for its conclusions.

(1). The writing must be in accordance with its supposed historical position as to time and place and circumstances.

(2). Differences of style imply differences of experience and age of the same author, or, when sufficiently great, differences of author and of period of composition.

(3). Differences of opinion and conception imply differences of author when these are sufficiently great, and also differences of period of composition.

(4). Citations show the dependence of the author upon the author or authors cited.

(5). Positive testimony as to the writing in other writings of acknowledged authority is the strongest evidence.

(6). The argument from silence is often of great value. If the matter in question was beyond the scope of the author's argument, it either had certain characteristics which excluded it, or it had no manner of relation to the argument.

If the matter in question was fairly within the scope of the author's argument, he either omitted it for good and sufficient reasons, or else he was unconscious or ignorant of it, or else it had not come into existence.*

These lines of evidence are used in the Higher Criticism of all kinds of literature. They were tested and verified in the study of Greek and Roman literature, and of the ecclesiastical writers of the Church, long before

---

* See *Biblical Study*, pp. 87-91.

any Biblical scholar used them in his studies of Holy Scripture.

Our problem is the Higher Criticism of the Hexateuch. We shall first consider the evidences from Holy Scripture, then test the traditional theory, and finally trace the history of the Higher Criticism of the Hexateuch, and use the six lines of evidence for the solution of the four great questions, as to the Integrity, the Authenticity, the Literary Forms and the Credibility of the Hexateuch.

II.

THE TESTIMONY OF HOLY SCRIPTURE.

I.—*The Testimony of the Hexateuch.*

WE shall consider first those passages of the Hexateuch which give evidence as to authorship.

(1). "And Moses came and told the people all the words of Yahweh, and all the judgments: and all the people answered with one voice and said, All the words which Yahweh hath spoken will we do. And Moses wrote all the words of Yahweh, and rose up early in the morning, and builded an altar under the mount, and twelve pillars, according to the twelve tribes of Israel . . . . And he took the book of the covenant, and read in the audience of the people: and they said, All that Yahweh hath spoken will we do, and be obedient." (Ex. xxiv. 3, 4, 7.)

This passage speaks of the Book of the Covenant in which Moses wrote all the words of Yahweh. These words of Yahweh were evidently those which Yahweh said unto Moses at Horeb, and which are given in Ex. xx. 22–26, and probably also the judgments of chapters xxi.–xxiii. There can be little doubt that the editor of the Hexateuch designed to give the essential contents of the Book of the Covenant in that series of pentades and decalogues which seem to have been the original contents of this code of the Ephraimitic writer. A critical study of this code shows that there have been omissions, insertions, transpositions, and revisions; but the substance of this original code of the twelve decalogues is there.*

This passage proves that Moses wrote a Book of the Covenant; but it does not prove that he wrote the Pentateuch, of which this Book in its present form takes less than four chapters.

(2). "And Yahweh said unto Moses, Write thou these words: for after the tenor of these words I have made a covenant with thee and with Israel." (Ex. xxxiv. 27.)

These words written at this time by Moses refer without doubt to the words which precede, that is the decalogue, which may be called the Little Book of the Covenant. This decalogue of the Little Book of the Covenant is parallel for the most part with one of the decalogues of the Greater Book of the Covenant. The one of these books is mentioned by the Ephraimitic writer, the other by the Judaic writer. The question thus arises whether there were two law codes in two different books, given within a few weeks of each other, or whether these are two different codifications of one and the same Book of the Covenant. At all events, this passage proves no more than that Moses wrote the decalogue of the Little Book of the Covenant, and by no means implies that he wrote the chapter which contains this narrative, still less the entire Pentateuch.†

(3). "But as for thee, stand thou here by me, and I will speak unto thee all the commandment, and the statutes, and the judgments, which thou shalt teach them, that they may do them in the land which I give them to possess it." (Dt. v. 31.)

This passage proves no more than that Moses spoke at Mt. Horeb, commandments, statutes and judgments.

---
*See Appendix VI. †See Appendix V.

No mention is made of committing any of these to writing. It is probably a parallel statement to Ex. xxiv. 12.

(4). "And Moses wrote this law, and delivered it unto the priests, the sons of Levi, which bare the ark of the covenant of Yahweh, and unto all the elders of Israel." .... "Take this book of the law, and put it by the side of the ark of the covenant of Yahweh your God, that it may be there for a witness against thee." (Dt. xxxi. 9, 26.)

Verse 26 tells us what precisely it was which Moses wrote, namely, the book of the Thorah, the book of instruction. This law book, as all modern Biblical scholars recognize, is what we call the Deuteronomic code. The code comprehends the laws in Deuteronomy xii.–xxvi. This code is in the rhetorical form and not in the form of decalogues and pentades as are the covenant codes. The question then arises whether this rhetorical form belongs to the original code or whether the original code of this law book has not been put in this rhetorical form by the Deuteronomist.* Whatever opinion we may form on this question, it is evident that the most that you can prove from this passage is that Moses wrote a law book which for substance is given in the legal chapters of Deuteronomy. It does not prove that Moses wrote Deuteronomy, still less that he wrote the other four books of the Pentateuch.

(5). "Only be strong and very courageous, to observe to do according to all the law, which Moses my servant commanded thee: turn not from it to the right hand or to the left, that thou mayest have good success whithersoever thou goest. This book of the law shall not depart out of thy mouth, but thou shalt meditate therein day and night, that thou mayest observe to do according to all that is written therein: for then thou shalt make

---

* See p. 85 *seq.*

thy way prosperous, and then thou shalt have good success." (Josh. i. 7, 8.)

"As Moses the servant of Yahweh commanded the children of Israel, as it is written in the book of the law of Moses, an altar of unhewn stones, upon which no man had lifted up any iron: and they offered thereon burnt offerings unto Yahweh, and sacrificed peace offerings." (Josh. viii. 31.)

These passages evidently refer to the law book already mentioned in Deuteronomy. They confirm the evidence as to the composition of that law book by Moses, but they do not give any additional evidence. There is nothing in them that implies that Moses wrote anything else.

From all these passages it is plain that Moses wrote one or more codes of law, but they give no evidence that Moses wrote all the laws of the Pentateuch contained in the other codes, and those which are embedded in the historical narratives.

(6). "So Moses wrote this song the same day, and taught it the children of Israel." (Deut. xxxi. 22.)

The song referred to is given in Deut. xxxii. and it is one of the finest pieces of poetry in the Old Testament, called by Schultz the Magna Charta of prophecy. Whether the song in its present form came from the pen of Moses is doubted by many evangelical scholars; but, whether it did or not, the most we can prove from this passage is that Moses wrote a song which the compiler of the Hexateuch proposes to give in Deuteronomy xxxii., in the form in which he knew of it.

(7). "And Moses wrote their goings out according to their journeys by the commandment of Yahweh: and these are their journeys according to their goings out." (Num. xxxiii. 2.)

This passage definitely states what it was that Moses

wrote, namely, the list of stations of the journeys of Israel from Egypt to the valley of the Jordan. It requires one to spring over too wide a stretch of reasoning to conclude from this list of journeys contained in a single chapter that Moses wrote the entire Pentateuch.

(8). "And Yahweh said unto Moses, Write this for a memorial in a book, and rehearse it in the ears of Joshua: that I will utterly blot out the remembrance of Amalek from under heaven." (Ex. xvii. 14.)

Here it is distinctly stated what Moses was to write, namely, the words, "I will utterly blot out the remembrance of Amalek from under heaven." The Revised Version correctly renders "in a book" taking the Massoretic pointing as giving the generic article in accordance with usage elsewhere (cf. Job xix. 23). But the American revisers insisted on giving the article a definite force "in *the* book" in order to support the theory that Moses kept a journal in which he wrote down from time to time the events recorded in the Pentateuch. This crude conceit as to the method of the composition of the Pentateuch may now be regarded as antiquated.

The passages usually cited from the Pentateuch to prove its Mosaic authorship have been examined. Such statements in any other historical writing would imply that the author or compiler was referring to some of the written sources from which he derived the materials for his own work. When the author of the Pentateuch says that Moses wrote one or more codes of law, that he wrote a song, that he recorded a certain memorandum, it would appear that having specified such of his materials as were written by Moses, he would have us infer that the other materials came from other sources of information. But it has been argued the other way, namely, that, because it is said Moses wrote the codes of the covenant and the Deuteronomic code, he also wrote all the laws of the Pentateuch ; that because he wrote the song Deut. xxxii., he wrote all the other pieces of poetry in the Pentateuch; that because he recorded the list of stations and the memorial against Amalek, he recorded all the other historical events of the Pentateuch. It is probable that no one would so argue did he not suppose it was necessary to maintain the Mosaic authorship of the Pentateuch at every cost. All that the Pentateuch says as to Mosaic authorship we may accept as valid and true; but we cannot be asked to accept such a comprehensive inference as that Moses wrote the whole Pentateuch from the simple statements of the Pentateuch that he wrote out the few things distinctly specified.

We shall now consider some passages of the Hexateuch which tell a different story.

(9). In Josh. xxiv. 26, it is said that Joshua wrote the words of his last discourse in the book of the instruction or law of God. The name of this book differs from the name of the book containing the Deuteronomic code only by the substitution of Elohim, God, for Yahweh. This statement in the Ephraimitic writer seems to imply that there was an official divine law book to which Joshua made this addition. But what has become of it? If it was the same book as the Deuteronomic code, why are not these words in that code at the present time? Is not the view more reasonable on the basis of this passage, that this old law book was used for the most part by the Deuteronomist in the book of Deuteronomy, but by the Ephraimitic writer in the passage Josh. xxiv. 26, and that the compiler of the present Hexateuch has given us both extracts from this same original law book in the words of these two different authors? Will any now argue from the statement, that Joshua wrote his last discourse in this law book, that Joshua wrote the whole of the book which bears his name? It used to be so argued. The day is not distant when we shall say "it used to be so" for the argument for the Mosaic authorship of the Pentateuch.

(10). In Num. xxi. 14, a piece of poetry is cited from the Book of the Wars of Yahweh. This book, which, like Joshua's law book, is no longer in existence, was probably an anthology of national Hebrew poetry. Its other contents are unknown. Possibly some of them are to be found among the other poetic extracts in the Hexateuch. It is not said who was the author or compiler of this book. Is there any reason to think of Moses? Or shall we not rather conclude, in accordance with the methods of reasoning of the anti-critics, that because this piece of poetry was taken from the Book of the Wars of Yahweh the whole Pentateuch was taken from that book, and was written by its author?

(11). In Josh. x. 12, 13, a strophe is cited from the book of Jasher, describing the theophany at the battle of Beth-Horon.

> "Sun, stand thou still upon Gibeon;
> And thou, moon, in the valley of Aijalon,
> And the sun stood still, and the moon stayed,
> Until the nation had avenged themselves of their enemies."

This book seems to have been another collection of poetry. Two other extracts from this book are given in the Old Testament. The one, 2 Sam. i. 18, is the lament of David over Jonathan and Saul, a dirge of wonderful beauty and power; the other is a little piece of four lines in 1 Kings viii. 12, 13, which, according to the LXX. was also taken from the book of Jasher, although this reference to the book of Jasher, and one line of the poem, is missing from the Massoretic text.

> "The sun is known in the heavens,
> But Yahweh said he would dwell in thick darkness.
> I have built up a house of habitation for thee;
> A place for thee to dwell in forever."

This passage is cited in the words of Solomon at the dedication of the temple. If now the book of Jasher contains, besides the ode of the battle of Beth-Horon of the time of Joshua, a dirge of David, and a piece of poetry of Solomon, that book could not be earlier than the dedication of the temple of Solomon. The compiler who cites from that book could not have compiled the book of Joshua before the book from which he cites was written. Therefore, the book of Joshua could not have been compiled in its present form before the dedication of the temple. If now the book of Joshua is inseparable from the Pentateuch and makes with it a Hexateuch, and if the four documents from the Pentateuch run right on through the book of Joshua, then it is evident that the Pentateuch could not have been compiled by Moses, but must have been compiled subsequent to the dedication of the temple of Solomon. But this connection of Joshua with the Pentateuch can be established by indubitable evidence from the Pentateuch and the book of Joshua,* therefore it is the evidence of the Hexateuch itself that Moses did not write the Pentateuch.

II.—*The Testimony of the Prophets.*

We are surprised by a lack of reference to the Mosaic law in the prophets of Israel. The most important passage in the discussion is Hos. viii. 12. This is rendered

---

* See pp. 61, 68, 70 *seq.*

by the Revised Version correctly: "Though I write for him my law in ten thousand precepts, they are counted as a strange thing." The American revisers would translate, "I wrote for him the ten thousand things of my law." The American revisers wish to hold to the traditional interpretation of this passage, that it refers to the ten thousand precepts contained in the Pentateuch. This would imply a very extensive body of law or doctrine written in or before the time of Hosea, and here referred to by him. But unfortunately for the American revisers, the tense of the verb is against them. It is the Hebrew imperfect tense. It is incorrect to render that tense as an aorist referring it to the Mosaic legislation. It is possible to render it as a frequentative. But this would refer it to a series of divine laws reaching up to the prophet's time, and that would not suit their purpose. The English revisers give the translation which is best suited to the Hebrew tense and the context of the passage, in rendering it as hypothetical. In this case there is no more than a general reference to the fact that divine laws were recorded, and that if such laws were given to an indefinite extent so as to run up to myriads of laws, they would only multiply the transgressions of a rebellious people. The laws were really prophetic instructions, including those of Hosea himself. That this is the true interpretation, we see from the usage of other prophets. Jeremiah viii. 8 refers to a law of Yahweh as coming through false prophets. Thorah is indeed divine instruction or doctrine, rather than divine law, and hence in the usage of the Old Testament it refers to any divine instruction, any teaching from God. It was not until the reign of rabbinical tradition that the law became a technical term for the Pentateuch. As Delitzsch says: "The recognition of this fact opens the eyes and delivers from the bondage of prejudice." The older scholars were blinded by the technical usage of rabbinical theology to the historic usage of Holy Scripture; and unfortunately the same veil lieth upon the heart of some modern scholars whensoever Moses is read.

III.—*The Law Book of Josiah*.

The most important passages in the Old Testament in evidence for the composition of the Pentateuch are 2 Kings xxii. 8, 11; xxiii. 2, 21, 25; and their parallels 2 Chron. xxxiv. 14, 15, 19, 30, xxxv. 3, 6.

II. KINGS XXII.–XXIII.	II. CHRONICLES XXXIV.–V.
"And Hilkiah the high priest said unto Shaphan the scribe, I have found the book of the law in the house of Yahweh. And Hilkiah delivered the book to Shaphan, and he read it." (xxii. 8.)	"And when they brought out the money that was brought into the house of Yahweh, Hilkiah the priest found the book of the law of Yahweh given by Moses. And Hilkiah answered and said to Shaphan the scribe, I have found the book of the law in the house of Yahweh. And Hilkiah delivered the book to Shaphan." (ver. 14, 15.)
. . . . . .	. . . . . .
"And it came to pass, when the king had heard the words of the book of the law, that he rent his clothes." (ver. 11.)	"And it came to pass, when the king had heard the words of the law, that he rent his clothes." (ver. 19.)
. . . . . .	. . . . . .
"And the king went up to the house of Yahweh, and all the men of Judah and all the inhabitants of Jerusalem with him, and the priests, and the prophets, and all the people, both small and great: and he	"And the king went up to the house of Yahweh, and all the men of Judah and the inhabitants of Jerusalem, and the priests, and the Levites, and all the people, both great and small: and he read in their ears

read in their ears all the words of the book of the covenant which was found in the house of Yahweh." (xxiii. 2.)	all the words of the book of the covenant that was found in the house of Yahweh." (ver. 30.)
. . . . . .	. . . . . .
"And the king commanded all the people, saying, Keep the passover unto Yahweh your God, as it is written in this book of the covenant." (ver. 21.)	"And he said unto the Levites that taught all Israel, ... kill the passover, and sanctify yourselves, and prepare for your brethren, to do according to the word of Yahweh by the hand of Moses." (xxxv. 3, 6.)
. . . . . .	
"And like unto him was there no king before him, that turned to Yahweh with all his heart, and with all his soul, and with all his might, according to all the law of Moses ; neither after him arose there any like him." (ver. 25.)	

Critical scholars are agreed that this law book was the Deuteronomic code. The older view was that it was the entire Pentateuch. There are a few anti-critics who adhere to this traditional theory as they do to all others. It is sufficient to cite the careful statement of the Hulsean professor of divinity at Cambridge, England, Herbert E. Ryle:

"When we enquire what this 'Book of the Law' comprised, the evidence at our disposal is quite sufficiently explicit to direct us to a reply. Even apart from the knowledge which we now possess of the structure of the Pentateuch, there was never much probability in the supposition, that the book discovered by Hilkiah was identical with the whole Jewish 'Torah,' our Pentateuch. The narrative does not suggest so considerable a work. Its contents were quickly perused and readily grasped. Being read aloud, it at once left distinct impressions upon questions of national duty. Its dimensions could not have been very large, nor its precepts very technical. The complex character of the Pentateuch fails to satisfy the requirements of the picture. Perhaps, too (although the argument is hardly one to be pressed), as it appears that only a single roll of the Law was found, it may not unfairly be remarked, that the whole Torah was never likely to be contained in one roll; but that, if a single roll contained any portion of the Pentateuch, it was most probably the Deuteronomic portion of it; for the Book of Deuteronomy, of all the component elements of the Pentateuch, presents the most unmistakable appearance of having once formed a compact independent work.

"But, there is no need to have recourse to arguments of such a doubtful kind. For while the evidence shows that a completed Torah could not have existed at this time, we seem to have convincing proof that 'the Book of the Law' was either a portion of our Deuteronomy or a collection of laws, Deuteronomic in tone, and, in range of contents, having a close resemblance to our Book of Deuteronomy. The evidence is twofold. (1). The description which is given of the book found in the Temple shows, that, in its most characteristic features, it approximated more closely to portions of Deuteronomy than to any other section of the Pentateuch. (2). The historian, from whom we obtain the account, appears, when he speaks of 'the law,' to have in view the Deuteronomic section, and scarcely to be acquainted with any other. These arguments have been frequently and fully discussed in other works, so that we need not here do more than summarize them very briefly.

"(1). The description of the book shows that, in its most conspicuous features, it was in close agreement with the contents of Deuteronomy.

"(a). The book contained denunciations against the neglect of the covenant with Jehovah. (2 Kings xxii. 11–13, 16, 17).

"Now the Pentateuch contains two extensive passages describing the fearful visitations that should befall the people of Israel for following after other gods (Lev. xxvi.; Deut. xxviii.–xxxi.). Of these, the passage in Deuteronomy is the longest, and while the passage in Leviticus would be calculated to produce a very similar impression, it may be noticed that the words of Huldah, in referring to the curses contained in the 'Book of the Law,' possibly contain a reference to Deut. xxviii. 37, xxix. 24 (cf. 2 Kings xxii. 19). It cannot be doubted that one or other, or both of these denunciations, must have been included in Josiah's 'Book of the Law.'

"(*b*). The reforms carried out by the king and his advisers, in order to obey the commands of 'the Book of Law,' deal with matters all of which are mentioned, with more or less emphasis, in the Deuteronomic legislation. (i.) The principal religious reform carried out by Josiah was the suppression of the worship at the high places, and the concentration of worship at the Temple. No point is insisted on so frequently and so emphatically in the Deuteronomic laws as that all public worship is to be centralised at the one place which Jehovah himself should choose (Deut. xii. 5 and *passim*). (ii.) Josiah took measures to abolish the worship of the heavenly bodies, a form of idolatry distinct from the worship of Baal and Ashtoreth. His action is in obedience to the commands of Deuteronomic laws (Deut. iv. 19, xvii. 3). There alone in the Pentateuch this particular form of idolatry is combated. For, although it had existed in an earlier time, it does not seem to have infected the religion of Israel until late in the monarchical period (cf. 2 Kings xxi. 3, 5, xxiii. 4, 5, 11, 12). (iii.) Josiah celebrated the Feast of the Passover (2 Kings xxiii. 21-23) in accordance with 'the Book of the Law':—we find the Law of the Passover laid down in Deut. xvi. 1-8. (iv.) Josiah expelled the wizards and diviners from the land in express fulfilment of 'the Book of Law' (2 Kings xxiii. 24): we find the prohibition of this common class of impostor in Oriental countries expressed in strong language in Deut. xviii. 9-14.

"It is not, of course, for a moment denied that laws, dealing with these last two subjects, are to be found elsewhere in the Pentateuch. But as in all four cases Josiah's action was based upon 'the law,' whatever 'the law' was, it must have dealt with 'feasts' and with 'wizards' as well as with 'concentration of worship' and 'star-worship.' In the Deuteronomic laws all four points are touched upon.

"(*c*). The book found in the Temple is designated 'the Book of the Covenant' (2 Kings xxiii. 2, 21), and it appears that it contained a covenant, to the observance of which the king solemnly pledged himself (*id*. 3). In the Pentateuch we find, it is true, a mention of 'the Book of the Covenant' (Ex. xxiv. 7), by which the substance of the Sinaitic legislation (Ex. xx.-xxiii.)

seems to be denoted. But it is clear, from the fact that the section, Ex. xx.–xxiii., contains no denunciation; from the fact that it contains only the very briefest notice of the Feast of the Passover, and then under another name 'the Feast of Unleavened Bread' (Ex. xxiii. 15); from the fact that it makes no mention of either wizards or star-worship;—that this portion of the Israelite law cannot be 'the covenant' referred to in 2 Kings xxiii. On the other hand, an important section at the close of our Book of Deuteronomy is occupied with a 'Covenant'; and it can hardly be doubted, that a 'Book of the Law,' which was also 'the Book of the Covenant,' must have included such passages as Deut. xxix. 1, 'These are the words of the covenant which the Lord commanded Moses to make with the children of Israel'; ver. 9, 'Keep therefore the words of this covenant'; ver. 14, 'Neither with you only do I make this covenant and this oath'; ver. 21, 'According to all the curses of the covenant that is written in the book of the law'; vers. 24, 25, 'Even all the nations shall say, Wherefore hath the Lord done thus unto this land? .... Then men shall say, Because they forsook the covenant of the Lord.'

"(2). The historian who has preserved to us the narrative of the finding of 'the Book of the Law' himself quotes directly from 'the law' in two passages, and in both instances from Deuteronomic writing. In 1 Kings ii. 3, 'And keep the charge of the Lord thy God to walk in His ways, to keep His statutes and His commandments and His judgments and His testimonies, according to that which is written in the law of Moses, that thou mayest prosper in all that thou doest and whithersoever thou turnest thyself,' the words used are characteristically Deuteronomic, and the thought is possibly based on Deut. xvii. 18-20 (cf. Josh. i. 8). In 2 Kings xiv. 6, 'But the children of the murderers he put not to death; according to that which is written in the book of the law of Moses, as the Lord commanded, saying, The fathers shall not be put to death for the children,' the citation is taken almost word for word from Deut. xxiv. 16. In numerous characteristic expressions and phrases the compiler of the Books of Kings shows a close acquaintance with the Deuteronomic portion of the Pentateuch, though nowhere, perhaps, so frequently as in 1 Kings viii., ix., *e.g.* viii. 51 (cf. Deut. iv. 20), ix. 3 (cf. Deut. xii. 5), ix. 7, 8 (cf. Deut. xxviii. 37, xxix. 24).

Generally speaking, where reference is made to 'the law' in the Books of Kings, the allusion can only be satisfied by a reminiscence of a Deuteronomic passage. Thus, exclusive of the two passages already quoted, may be noted 1 Kings viii. 9 (cf. Deut. x. 5, xxix. 1), 53 (cf. Deut. iv. 20), 56 (cf. Deut. xii. 9, 10, xxv. 19), 2 Kings x. 31, xviii. 12, xxi. 8, xxii. 8, xxiii. 25.

"If, therefore, the compiler of the Books of Kings identified 'the law of Moses' and 'the book of the law' with Deuteronomy, or, at least, with a Deuteronomic version of the law, we may nearly take it for granted, that, in his narrative of the reign of Josiah, when he mentioned 'the Book of the Law' without further description, he must have had in his mind the same Deuteronomic writings with which he was so familiar." (*Canon of the Old Testament*, pp. 48–53.)

This long extract gives the critical argument compactly and thoroughly, and in the course of it gives the true meaning of the several passages in the book of Kings bearing on the composition of the Pentateuch, making it clear that these give no proof of the Mosaic authorship of the Pentateuch.

Jeremiah, the great prophet of the age of Josiah, makes reference to this law of Yahweh, and it is admitted that he is full of the spirit and ideas of the book of Deuteronomy. But he shows no knowledge of those parts of the Pentateuch which are now generally attributed to a priestly writer, and presents no evidence of the existence of a Pentateuch in his day, still less of a Pentateuch written by Moses.

IV.—*The Testimony of the Exilic and Postexilic Literature.*

In the Psalter the only sacred writing referred to is the roll of the book concerning the king, Ps. xl. 8. This doubtless points to the law contained in Dt. xvii. 14 *sq.*, and gives evidence of a knowledge of the Deuteronomic code by the writer of this exilic psalm. "Law" in the Psalter is for the most part used in psalms of a very late postexilic date.

We have thus far found no recognition of a Mosaic Pentateuch in any writing prior to the restoration from exile. We have found nothing more than the Pentateuch itself gives us in the passages cited, a Mosaic law book of limited dimensions, a covenant code and the code of Deuteronomy.

I shall first refer to a passage from the last of the prophets:

"Remember ye the law of Moses my servant, which I commanded unto him in Horeb for all Israel, even statutes and judgments." (Malachi iv. 4.)

This reference to the law of Moses coupled as it is with the name Horeb, if it imply a written law, refers to the Deuteronomic code where Horeb is used for Sinai of the priestly document of the Hexateuch. It seems probable that in the time of Malachi, the Deuteronomic code still existed as a separate writing.

The Chronicler is a late writer, not earlier than the Greek period, some considerable time subsequent to the reforms of Ezra and Nehemiah, when it is admitted that the Pentateuch existed in its present form. What then is the evidence of the Chronicler on this subject? It is evident that a great variety of phrases is used for law by the Chronicler. We shall divide them into groups.

(a). Words of the Law. Neh. viii. 9, 13.
Portions of the Law. Neh. xii. 44.
The Law of Yahweh. Ez. vii. 10; 1 Chron. xvi. 40; 2 Chron. xii. 1, xxxi. 3, 4, xxxv. 26.
The Law of God. Neh. x. 29, 30.
The Law of Yahweh thy God. 1 Chron. xxii. 12.

Book of the Law. Neh. viii. 3 ; 2 Chron. xxxiv. 15.

Book of the Law of Yahweh their God. Neh. ix. 3.

Book of the Law of God. Neh. viii. 18.

Book of the Law of Yahweh. 2 Chron. xvii. 9, xxxiv. 14.

Written in the Law. Neh. x. 34, 37.

In the Book in the Law of God. Neh. viii. 8.

It is evident that Mosaic authorship cannot be proven from these phrases.

(*b*). In the Law which Yahweh commanded by the hand of Moses. Neh. viii. 14.

The Word that thou commandest thy servant Moses. Neh. i. 8.

All that Moses the servant of God had commanded. 1 Chron. vi. 34.

There is nothing in these statements which is not contained already in the Pentateuch itself with regard to the matters referred to. They do not prove the Mosaic authorship of the Pentateuch, but only the connection of Moses with certain things in the way of law and prediction recorded in the Pentateuch.

(*c*). The third group needs more careful consideration:

Law of Moses. 2 Chron. xxx. 16; Ez. vii. 6.

Book of the Law of Moses. Neh. viii. 1.

Written in the Law of Moses. 2 Chron. xxiii. 18 ; Ez. iii. 2 ; Dan. ix. 11, 13.

Written in the Book of Moses. 2 Chron. xxxv. 12; Ez. vi. 18.

Written in the Law in the Book of Moses. 2 Chron. xxv. 4.

The question here arises whether the attachment of the name of Moses to this law book implies Mosaic authorship of the book and all its contents. (1). Is it certain that it refers to. our Pentateuch? Delitzsch, who has resisted the progress of the Higher Criticism as an honest, God-fearing man, and who has yielded only when convinced by irresistible arguments, says no. In his last volume on Genesis, he says:

"Nowhere in the canonical literature of the Old Testament do the terms 'the law,' 'the book of the law,' 'the law of Moses,' cover the Pentateuch in its present form, not in the history of Joshua, Jos. i. 8, or Jehoshaphat, 2 Chron. xvii. 9, not altogether even in the history of Ezra and Nehemiah, Neh. viii. 1b." *

But admitting that it refers to the priestly document, or to the whole Pentateuch, does it imply Mosaic authorship in all respects? We urge that it does not imply this. If the Chronicler had known the historic origin and successive stages of development in the composition of the Hexateuch as we know them, *e. g.* that we have in our Hexateuch a Mosaic code written by Moses in a book of the covenant which appears in one form in Ex. xx.–xxiii., and in another form in Ex. xxxiv., and in a book of law in Dt. xii.–xxvi., and which lies at the basis of the code of Holiness in Leviticus and the priest's code in the middle books of the Pentateuch; and that these codes existing in four different historic writings had been compiled in the more comprehensive codification of our Pentateuch; would he not have been justified in speaking of the Pentateuch as the book of Moses, the law of Moses, the book of the law of Moses? So it seems to some who have carefully considered the whole

---

* P. 13.

subject. Others may think differently, but have they any right to force their interpretation upon us? The critics base their opinion upon important considerations. There is a sufficient number of parallels in the Old Testament. Take for example the name David in the titles of the Davidic psalms. The older theory was that David wrote the entire Psalter, then the theory was proposed that David, in the titles of the psalms, implied the Davidic authorship of those particular psalms. But this theory has to be abandoned because many of these psalms which bear the name of David are postexilic. It seems altogether probable that these psalms were all taken from the earliest of the minor psalters, which were collected under the name of David because David was the traditional master of sacred song. The Psalter of David in this ancient collection did not imply that David wrote all these psalms, but that his was an appropriate name under which to compile them. The same is true with regard to that ancient collection of distichs which bears the title " Proverbs of Solomon." (Pr. x.–xxii. 16.) Who can believe that Solomon was the author of them all? He was the master of sacred wisdom and under his name it was appropriate to compile a collection of wisdom. Why may we not conclude that the Chronicler, who wrote after these three compilations had been made, of the minor psalter of David, the proverbs of Solomon, and the laws of Moses, used these three names in exactly the same way ; and that he knew that no one of the three implied authorship, but only that Moses was the father of the law, as David was the father of the psalmody, and Solomon the father of the wisdom? Some may not be able to explain these things as we do, but if they do not, have they any right to force their interpretation of these facts upon us? All these phrases refer to the law. But what about the history? If the book is called the law of Moses, the book of the law of Moses, does that imply that all the history in the book was written by Moses? Are we compelled to conclude that nothing could have been written in the book except what came from Moses or was compiled by Moses? Those who insist upon interpreting such phrases in such a way as to force belief in the Mosaic authorship of the Pentateuch, when they are capable of another interpretation and are given that explanation by Christian scholars of the highest rank, and by those pre-eminent in Biblical learning, should beware lest they risk the canonicity of the writings of the Chronicler by bringing him in conflict with the mass of evidence that may be presented from the Pentateuch itself to show that, if the Chronicler held their opinion, he was altogether mistaken.

V.—*The Testimony of the New Testament.*

The evidence from the New Testament may be distributed in five sections and summed up as follows:

(1). Jesus speaks of the law of Moses, Luke xxiv. 44, John vii. 23; and the book of Moses, Mark xii. 26. Moses is used for the Pentateuch, Acts xv. 21; 2 Cor. iii. 15. These are all cases of naming books cited.

These passages must be interpreted in accordance with usage. It is the custom in literature to name anonymous writings after the name of the chief character in it, or the theme of it; and then in that case it is quite common to personify the book and represent it as saying or teaching this or that. When Jesus uses Moses as another name for the Law or Pentateuch, it is by no means certain that Jesus meant to say that Moses wrote the Pentateuch. The Book of Esther is named Esther not because any one ever supposed that she wrote it; but because she is the heroine, the theme of the book, and when one says, as it is often said, "Esther never uses the name of God, or teaches any doctrine of faith," you understand him as using Esther for the book Esther.

No one ever supposed that Ruth wrote the book of Ruth, or would suppose that she was regarded as its author if one should say, as it has often been said," Ruth teaches a doctrine different from Deuteronomy and Ezra in representing that even a Moabitish woman may enter the kingdom of God." The usage of the New Testament is also sufficiently clear at these points. Thus the epistle to the Hebrews iv. 7 uses David as a name of the Psalter. It was a common opinion until the 18th century that David wrote all the psalms, but no Biblical scholar at present, so far as is known, thinks that the epistle to the Hebrews forces him to hold that David is the author of the entire Psalter. Why then should any one insist that when the name Moses is given to the Pentateuch, it implies that Moses wrote all the writings attributed to him by tradition?

(2). Jesus represents Moses as a law-giver, giving the Ten Commandments, Mark vii. 10; the law of the lepers' offering, Mark i. 44, etc.; the law of divorce, Matt. xix. 7-8; the law of raising up seed for the brother's wife, Luke xx. 28; the law in general, John vii. 19. The epistle to the Hebrews represents Moses as giving the law of priesthood, Heb. vii. 14, and as a law-giver whose law could not be disobeyed with impunity, Heb. x. 28. These passages all represent Moses to be the law-giver that he appears to be in the narratives of the Pentateuch, but do not, by any means, imply the authorship of those narratives that contain these laws, any more than the reference in 1 Cor. ix. 14, to the command of

Christ in Luke x. 7, and the institution of the Lord's supper by Jesus, 1 Cor. xi. 23 *seq.*, imply that Jesus was the author of the gospels containing his words.

(3). Jesus represents Moses as a prophet who wrote of him, John v. 46, 47, so Philip, John i. 45, Peter, Acts iii. 22–24, Stephen, Acts vii. 37, Paul, Acts xxvi. 22; and in Rom. x. 5, 19, the apostle refers to the address in Deut. xxx., and the song, Deut. xxxii. These passages may prove that certain prophecies came from Moses, but do not prove that the Pentateuch as a whole, or the narratives in which these prophecies occur, were written by Moses.

(4). Certain historical events narrated in the Pentateuch in which Moses takes the lead are mentioned in Luke xx. 37; Heb. viii. 5; ix. 19, xii. 21, etc., but these simply teach the historical character of the transactions, not the exclusive Mosaic authorship of the writings containing these historical incidents.*

(5). In Acts iii. 24, it is said, "All the prophets from Samuel and them that followed after, as many as have spoken, they also told of those days." But Samuel uttered no Messianic prophecy in the book of Samuel. The name Samuel is used as the name of the book, and the name of the book is personified and represented as speaking the prophecy which in the book is attributed to the prophet Nathan. If now Samuel as the name of the book may be represented by the apostle Peter as speaking the prophecy of Nathan, why may not Moses as the name of the book of Moses be represented as giving the exhortations of an unknown prophet contained in the book which bears his name? It is quite true that an ancient Jewish tradition in the

---

* See *Biblical Study*, pp. 192–193.

Talmud represents that Samuel wrote his book, but a later writer in the Talmud itself comments on the statement that Samuel wrote his book thus: "'But it is written there: and Samuel died, and they buried him in Rama.' Gad the seer and Nathan the prophet finished it." In other words, the book was begun by Samuel and completed by Nathan and Gad. It may be that there are some persons at the present time who would accept this Talmudic comment on the older Talmudic tradition, but certainly no one believes that Samuel recorded Nathan's prophecy delivered long after Samuel's death, and this is just the prophecy that Peter represents Samuel as speaking.

But some one will say, "Was it not the common opinion in the days of our Lord that Moses wrote the Pentateuch?" We answer that, so far as we know, it was the common opinion that David wrote the Psalter. As to the Pentateuch, opinion was divided whether it was lost when the temple was destroyed by the king of Babylon, and restored or recast by Ezra, or not. If you insist upon interpreting the New Testament by the opinion of the Jews at the time as regards the Pentateuch you must follow it also as regards the Psalter. But why should we interpret Jesus and His apostles by the opinions of the Jews of His time? Why should we suppose that He shared with them all the errors He did not oppose and refute? Jesus either knew that Moses wrote the Pentateuch or He did not know. (*a*). If we should say Jesus did not know whether Moses wrote the Pentateuch or not, we would not go beyond His own saying that He knew not the time of His own advent. Those who understand the doctrine of the humiliation of Christ and the incarnation of Christ, find no more difficulty in supposing that Jesus did not know the author of the Pentateuch than that He did not know the day of His own advent. As Charles Gore says:

"When he speaks of the 'sun-rising' He is using ordinary language. He shows no signs at all of transcending the science of His age. Equally He shows no signs of transcending the History of His age. . . . The utterances of Christ about the Old Testament do not seem to be nearly definite or clear enough to allow of our supposing that in this case He is departing from the general method of the incarnation, by bringing to bear the unveiled omniscience of the Godhead to anticipate or foreclose a development of natural knowledge." (*Lux Mundi*, p. 360.)

(*b*). If on the other hand any one should say Jesus must have known all things and He ought not to have used language that might deceive men, we respond that His language does not deceive men. Literary usage in all ages and in the Bible itself shows that it is equally true and good language for the critics as for the anti-critics. The question is, shall we interpret the words of Jesus by the opinions of His contemporaries? This we deny. Jesus was not obliged to correct all the errors of His contemporaries. He did not correct their false views of science. He was the great physician, but He did not teach medicine. He was greater than Solomon, and yet He declined to decide questions of civil law and politics. He never rebuked slavery. Is He responsible for slavery on that account? The Southern slaveholders used to say so. But even they are now convinced of their error. The signs of the times indicate that in a few years the anti-critics will disappear as completely as the slaveholders. The attempt to bar the way of the Higher Criticism of the Old Testament by interposing the authority of the New Testament is an unworthy attempt to make our Lord and

His apostles responsible for those conceits and follies of ancient tradition which modern traditional dogma has with great unwisdom accepted and endorsed.

We have gone over the evidence from Holy Scripture and have found no direct testimony sufficiently explicit to prove the Mosaic authorship of the Pentateuch. But we have found indirect evidence to show that much of the Pentateuch is of a date considerably later than Moses.

III.

THE TRADITIONAL THEORIES.

WE shall now consider the evidence from Tradition. The earliest Rabbinical theory of the Old Testament Literature known to us is contained in the Tract Baba Bathra of the Talmud. The Beraitha reads as follows:

"Moses wrote his book, the chapter of Balaam, and Job; Joshua wrote his book and the eight verses of the Law;* Samuel wrote his book and Judges and Ruth; David wrote the book of the Psalms with the aid of ten ancients, with the aid of Adam the first, Melchizedek, Abraham, Moses, Heman, Jeduthun, Asaph and the three sons of Korah; Jeremiah wrote his book, the book of Kings and Lamentations; Hezekiah and his company wrote Isaiah, Proverbs, Song of Songs and Ecclesiastes; the men of the great synagogue wrote Ezekiel, and the twelve (minor prophets), Daniel and the roll of Esther; Ezra wrote his book and the genealogy of Chronicles until himself."*

Thus this tract assigns writers to all the Biblical books. But it is very clear that "write" in this passage does not mean compose of authorship, but commit to writing, whether by the author himself or others. Thus only can we explain the writing of Isaiah, Proverbs, Song of Songs, and Ecclesiastes by Hezekiah and his company; and of Ezekiel, the minor prophets and the roll of Esther,

---
* See *Biblical Study*, p. 176.

by the men of the great synagogue. If this be true in these cases we cannot be sure that it is not true in the other cases also. This statement of the Mishna is enlarged upon by the Gemara.

"The author (of the Beraitha) said, Joshua wrote his book and the eight verses of the law; this is taught according to him who says of the eight verses of the law, Joshua wrote them. For it is taught: And Moses, the servant of the Lord, died there. How is it possible that Moses died and wrote: and Moses died there? It is only unto this passage Moses wrote, afterwards Joshua wrote the rest. These are the words of Rabbi Jehuda. Others say of Rabbi Nehemiah. But Rabbi Simeon said to him: Is it possible that the book of the law could lack one letter, since it is written: Take this book of the law? It is only unto this the Holy One, blessed be He! said, and Moses said and wrote. From this place and onwards the Holy One, blessed be He! said, and Moses wrote with weeping."

The Talmud elsewhere contains other conflicting statements, which cannot, however, claim the antiquity or authority of the passage cited above.

The ordinary Jewish view is that Moses also wrote the last eight verses by divine dictation.*

A still more ancient and higher authority in some respects is the Apocalypse of Ezra † from the first Christian century, printed among the Apocryphal books in the English Bible, and preserved in five versions, and used not infrequently by the Fathers as if it were inspired Scripture. This tradition represents that the Law and all the holy books were burned at the destruction of Jerusalem by Nebuchadnezzar and lost; that Ezra under divine inspiration restored them all, and also composed seventy others to be delivered to the wise as the

---

* See Wogue, *Histoire de la Bible*, 1881, p. 21, *sq.*; Josephus, *Antiquities*, iv. 8, 48; Philo, *Life of Moses*, iii., 39.

† xiv. 19-46.

esoteric wisdom for the interpretation of the twenty-four.

This view of the restoration of the Old Testament writings by Ezra was advocated by some of the Fathers such as Clement of Alexandria,* Tertullian,† Chrysostom,‡ in an anonymous writing wrongly attributed to Augustine,§ and the Clementine Homilies.‖ Another common opinion of the Fathers is represented by Irenæus.¶

"During the captivity of the people under Nabuchadnezzar, the Scriptures had been corrupted, and when, after seventy years, the Jews had returned to their own land, then in the time of Artaxerxes, King of the Persians, (God) inspired Esdras, the priest of the tribe of Levi, to recast all the words of former prophets, and to re-establish with the people the Mosaic legislation."

With him agree Theodoret ** and Basil.†† Jerome ‡‡ says with reference to this tradition : " Whether you wish to say that Moses is the author of the Pentateuch, or that Ezra restored it, is indifferent to me." Bellarmin §§ is of the opinion that the books of the Jews were not entirely lost, but that Ezra corrected those that had become corrupted, and improved the copies he restored. Junilius, in the sixth century, author of the first extant Introduction,‖‖ a reproduction of a lost work of his instructor, Paul of Nisibis, of the Antiochian school of Exegesis, makes the wise discrimination between those Scriptures having their authors indicated in their titles and introductions, and those whose authorship rested

---

* *Stromata*, i., 22. † *De cultu foeminarum*, c. 3.
‡ Hom. viii., in *Epist. Hebraeos*, Migne's edition, xvii., p 74.
§ *De Mirabilibus Sacræ Scripturæ*, ii., 33. ‖ iii., c. 47.
¶ *Adv. Haereses*, iii., 21, 2. ** *Praef in Psalmos*.
†† *Epist. ad Chilonem*, Migne's edition, iv., p. 358. ‡‡ *Adv. Helvitium*.
§§ *De Verbo Dei*, lib. 2. ‖‖ *Institutio regularis Divinæ Legis*.

purely on tradition, in the latter including the Pentateuch and Joshua.* This position of Junilius is the true scholarly position. It puts the authorship of the Pentateuch on the same level as the authorship of the other historical books of the Old Testament. This work of Junilius held its own as an authority in the Western Church until the Reformation. It would be difficult to define a consensus of the Fathers in regard to the authorship of the historical books of the Old Testament.

Little attention was given to such topics in the sixteenth century. How the Reformers would have met these questions we may infer from their freedom with regard to traditional views in the few cases in which they expressed themselves.

Luther denied the Apocalypse to John, and Ecclesiastes to Solomon. He maintained that the epistle of James was not an apostolic writing. He regarded Jude as an extract from 2d Peter, and asks what it matters if Moses should not himself have written the Pentateuch.† Calvin denied the Pauline authorship of the epistle to the Hebrews and doubted the Petrine authorship of 2d Peter. He held that Ezra or some one else edited the Psalter, and regarded Ezra as the author of Malachi, Malachi being his surname. He also constructed a harmony of the Pentateuchal legislation after the model of the Harmony of the Gospels.

Questions of human authorship and date of Biblical writings troubled the Reformers but little. They had to battle against the Vulgate for the original text and popular versions, and for a simple grammatical exegesis over against traditional authority and the manifold

---
* See Kihn, *Theodor von Mopsuestia*, ss. 319-330, § viii., 2.

† *Vorreden* in Walch's edition of Luther's *Werken*, xiv., pp. 35, 146-153, *Tischreden*, I., p. 28.

sense. Hence it is that on these literary questions the symbols of the Reformation take no position whatever except to lay stress upon the sublimity of the style, the unity and harmony of Scripture, and the internal evidence of its inspiration and authority.

The Westminster standards are in entire accord with the other Reformed Confessions and the faith of the Reformation on these subjects. They express a devout admiration and profound reverence for the holy, majestic character and style of the divine Word, but do not define the human authors and dates of the various writings. As Prof. A. F. Mitchell, of St. Andrew's, well states:

"Any one who will take the trouble to compare their list of the canonical books with that given in the Belgian Confession or the Irish articles, may satisfy himself that they held with Dr. Jameson that the authority of these books does not depend on the fact whether this prophet or that wrote a particular book or parts of a book, whether a certain portion was derived from the Elohist or the Jehovist, whether Moses wrote the close of Deuteronomy, Solomon was the author of Ecclesiastes, or Paul of the Epistle to the Hebrews, but in the fact that a prophet, an inspired man, wrote them, and that they bear the stamp and impress of a divine origin." *Minutes of the Westminster Assembly,* p. xlix.

And Matthew Poole, the great Presbyterian critic of the seventeenth century, quotes with approval the following from Melchior Canus:

"It is not much material to the Catholick faith that any book was written by this or that author, so long as the Spirit of God is believed to be the author of it; which Gregory delivers and explains: For it matters not with what pen the King writes his letter, if it be true that he writ it." *Blow at the Root,* 4th ed., 1671, p. 228.

IV.

THE RISE OF CRITICISM.

THE Mosaic authorship of the Pentateuch was first questioned in modern times by Carlstadt,* who left the author undetermined. The Roman Catholic scholar Masius, and the British philosopher Hobbes distinguished between Mosaic originals and our present Pentateuch, but the Roman Catholic priest Peyrerius,† and especially Spinoza,‡ first arranged the objections to the Mosaic authorship in formidable array, the latter reviving the doubts of Aben Ezra.

They presented evidence against the Mosaic authorship from 18 different passages as follows. We shall classify them and test them.

I.— *Historical Objections.*

(1). Gen. xii. 6. "The Canaanite was then in the land" implies a time when this was not the case, that is centuries after the conquest by Joshua.

(2). Gen. xiv. 14. "And pursued as far as Dan." But Dan did not receive this name until long after the death of Moses; for Judges xviii. 29 tells us that the

---
* *De Scriptor. Canon*, § 85, 1521.
† In his *Syst. Theo. Praead.*, 1660, liv., cap. 1.
‡ In his Tract, *Theo. Polit.*, 1670, c. 8.

Danites in the times of the Judges "called the name of the city Dan, after the name of Dan their father who was born unto Israel; howbeit the name of the city was Laish at the first."

(3). Gen. xxxvi. gives a list of kings reigning in Edom: "before there reigned any king over the children of Israel." (Ver. 31). This implies an author living after the establishment of kings in Israel not earlier than the Hebrew monarchy.

(4). Ex. xvi. 35. "And the children of Israel did eat the manna forty years, until they came to a land inhabited; they did eat the manna, until they came unto the borders of the land of Canaan." This passage implies the entrance into Canaan after the death of Moses and the author's knowledge of the event described in Jos. v. 12.

(5). Deut. i. 1. "These be the words which Moses spake unto all Israel beyond Jordan" implies an author who was in Palestine, for only such an one could write "beyond Jordan."

(6). Deut. ii. 12. The children of Esau destroyed the Horites and dwelt in their stead "as Israel did unto the land of his possession which Yahweh gave unto them." This implies the conquest of Canaan.

(7). Deut. iii. 11. "For only Og, king of Bashan, remained of the remnant of the Rephaim; behold, his bedstead was a bedstead of iron; is it not in Rabbah of the children of Ammon?" This implies a writer looking back upon the story of the conquest of Bashan from a date much later than Moses.

(8). Deut. iii. 14. "And called them after his own name Havvoth-jair unto this day." This implies a day long after this naming which was made in the last days of Moses.

(9). Deut. xxxiv. 10. "And there hath not arisen a prophet since in Israel like unto Moses." This implies a time long subsequent to Moses.

These are all historical statements which are inconsistent with Mosaic authorship. Either then they are notes of later editors, or else the writings which contain them must be later than the history implied in them. Two other instances have not altogether stood the test of criticism.

(10). Gen. xxii. 14. Mt. Moriah is called the mount of God, which could not be so called until the erection of the temple. This objection rests upon a mistake. It is not called the Mount of Yahweh, but the place is called "Yahweh sees." As it is said to this day, "in the mount where Yahweh appears." This proverbial expression, however, implies a long sojourn in the Holy Land, and, therefore, a period long subsequent to Moses.

(11). Deut. ii. 5. "Not so much as for the sole of the foot to tread on," when compared with 1 Chron. xviii., where David conquers Edom, shows an inconsistency, and doubtless implies a time when Israel was friendly with Edom, but does not in itself imply a later date than Moses.

II.—*Indications of Special Authorship.*

(12). Num. xxi. 14. The citation of the book of the wars of Yahweh implies another author than Moses.

(13). Deut. xxvii. 2 *seq.*, comp. Jos. viii. 30 *seq.*, where the law was written on an altar, implies a law much less extensive than the Pentateuch. It is now generally agreed that the reference here is to the Deuteronomic code.

III.— *Inconsistencies.*

(14). Deut. x. 8, which narrates the separation of the Levites at Jotbathah is inconsistent with their separation before the death of Aaron as reported in Leviticus and Numbers.

(15). Ex. iv. 20, which represents that Moses took his family with him to Egypt, is inconsistent with Ex. xviii. 2 *seq.*, which states that they remained with his father-in-law in Midian. Modern critics explain these variations as due to the different stories of the same thing recorded in different documents.

IV.— *Personal Considerations.*

(16). Ex. xxxiii. 11. "Yahweh spake unto Moses face to face."

(17). Num. xii. 3. "Now the man Moses was very meek, above all the men which were upon the face of the earth."

(18). Deut. xxxi. 9. "And Moses wrote this law."

Several other passages—Num. i. 1; ii. 2; v. 1; xxxi. 14; Deut. xxxi. 1; xxxiii. 1, where Moses is spoken of in the third person and sometimes in flattering terms.

Some of these might be accounted for after the analogy of the classic historians as a variation of style, but the laudatory references are not to be explained in this way and therefore count against the Mosaic authorship of them. We are therefore compelled either to take them as editorial notes, or, as this is difficult if not impossible in many of these cases, to regard them as from documents written by other persons than Moses.

These objections of Peyrerius and Spinoza are of an external character. A few of them have been satisfactorily explained and their force dulled; others have been admitted as implying the work of later editors. The most of them have maintained their validity.

Soon after Spinoza, Richard Simon, a Roman Catholic, published his work on the Historical Criticism of the Old Testament.* He first began to apply historical criticism in a systematic manner to the study of the books of the Old Testament. He represented the historical books as made up of the ancient writings of the prophets, who were public scribes, and who wrote down the history in official documents on the spot, from the time of Moses onward, so that the Pentateuch in its present shape is not by Moses. Simon distinguished in the Pentateuch between that which was written by Moses, *e.g.*, the commands and ordinances; and that written by the prophetical scribes, the greater part of the history. As the books of Kings and Chronicles were made up by abridgments and summaries of the ancient acts preserved in the archives of the nation, so was the Pentateuch.† The later prophets edited the works of the earlier prophets and added explanatory statements. Simon presents as evidences that Moses did not write the Pentateuch: (1). The double account of the deluge. (2). The lack of order in the arrangement of the narratives and laws. (3). The diversity of the style.

It is evident that the Roman Catholic scholar goes deeper into the subject than the philosopher Spinoza had gone. He presents another class of evidences. These three lines were not sufficiently worked by Simon. He fell into the easy temptation of expending his strength on the elaboration and justification of his theory. The facts he discovered have proved of permanent value, and have been worked as a rich mine by later

---

* *Histoire Critique de Vieux Testament*, 1678. † *l. c.*, p. 17, *seq.*

scholars, but his theory was at once attacked and destroyed. The Arminian Clericus, in an anonymous work,* assailed Simon for his abuse of Protestant writers, but really went to greater lengths than Simon. He distinguishes in the Pentateuch three classes of facts, those before Moses, those during his time, and those subsequent to his death,† and represents the Pentateuch in its present form as composed by the priest sent from Babylon to instruct the inhabitants of Samaria in the religion of the land, 2 Kings xvii.‡ Afterward he gave up this theory and took the ground § of interpolations by a later editor. Anton Van Dale,‖ distinguishes between the Mosaic code and the Pentateuch, which latter Ezra composed from other writings, historical and prophetical, inserting the Mosaic code as a whole in his work. This was also essentially the view of Semler.¶

These various writers brought to light a most valuable collection of facts which demanded the attention of Biblical scholars of all creeds and phases of thought. They all made the mistake of proposing untenable *theories* of various kinds to account for the facts, instead of working upon the facts and rising from them by induction and generalization to permanent results. Some of them, like Spinoza and Hobbes, were animated by a spirit more or less hostile to the evangelical faith. Others, like Carlstadt and Clericus, were heterodox in other matters. The most important investigations were

---

* *Sentimens de quelques theologiens de Holland sur l'Histoire Critique*, Amst., 1685.

† *l. c.*, p. 107.   ‡ P. 129.

§ *Com. on Genesis, introd. de Scriptore Pent.*, § 11. Simon replied to Clericus in *Réponse au Livre intitule Sentimens*, etc. Par Le Preur de Bolleville, Rotterdam, 1686.

‖ *De origine et progressu idol.*, 1696 (p. 71), and *epist. ad Morin.* (p. 686).

¶ *Apparatus ad Liberalem Vet. Test. Interp.*, 1773 (p. 67).

those of the Roman Catholics, Masius and Simon. These authors, in a Church noted for its adherence to tradition, felt that they were free on this question of the authorship of the Pentateuch, there being no consensus of the Fathers against them.

The Mosaic authorship of the Pentateuch was defended by Huet, a Jesuit;* Heidegger, a divine of the Reformed Church of Switzerland;† the Dutch Reformed, Maresius,‡ and the German Lutheran, Carpzov.§ These scholastic divines, instead of seeking to account for the facts brought to light by the critics, proceeded to defend the Mosaic authorship of the entire Pentateuch and to explain away these facts. Thus, Huet is unwilling to admit that Moses did not write the account of his own death. Maresius insists that the testimony of Christ decides the matter for us. Heidegger argues that the whole Pentateuch was found by Hilkiah in the temple in the time of Josiah, that Christ and His apostles ascribe the Pentateuch to Moses as author, and he follows the Rabbinical tradition, rejecting the traditions prevalent with the Christian fathers. He admits that the last verses of Deuteronomy were added by Joshua or some one else, but explains Gen. xxii. 14 as a prophecy of the temple or of seeing Christ in the flesh, and the kings of Edom prior to kings in Israel, Gen. xxxvi. 31, as a line of kings prior to Moses as king. He meets the argument from diversity of style by the remark that the Holy Spirit might inspire the same author to use a

---

* *Demonstratio Evangelica,* 1679, iv., cap. xiv.

† *Exercitiones Biblicæ,* 1700, Dissert. ix.

‡ *Praef. apol. pro authentia script.*, pp. 23-36. And in his *Refutatio Fabulæ Præadamiticæ,* Groniga, 1656, he meets the various arguments of Peyrerius.

§ *Introductio ad Libros Canonicos, Bib. Vet. Test.*, Edit. 2, Lipsae 1731. See also Du Pin *Dissert. prelim. Bib. des auteurs eccl.*, Paris, 1688.

variety of styles.* He meets the argument from defective arrangement by representing it as a charge against the Holy Spirit.† Carpzov calls in the spirit of prophecy to account for the kings of Edom (Gen. xxxvi. 31), and the account of the continuation of the manna until the conquest (Ex. xvi. 35). Such special pleading and arbitrary conjectures were as hurtful from the scholastic side as were the hasty and ill-adjusted theories from the other.

There were, however, in those times, other divines who looked the facts in the face and took a better way. Thus Witsius ‡ admits *four* interpolations, after carefully considering the objections that were urged to the Mosaic authorship, and is followed by Dr. Graves,§ who admits six additions by a later hand, and also by Adam Clarke,‖ who, in general, admits additions by Ezra. Prideaux¶ represents Ezra as editing the Pentateuch and making additions in a number of places— illustrating, connecting and completing the narratives.**

---

* " In Spiritus s. quinetiam calamus dirigentis arbitrio fuit, verba et verborum ordinem suggere, prout ipsi, visuum est. Sicut diversos Scriptores diversi modo ita inspiravit, ut diverso stylo uterentur: ita eundem Scriptorem quo minus diversi modo inspiraret, nihil vetabat equidem," p. 269.

† Nam spiritus prophetiæ et infallibilitatis si in uno, veluti scriba, revisore peccare, abberrare potest, poterit etiam in altero, puta in Mose," p. 270.

‡ *Misc. Sacra*, 1692, pp. 104, 130.

§ *Lectures on the Four Last Books of the Pentateuch*, 1807, 4th Edit., 1831, p. 439 *sq.*

‖ *Holy Bible*, 1810-26.

¶ *Old and New Testaments connected*, 1716-18, Part I., Book V. (3).

** " The third thing which Ezra did about the holy Scriptures in his edition of them was, that he added in several places throughout the books of this edition what appeared necessary for the illustrating, connecting, or completing of them ; wherein he was assisted by the same Spirit by which they were at first wrote. Of this sort we may reckon the last chapter of Deuteronomy, which, giving an account of the death and burial of Moses, and of the succession of Joshua after him, it could not be written by Moses himself, who undoubtedly was the penman of the rest of that book. It seems most probable that it was added by

Vitringa* gave a more careful consideration to the facts, and taught that Moses collected, digested, and embellished the documents of the patriarchs and supplied their deficiencies. This, he argues, does not destroy the authority of the book, for Moses was aided by the Holy Spirit. So Luke prepared his history of the Gospel from the narratives of others and annotations of eye-witnesses, and these are of no less authority than the narratives of Matthew and John. The aid of the Holy Spirit was given to them, whether they composed as eye-witnesses or digested the narratives of others. This view of Vitringa was advocated by Calmet,† Bishop Gleig,‡ and others. About the same time several Roman Catholic divines took ground independently in favor of the theory of the use of written documents by Moses in the composition of Genesis, namely, Abbé Fleury,§ and Abbé Laurent François.∥ Prideaux, Calmet, Vitringa and their associates represented the true schol-

---

Ezra at this time. And such we may also reckon the several interpolations which occur in many places of the holy Scriptures." He refers especially to Gen. xii. 6; xiv. 14; xxii. 14; xxxvi. 3; Ex. xvi. 35; Deut. ii. 12; iii. 11, 14; and concludes: "Of which interpolations undoubtedly Ezra was the author, in all the books which passed his examination, and Simon the Just of all the rest which were added afterward, for they all seemed to refer to those latter times. But these additions do not detract anything from the divine authority of the whole, because they were all inserted by the direction of the same Holy Spirit which dictated all the rest."

* *Observ. Sacra*, c. IV., 2, 1722.

† *Com. Litterale*, 1722, *tom.* I., p. xiii.

‡ Stackhouse's *History of the Bible*, corrected and improved, 1817, Vol. I., p. xx.

§ *Moeurs des Israelites*, p. 6, Bruxelles, 1701. This was translated into English and enlarged by Adam Clarke; 3d edition, 1809.

∥ *Preuves de la Religion de Jesus Christ, contra les Spinosistes et les Deistes*, 1751, I. 2, c. 3, art. 7. "Il est plus que vrai-semblable que dans la lignée, ou s'est conservée la connoissance de Dieu on conservit aussi par écrit, des mèmoires des anciens temps; car les hommes n' ont jamais êté sans ce soin."

arly position. They presented a reasonable solution, in view of the facts then adduced. They laid the foundations for Evangelical Criticism in the great revival of *Higher Criticism*, which was about to begin and run a long and successful course. We shall divide the history of this movement of Higher Criticism into three stadia: the documentary, supplementary, and development hypotheses.

V.

THE DOCUMENTARY HYPOTHESIS.

JEAN ASTRUC, a Roman Catholic physician, opened a new era for the study of the Pentateuch. In 1753 he made it evident that Genesis was composed of several documents. He presented to the learned world, with some hesitation and timidity, his discovery that the use of the divine names Elohim and Yahweh divided the book of Genesis into two great memoirs and nine lesser ones, as follows: vii. 20–23; xiv., xix. 29–38; xxii. 20–24; xxv. 12–18; xxvi. 34–35; xxviii. 6–9; xxxiv., xxxv. 28–xxxvi. The advantages of this discovery are admirably presented: (1). It explains the singularity of the use of these two divine names. (2). It explains the repetitions of the same subject by distributing these among the memoirs. (3). It excuses Moses from negligence in composition by the supposition that he arranged these memoirs in four different columns, as Origen did the ancient versions in his Hexapla and as Harmonists arrange the four Gospels.

This was a real discovery, which, after a hundred years of debate, has won the consent of the vast majority of Biblical scholars. His analysis is in some respects too mechanical, and, in not a few instances, is defective and needed rectification, but as a whole it has been maintained. He relies also too much upon the different use of the divine names, and too little upon variations in style, language, and narrative. Since his date his line of argument has been more thoroughly worked out. Every use of the divine names throughout the Hebrew Bible, has been carefully examined in the preparation of the new Hebrew Lexicon, edited by Dr. Brown, with the co-operation of Canon Driver and the author, and a fresh and exhaustive investigation has been made of the whole subject. These are the facts: In Ex. vi. 2-3 it is written: "And *Elohim* spake unto Moses, and said unto him, I am *Yahweh:* and I appeared unto Abraham, unto Isaac, and unto Jacob as *'El Shadday*, but by my name *Yahweh* I was not known to them." Turning now to Genesis we find *'El Shadday* used in connection with the covenants made with Abraham and Jacob; but we also find that the divine name Yahveh is placed in the mouth of the antediluvians and patriarchs from Genesis, chap. ii., onward. Here is a glaring inconsistency not invented by critics, but on the surface of Genesis itself. The discovery of Astruc, that this inconsistency is due to a usage of different documents, removed the difficulty. Criticism has found that the priestly writer who wrote Ex. vi. never uses the divine name Yahweh in his document prior to Ex. vi., when he states that it was revealed to Moses for the first time. The use of the divine name Yahweh in Genesis is in the Judaic document, which nowhere mentions or seems to know anything about the revelation of the name Yahweh to Moses. He uses it as the name of God from the beginning. The early analysts were confronted with the difficulty that there was a very singular and apparently capricious use of the divine name left in the Judaic document after the Elohistic document had been eliminated.

This led to a more thorough study of that document which resulted in the discovery that it had been closely connected with another document which uses the divine name Elohim. This discovery was made by Ilgen in 1798;* but the discovery was ignored until a much later date when it was rediscovered by Hupfeld.

Looking now at Exodus iii., we observe that it tells of a revelation of the divine name Yahweh to Moses, at Horeb. This is a parallel narrative to chapter vi., and is now recognized by criticism as from the Ephraimitic author. Thus the whole difficulty of the use of the divine names is solved. The critics did not make the difficulty. They have removed the difficulty by the science of criticism. This Ephraimitic author not only uses the divine name Elohim, but it is his style to use it with the definite article, and it is also his style to use it by preference, even after the divine name Yahweh was revealed; whereas the priestly writer seldom uses Elohim after he tells of the revelation of Yahweh to Moses.†

In the book of Deuteronomy we find a fourth document which also extends through Joshua, and appears occasionally in the earlier narratives. It is the style of this writer to use the terms Yahweh thy God, or Yahweh your God. He uses Yahweh thy God 238 times. This phrase is used elsewhere in the Hexateuch, 5 times in the Ten Words; 3 times in the ancient law of worship, in the covenant codes and in two passages Gen. xxvii. 20, Ex. xv. 26, in verses which present other reasons for being considered editorial seams.

Other peculiarities in the use of divine names may be mentioned here. *Adonay*, " my Lord," as applied to God, is used in J 13 times, elsewhere in the Hexateuch only

---

* *Urkunden des Jerusalemer Tempel-archivs.* † See Appendix I.

in Gen. xx. 4; (E?) and Ex. xv. 17, (Song of Red Sea, where the Samaritan codex has Yahweh). *Adonay Yahweh* is used only in Gen. xv. 2, 8; Jos. vii. 7 (J) and Dt. iii. 24; ix. 26 (D). "God of Abraham" is a phrase of J. "Israel's God" is a phrase of E, used 9 times. It is also used in Ex. xxxiv. 23 (covenant code of J) and Jos. vii. 13, 19, 20, where JE are so mixed that it is difficult to disentangle them, and by R in Num. xvi. 9; Jos. ix. 18, 19, xxii. 24; x. 40, 42; xiii. 14, 33. "God of the Hebrews" is a phrase of JE, used 5 times. "Other gods" is a phrase of D, used in the Hexateuch besides only in the Ten Words, in the Deuteronomic expression Ex. xx. 3=Dt. v. 7; and in the covenant code of E, Ex. xxiii. 18= "other God," of the covenant code of J, Ex. xxxiv. 14, possibly by editorial change; and Jos. xxiv. 2, 16 (E); Dt. xxxi. 18, 20 (JE). Elohim is construed with the plural verb only in E, Gen. xx. 13, xxxv. 7, Jos. xxiv. 19.

The attention of German scholars was called to this discovery of the use of the divine names by Jerusalem. Eichhorn was independently led to the same opinion. In 1780 he published his Introduction to the Old Testament.

Eichhorn combined in one the results of Simon and Astruc, embracing the various elements in an organic method which he called the Higher Criticism.

In the preface to his 2d edition, 1787, he says:

"I am obliged to give the most pains to a hitherto entirely unworked field, the investigation of the internal condition of the particular writings of the Old Testament by help of the Higher Criticism (a new name to no Humanist). Let any one think what they will of these efforts, my own consciousness tells me, that they are the result of very careful investigation, although no one can be less wrapt up in them than I their author.

The powers of one man hardly suffice to complete such investigations so entirely at once. They demand a healthful and ever cheerful spirit, and how long can any one maintain it in such toilsome investigations? They demand the keenest insight into the internal condition of every book; and who will not be dulled after a while?"

Eichhorn separated the Elohistic and Jehovistic documents in Genesis with great pains and wonderful success, recognizing besides as separate documents ii. 4–iii. 24; xiv.; xxxiii. 18–xxxiv. 31; xxxvi.; xlix. 1–27. This analysis of Eichhorn has been the basis of all critical investigation since his day, and notwithstanding the subsequent distinction of a second Elohist and Redactor, the results of Eichhorn have been maintained.*

The great advantages of this analysis are admirably stated by Eichhorn (ii., p. 329):

" For this discovery of the internal condition of the first books of Moses, party spirit will perhaps for a pair of decennials snort at the Higher Criticism instead of rewarding it with the full thanks that are due it, for (1) the credibility of the book gains by such a use of more ancient documents. (2) The harmony of the two narratives at the same time, with their slight deviations,

---

* Thus Prof. Henry P. Smith, in his article in the *Presbyterian Review*, iii., p. 375, in showing the present consensus of the critics, says: "If we find, however, that the recognized leaders, though far apart on the question of the 'order of production' of different documents, are substantially agreed as to what makes up each document, we ought to recognize that the unanimity *here* is so much the stronger on account of the diversity *there*. An examination shows that in the first thirty chapters of Genesis the following passages are *unanimously* accepted by Hupfeld, Nöldeke, Dillmann, Wellhausen, and Kayser, as making up one of the documents called by Dillmann A ; by Wellhausen Q ; to wit : i. 1—ii. 3 ; v. 1-28, 30-32; vi. 9-22; viii. 1-4, 13-19; ix. 1-17, 28, 29; xi. 10-26, 32; xii. 4, 5; xiii. 6, 11, 12; xvi. 3, 15, 16; xvii. 1-27; xix. 29; xxi. 2-5; xxiii. 1-20; xxv. 7-11, 17, 20, 26; xxvi. 34, 35; xxviii. 1-9 (I have disregarded fractions of a verse)." Now it shows the keenness and accuracy of Eichhorn as well as the *invincible* strength of the evidence that in his first effort, his *Elohist* embraces all of the passages given above except the detached verses, xii. 4, 5; xiii. 6, 11, 12; xvi. 3, 13, 16; xxv. 26.

proves their independence and mutual reliability. (3) Interpreters will be relieved of difficulty by this Higher Criticism which separates document from document. (4) Finally the gain of Criticism is also great. If the Higher Criticism has now for the first distinguished author from author, and in general characterized each according to his own ways, diction, favorite expressions, and other peculiarities, then her lower sister who busies herself only with words, and spies out false readings, has rules and principles by which she must test particular readings." *

Eichhorn regarded Exodus, Leviticus, and Numbers as having grown from the collection of particular writings which the redactor connected by historical narratives: Exodus and Leviticus composed at Mt. Sinai; Numbers in the land of Moab. He thought that Moses was the author of Deuteronomy, except the last chapter. Deuteronomy is characterized as the law book for the people, and the legislation of the other books as the priests' code. He remarks that the Pentateuch only claims Moses as the author of particular sections, and that the middle books are not cited in the Old Testament under the name of Moses. He explains it from the fact that they constituted the priests' code over against Deuteronomy, the people's book. This important distinction of Eichhorn was also a valuable discovery for Higher Criticism. Long neglected, it has in recent times again come into play, as we shall see further on. Eichhorn also admits many glosses by a late hand, but in general abides by the authorship in the Mosaic period, and chiefly by Moses himself.

---

* See also *Urgeschichte* in the *Repertorium*, 1779, v., p. 187.

We cannot help calling attention to the fine literary sense of Eichhorn, as manifest in the following extract : " Read it (Genesis) as two historical works of antiquity, and breathe thereby the atmosphere of its age and country. Forget then the century in which thou livest and the knowledge it affords thee; and if thou canst not do this, dream not that thou wilt be able to enjoy the book in the spirit of its origin."

Eichhorn carried his methods of Higher Criticism into the entire Old Testament with the hand of a master, and laid the foundation of views which have been maintained ever since with increasing determination. But we do not find that in all cases he grasped the truth. He sometimes chased shadows, and framed, in some cases, visionary theories in relation to both the Old and the New Testaments, like others who have preceded him and followed him. He could not transcend the limits of his age, and adapt himself to future discoveries. The labors of a large number of scholars, and the work of a century and more were still needed, as Eichhorn modestly anticipated.

Eichhorn's Higher Criticism swept the field in Germany in his day, meeting but feeble opposition. Even J. D. Michaelis, one of the chief scholars of Germany, "the pillar of supernaturalism," who sought to modify some of the positions of Eichhorn,* although he was willing to accept the analysis of Astruc and Eichhorn with certain modifications,† met with little favor. He died, leaving his work incomplete.‡ As J. G. Gabler, the father of Biblical Theology, says: § The analysis of the two documents by Astruc, Jerusalem, and especially by Eichhorn, is so masterly, and the combination of the various documents in one by Moses has been made so

---

* *Einleit. in d. göttlichen Schriften d. Alt. Bundes*, 1787.

† P. 267.

‡ Michaelis denies that Ex. i.-ii. can belong to the Elohist. "I suppose that what Moses wrote of himself he took from no books" (p. 269); and claims that Genesis i., the account of the Creation, must have been given to Moses by inspiration directly from God (p. 269). He objects to the artificial analysis of Astruc, but claims that when אלהים and יהוה are used throughout entire chapters, a difference of style is evident (p. 277). He recognizes that Moses must have used written as well as traditional and monumental sources.

§ In his Introduction to his edition of Eichhorn's *Urgeschichte*, 1790.

evident that, "in our day it can be regarded as settled and presupposed without fear of any important opposition."

G. L. Bauer, in 1794,* followed Eichhorn in his analysis, but held that the Pentateuch was composed in the time of David.† Rosenmüller ‡ also followed Eichhorn, but subsequently § changed his view, influenced chiefly by J. G. Hasse,‖ and the overdoing of the analysis by Ilgen. Jahn¶ also followed Eichhorn in part. Fulda** distinguishes between law codes, and Pentateuch, and puts the codes first, in the time of David, the present Pentateuch in the Restoration. Ottmar (Nachtigal),†† makes Jeremiah the last collector and arranger of the Pentateuch.

These discussions produced little impression upon Great Britain. The conflict with Deism had forced the majority of her divines into a false position. If they had maintained the internal divine evidence for the authority of Holy Scripture and the evangelical critical position of the Reformers and Westminster divines, they would not have hesitated to look the facts in the face, and strive to account for them; they would not have committed the grave mistakes by which Biblical learning was almost paralyzed in Great Britain for half a century. Eager for the defence of traditional views, they, for the most part, fell back again on Jewish Rabbinical tradition and external evidence, contending with painful anxiety for authors and dates, and so antagonized Higher Criticism itself as Deistic Criticism and Rationalistic Criticism,

---

* *Entwurf einer Einleit.*, 3d Edit. *Entwurf ein. hist.-krit. Einleit.*, 1806.
† P. 328.   ‡ *Scholia*, 1795, i., pp. 7-12.   § In Edition iii., 1821.
‖ *Entdeckungen im Felde der ältesten Erd-u.-Menschengeschichte*.
¶ *Int. ad Vet. Foed.* 1793, pp. 209-224.   ** Paulus, *Repert.* iii., p. 180.
†† *Über d. allmählige Bildung*, etc., in Henke's *Magazin*, ii., 433, iv, 1-36 (p. 30).

not discriminating between those who were attacking the Scriptures in order to destroy them, and those who were *searching* the Scriptures, in order to defend them. Mozley says: * "There was hardly such a thing as Biblical Criticism in this country (Great Britain) at the beginning of this century. Poole's Synopsis contained all that an ordinary clergyman could wish to know. Arnold is described as in all his glory at Rugby, with Poole's Synopsis on one side and Facciolati on the other."

Thus Bishop Marsh, in 1792, in a brief address at Cambridge,† takes the position:

"The Pentateuch contains a system of ceremonial and moral laws which, unless we reject the authority of *all* history, were observed by the Israelites from the time of their departure out of Egypt till their dispersion at the taking of Jerusalem. These *laws*, therefore, are as ancient as the conquest of Palestine. It is also an undeniable historical fact that the Jews in every age believed their ancestors had received them from the hands of Moses, and that these laws were the basis of their political and religious institutions as long as they continued to be a people. We are therefore reduced to this dilemma, to acknowledge either that these laws were actually delivered by Moses, or that a whole nation, during fifteen hundred years, groaned under the weight of an imposture, without once detecting or even suspecting the fraud" (p. 7).

This statement is, in part, quoted and approved by Horne in his Introduction.‡ But it is a weak position; indeed, the chief fault of the traditional theory, as we shall have occasion hereafter to show. The evidence from the Scriptures is all to the effect that these laws were *not* observed, and any argument for the composition of the Pentateuch that rests upon their observance " from the

---

* *Reminiscences*, 1882, American edit. ii, p. 41.
† *The Authenticity of the Five Books of Moses*, 4to, p. 16.
‡ Vol. ii. 19, 1st edit. 1818.

time of the departure out of Egypt till their dispersement," is an insecure argument. Bishop Marsh acknowledges a few alterations in the Pentateuch, "a circumstance at which we ought not to be surprised, when we reflect on the many thousands of transcripts that have been made from it in the course of three thousand years."* Faber† says: "At any one epoch during the whole existence of the Hebrew Polity, it would have been just as impossible to introduce a new and spurious Pentateuch, as it would be now impossible to introduce a new and spurious Bible. In each case the reason is the very same, the *general publicity of the book*."‡ "The general publicity" of the Pentateuch from the conquest to the exile is opposed by strong evidence to the contrary, as we shall see hereafter. T. Hartwell Horne, in 1818, issued his *Introduction to the Critical Study and Knowledge of the Holy Scriptures*, which passed through many editions,§ and has been highly esteemed for its many excellent qualities by several generations of students. Horne's statement in the Preface to the second edition of his work shows how far Great Britain was behind the continent at that time. He says:

"It (the work) originated in the author's own wants many years since, ... when he stood in need of a guide in reading of the Holy Scriptures. . . . . At this time the author had no friend to assist his studies,—or remove his doubts,—nor any means of procuring critical works. At length a list of the more eminent foreign Biblical critics fell into his hands, and directed him to some of the sources of information which he was seeking. He then resolved to procure such of them as his humble means would permit, with the design in the first instance of sat-

---

* Page 16. † *Horæ Mosaicæ*, 1801, 2d edit., 1818.
‡ An unknown reader of the copy we have examined, writes on the margin: "? 2 Chron. xxxiv. 14."
§ 4th, 1823; 10th, 1856.

isfying his own mind on those topics which had perplexed him, and ultimately of laying before the public the results of his inquiries, should no treatise appear that might supersede such a publication."

It is evident from Horne's work that he wrote it before he had fully read the literature of his subject, and before he had mastered its principles and its details. Horne passes lightly over the views of Eichhorn, simply remarking:

"On the Continent the hypothesis of Calmet was adopted by M. Astruc, who fancied that he discovered traces of *twelve* different ancient documents from which the earlier chapters of Exodus as well as the entire book of Genesis are compiled. These, however, were reduced by Eichhorn to two in number, which he affirms may be distinguished by the appellations of Elohim and Jehovah, given to the Almighty. The hypothesis of Eichhorn is adopted by Rosenmüller (from whom it was borrowed by the late Dr. Geddes), and is partially acceded to by Jahn. To this hypothesis there is but one objection, and we apprehend that it is a fatal one, namely, the *total silence* of Moses as to any documents consulted by him. . . . . Should the reader, however, be disposed to adopt the hypothesis of Calmet without the refinements of Eichhorn and his followers, this will not, in the smallest degree, detract from the divine authority of the book of Genesis." (vol. ii., p. 31, first edition.)

He also makes the following argument:

"Moreover, that the Pentateuch was extant in the time of David, is evident from the very numerous allusions made in his psalms to its contents; but it could not have been drawn up by him, since the law contained in the Pentateuch forbids many practices of which David was guilty." (4th edit., vol. i., p. 54.)

Little did he anticipate how soon the arguments from *silence* and from *violation* of law upon which he relies, would be turned against the Mosaic authorship of the Pentateuch, and prove so difficult to answer. Little did he and Bishop Marsh imagine that their main argument, "*the observance of the law from the conquest till the exile*," would prove the special weakness of the traditional theory.

Horne refers above to the Roman Catholic divine, Dr. Alex. Geddes, as holding the view of Eichhorn; but in fact Geddes differs radically from Eichhorn and his school, and is the real father of a variant theory of the composition of the Pentateuch, which has been called the fragmentary hypothesis. Thus Dr. Geddes says:*

"It has been well observed by Michaelis that all external testimony here is of little avail; it is from intrinsic evidence only that we must derive our proofs. Now, from intrinsic evidence, three things, to me, seem indubitable: (1) The Pentateuch in its present form was not written by Moses. (2) It was written in the land of Chanaan, and most probably at Jerusalem. (3) It could not be written before the reign of David, nor after that of Hezekiah. The long pacific reign of Solomon (the Augustan age of Judea) is the period to which I would refer it; yet I confess there are some marks of a posterior date, or at least of posterior interpolation. But although I am inclined to believe that the Pentateuch was reduced into its present form in the reign of Solomon, I am fully persuaded that it was compiled from ancient documents, some of which were coeval with Moses, and some even anterior to Moses. Whether all these were written records or many of them only oral traditions, it would be rash to determine." Also p. xxi.: "To the Pentateuch I have joined the book of Joshua, both because I conceive it to have been compiled by the same author, and because it is a necessary appendix to the history contained in the former books."

The fragmentary hypothesis of Geddes was introduced into Germany by Vater.† Vater's view is that the Pen-

---

* *The Holy Bible; or, The Books Accounted Sacred by Jews and Christians*, etc., *faithfully translated*, etc. London, 1792, vol. i., p. xviii.

† *Commentar über den Pentateuch mit Einleitungen zu den einzelnen Abschnitten, der eingeschalteten Übersetzung von Dr. Alexander Geddes's merkwürdigeren kritischen und exegetischen Anmerkungen*, etc. Halle, 1805.

tateuch and Book of Joshua are composed of a great number of separate fragments of different authors, loosely joined by a collector.* He puts the greater part of Deuteronomy at least as early as the Davidic age, but the composition of our Pentateuch toward the time of the exile.† Calling attention to the discrepancies in the codes of legislation and the non-observance of them in the history of Israel, he makes the important statement:

"Still in later times we find the most important laws of the Mosaic constitution either unknown or at least unobserved, so that the conclusion may be drawn therefrom that either the Pentateuch was not there, or at least not yet in its present extent the book of religion that was regarded as generally obligatory, which it must have been if it had been esteemed as such from the times of Moses." III., p. 652.

Vater takes the first alternative of the non-existence of the books. His other alternative was not sufficiently considered by himself or by others. The fragmentary hypothesis was also advocated by A. T. Hartmann,‡ Von Böhlen,§ and others. It was a radical and destructive theory, that called forth the determined opposition of all earnest men, and it was soon overthrown.

Comparing this fragmentary hypothesis of Geddes and others with the documentary hypothesis of Eichhorn's school and the Rabbinical view as advocated by Marsh and Horne, we remark that the documentary hypothesis of the school of Eichhorn, notwithstanding serious defects, is in the midst of two extremes. It gave the best solution of the facts that had been discovered in those times. The documentary hypothesis found representa-

---

* III., p. 504. † III., p. 680.
‡ *Historisch-krit. Forschungen*, 1831.
§ *Die Genesis historisch-krit. erläutert*, 1835.

THE DOCUMENTARY HYPOTHESIS

tion in Great Britain and America in Taylor's edition of Calmet's Dictionary of the Holy Bible,* and in the American edition by Edward Robinson in 1835. Taylor's statement, as revised by Robinson, is the following:

"It may be admitted, for instance, (1) that the Book of Genesis contains various repetitions or double narratives of the same early events; (2) that these duplicate narratives, when closely compared, present characteristic differences of style; (3) that these differences are too considerable and too distinct to admit of any other explanation than that of different originals, taken into association."

---

* Edition of 1832.

VI.

THE SUPPLEMENTARY HYPOTHESIS.

THIS stadium is characterized by the effort to determine the *genesis* of the various documents constituting the Pentateuch. De Wette is the man who chiefly influences the discussion.*

Reviewing the previous stadium Merx properly remarks that both the fragmentary and documentary hypotheses

—" have this in common that they seek to attain their aim chiefly by the way of Literary Criticism, and neglect or use only as a subsidiary help, the realistic, antiquarian and historical criticism of the contents of the Pentateuch. This element De Wette chiefly brought into the scientific investigation in his *Kritik der israelitischen Geschichte*, Halle, 1807."—P. lxxxii. of 2d Aufl. of Tuch's *Com. über Genesis*, Halle, 1871.

At first hovering between the documentary hypothesis of Eichhorn and the fragmentary hypothesis of Geddes, recognizing the features of truth and of error in them both, De Wette at last rises above them and presses for the *unity* of the Pentateuch in its present

---

* For an excellent account of the criticism of this stadium see the valuable articles of Prof. F. A. Gast, D.D., on Pentateuch Criticism, in the April and July Numbers of the *Reformed Quarterly Review*, 1882; also *Nachwort*, by Merx in 2d Aufl. of Tuch's *Genesis*, 1871, p. lxxviii. *sq.*, etc.

form as the *plan* of one mind. He first stated that Deuteronomy is an independent part of the Pentateuch, composed in the age of Josiah.* He subsequently adopted into his system the improvements suggested by other Biblical scholars who followed in his footsteps.†

In 1824 Bleek‡ adopted the view of Geddes and Vater, that the death of Moses was not the proper close of the history begun in Genesis, but that it aimed at the occupation of the Holy Land, and that the Book of Joshua therefore belonged with the Pentateuch, so that these should rather be considered as a Hexateuch. Bleek was the first to give shape to what has been called the *supplementary* hypothesis. He made the Elohist original and fundamental, the Jahvist the supplementer. Bleek also advanced in his position by subsequent investigations of himself and others. His final statement is presented in his posthumous Lectures on Introduction, 1860.§

In 1823 Ewald ‖ also insisted upon the *unity* of Genesis over against the fragmentary hypothesis, and in 1831,¶ showed that the Elohistic and Jahvistic documents extended through the *entire Pentateuch*. Soon after, the same was found to be the case with Joshua, and the unity of the Hexateuch in the midst of the diversity of documents was made manifest.

Over against these critical investigations the traditional theory was advocated by Ranke,** who sharply and successfully attacked the fragmentary hypothesis,

---

* 1805, *Dissert. zur Deut.*; 1806-7, *Beitr. zur Einleit.*; 1817, *Lehrb. d. hist.-krit. Einleitung.* 2d edition, trans. by Theo. Parker, Boston, 1843.

† 6th Aufl. *Einleit.* 1844. 7th, 1852.

‡ Rosenm., *Bib. Exeget. Repert. I.*

§ The 2d edition was translated into English by G. H. Venables, 1865.

‖ *Composition der Genesis*, 1823.

¶ *Stud. und Krit.* in a review of Stähelin on Genesis, 602 *sq.*

** *Untersuchungen*, 1834-40.

but did not squarely meet the position of the school of De Wette. Hengstenberg * made war upon the distinction of documents and sought to efface the differences by his theory of an intentional change of the divine names in accordance with their essential meaning and the circumstances of the case. Kurtz also † took a similar position, which, however, he subsequently abandoned.‡ Drechsler § also sharply attacked the methods of the Higher Criticism. But the ablest work on the scholastic side was produced by Hävernick.‖ Hävernick sturdily maintained the Rabbinical view after Carpzov and Heidegger, and declined to make concessions as to variety of documents in the Pentateuch. This revival of traditional views was very strong, and powerful efforts were put forth to overcome the advancing critics, but in vain, for it died away essentially with these distinguished champions. Kurtz soon went over to an intermediate position. Keil, in 1854, took up the work of Hävernick, but without any appreciable effect upon the discussion so far as Germany is concerned. In 1866 it was the author's privilege to study with Hengstenberg in the University of Berlin. His studies were at first chiefly on the traditional side. He can say that he worked over the chief authorities on that side, and they had all the advantages of his predilections in their favor. But Hengstenberg himself convinced him in his own lecture-room that he was defending a lost cause. He then turned away from the study of the Pentateuch and

---

* *Beiträge zur Einleitung ins Alte Testament:* Bd. ii.-iii., *Die Authentie des Pentateuchs*, 1836-39.

† *Beiträge*, 1844, and *Einheit der Genesis*, 1846.

‡ *Gesch. d. Alt. Bundes*, 1848, 2d Ed. 1864.

§ *Unwissenschaft. d. Kritik*, 1837.

‖ *Hist.-krit. Einleit.*, 1836. (2te Aufl. by Keil, 1854).

the Historical books and devoted himself to the study of the Poetical and Prophetical books, under the guidance of Roediger, and it was not until his fourth year in Germany that he returned to the study of the Pentateuch, and then worked under the guidance chiefly of Ewald. His experience corresponds with that of many other students of his time. We yielded against our wishes to insuperable arguments, and when compelled to adopt the analysis of the Hexateuch reserved our decision on the date of the documents until these could be definitely determined. Hengstenberg was the last great champion of traditionalism in the Old Testament. His successor, August Dillmann, a pupil of Ewald, has been the most painstaking critic of our times. Hermann Strack said in 1882 :* " Keil is now about the only prominent Old Testament scholar who holds to the Mosaic authorship of the entire Pentateuch." Keil died soon afterwards, and with him scholarly opposition ceased in Germany.

A more careful analysis of Genesis was undertaken by Tuch,† and this was extended by Stähelin to the entire Pentateuch.‡ Hupfeld § took up the analysis of Genesis, and, unaware of the work of Ilgen, came independently to essentially the same results, only that in his exceedingly careful discrimination of the various documents he made it clear that there were Elohist, 2d Elohist, Jahvist, and Redactor; the Redactor, differing from the other three, in that he is distinguished for the conscientiousness with which he reproduces the ancient documents, word for word, and the skill with which he combines them in the unity and order which characterize

---

* *Handb. d. Theol. Wissensch.*, 1882, I.　　† *Comm. ü. d. Genesis*, 1838.
‡ *Krit. Unters. in Genesis*, 1830. *Krit. Unters.*, 1843. *Specielle Einleit.*, 1862.
§ *Quellen d. Genesis*, 1853.

his work. This was a very great gain. Knobel* analyzed the Hexateuch and made the Elohist the fundamental writing, and found two other documents used by the Jahvistic supplementer, and combined with it. Ewald † gave a new turn to the question by taking the Elohistic document as the Book of Origins. This gathered into itself three older writings in part: the book of the wars of Yahweh, a biography of Moses, and the book of the Covenants, having the design to trace the history from the creation of the world until the erection of the temple of Solomon. It was composed in the first third of the reign of Solomon. The second Elohist is the third narrator, in the age of Elijah and Joel. The Jahvist is the fourth narrator, in the eighth century. The Redactor is the fifth narrator, who worked up the entire Hexateuch except Lev. xxvi. 3–45, Deut. i. 1—xxii. 47, xxxiv. 11–12, and xxxiii., which were three separate writings subsequently united with it. The Deuteronomist wrote his work in the second half of the reign of Manasseh. The last work upon the Pentateuch was done by the author of Deut. xxxiii. shortly before the destruction of Jerusalem. Thus our Pentateuch, in the course of centuries, gradually grew into its present form.‡

It became more and more evident that the problem was to determine the work of the Redactor. E. Böhmer§ followed Hupfeld and sought to define more

---

* *Comm. Gen.*, 1852, (2te *Aufl.*, 1860). *Exod. und Levit.*, 1857. *Krit. des Pent. und Josh.*, 1861.

† *Gesch. des Volkes Israel*, 1843-52. 2 Bde. 3te Ausg. 7 Bde., 1864–68, Bd. I., p. 94 *f.*

‡ We cannot pause to give the reasons of Ewald for his positions or to criticise them. We may remark that his positions are carefully taken and justified by plausible evidences. We will consider the most important of them in our criticism of the theories of this stadium as a whole.

§ *Liber Genesis Pent.*, 1860, *Das erste Buch d. Torah*, 1862.

THE SUPPLEMENTARY HYPOTHESIS

exactly the Redactor's part. Nöldeke * examined the Elohist with the utmost exactness, and represented it as a systematic work by itself, to a very large extent preserved in the Pentateuch. He held that it was written by a priest at Jerusalem in the ninth or tenth century B.C. Other materials were used by the Jehovist, especially the work of the second Elohist, from about the same time as the first Elohist. The Redactor, about 800 B.C., united the two together. In the reign of Josiah, the Deuteronomist added his book and worked over Joshua and gave the Pentateuch its present form.

Schrader † introduced the more recent investigations into the scheme of De Wette, and combined the documentary and supplementary hypotheses as follows: There are two chief documents: the Annalistic (Elohist) and Theocratic (2d Elohist), composed, the former in in the earlier part of the reign of David, the author a priest who used earlier written sources; the latter soon after the division of the kingdom in the northern realm, 975-950 B.C., also using ancient documents. The third prophetic narrator (Jehovist) combined the two, freely appropriating, and rejecting, and enlarging by numerous additions, making a complete and harmonious work, in the reign of Jeroboam II., 825-800 B.C., in the northern kingdom. The Deuteronomist in the prophetic spirit composed the law of Moses contained in Deuteronomy, and became the final *redactor* of the Pentateuch in its present form, immediately before the reform of Josiah, 622 B.C., being a man closely associated with the prophet Jeremiah. Schrader briefly and clearly sums up the various characteristic differences in the

---

* *Alttest. Lit.*, 1868, *Untersuch.*, 1869.
† 8th edition of De Wette's *Einleit.*, 1869.

documents: (1) a thoroughgoing difference of language; (2) a striking difference in style; (3) difference in religious conceptions; (4) discrepancy in historical statements; (5) difference of plan and method of narration.

The supplementary hypothesis passed over into England through Samuel Davidson.* Davidson places the Elohist, a Levite in Judah, in the time of Saul; the 2d Elohist in the time of Elisha, 880 B.C.; the Jehovist in the reign of Uzziah. These three were combined by a Redactor, "with considerable independence, adding occasionally a connecting link, omitting what seemed to stand in the way of the connection, abridging in different modes, and transposing pieces according to his own view." † The date of the completion of the Pentateuch coincides with the composition of Deuteronomy in the reign of Manasseh, whose author is also responsible for the present form of Joshua.‡ Dr. Perowne also adopted it in a mediating way; § Dean Stanley unreservedly,‖ and others in various forms.

---

* *Introduction to the Old Testament*, 1862.
† P. 51. ‡ Pp. 131 and 421.
§ "So far then the direct evidence from the Pentateuch itself is not sufficient to establish the Mosaic authorship of every portion of the five books. Certain parts of Ex., Lev., and Numbers, and the whole of Deut. to the end of chap. xxx., is all that is expressly said to have been written by Moses." "There is, therefore, it seems, good ground for concluding that, besides some smaller independent documents, traces may be discovered of two original historical works which form the basis of the Book of Genesis and of the earlier chapters of Exodus. Of these there can be no doubt that the Elohistic is the earlier." "On carefully weighing all the evidence hitherto adduced, we can hardly question without a literary scepticism which would be most unreasonable, that the Pentateuch is, to a very large extent, as early as the time of Moses, though it may have undergone many later revisions and corrections, the last of these being certainly as late as the time of Ezra. But as regards any direct and unimpeachable testimony to the composition of the whole work by Moses, we have it not."—Smith's *Dictionary of the Bible*, article, *Pentateuch*, 1863.

‖ *Lectures on the History of the Jewish Church*, Part II., p. 648. N. Y., 1869.

Delitzsch, Kurtz, and Kleinert, in Germany, also strove to mediate. Delitzsch* held that the legislation of Exodus, Leviticus, and Numbers was Mosaic legislation, but the codification of the various laws was made by a man like Eleazar, in the Holy Land after the conquest, who became the author of the Elohistic document. Joshua, or one of the elders, supplemented this work as the Jehovist, taking Moses' Book of Deuteronomy and incorporating it with the rest. Kurtz † abandoned his previous defence of the traditional theory, and took the ground that the two streams of history in the Pentateuch must be distinguished. He agreed with Delitzsch in the main, save that he put the codification of the various laws of the middle books by a man like Eleazar in the land of Moab. Kleinert ‡ maintained that the codification of the Deuteronomic law took place in the time of Samuel,§ and that it was set in its historical rim with the other discourses and songs by Samuel, the great reformer.∥ The redaction of our Pentateuch was placed in the time of Hezekiah.¶ Lange ** also took a mediating position.

In a critical examination of the supplementary hypothesis we must distinguish between the theory and the facts upon which it is grounded. We should not allow ourselves to be influenced by the circumstance that many of the scholars who have been engaged in these researches have been rationalistic or semi-rationalistic in their religious opinions; and that they have employed

---

* *Comm. on Genesis*, 1852. 3d edit., 1860. 4th ed., 1872.
† *Gesch. des Alten Bundes*, 1855, Bd. iii., p. 554.
‡ *Deuteronomium und der Deuteronomiker*, 1872.
§ P. 153. ∥ P. 242. ¶ P. 247.
** *Commentary on Genesis*. American 4th edition, 1870, p. 98. *Commentary on Exodus and Leviticus*, 1876, p. 10.

the methods and styles peculiar to the German scholarship of our century. Whatever may have been the motives and influences that led to these investigations, the questions we have to determine are: (1) What are the facts of the case? and (2) do the theories account for the facts?

(1). Looking at the facts of the case we note that the careful analysis of the Hexateuch by so large a number of the ablest Biblical scholars of the age has brought about general agreement as to the following points:

(*a*) An Elohistic writing extending through the Hexateuch, written by a priestly writer, commonly therefore designated by P. (*b*) A Jahvistic writing, also extending through the Hexateuch, designated by J. (*c*) A second Elohistic writing in close connection with the Jahvist, designated by E. (*d*) The Deuteronomic writing, chiefly in Deuteronomy and Joshua, with a few traces in the earlier books, designated by D. (*e*) These writings have been compacted by redactors who first combined J with E, then JE with D, and at last JED with P. Notwithstanding the careful way in which these documents have been compacted into a higher unity by these successive editings, the documents may be distinguished by characteristic differences, not only in the use of the divine names, but also in language and style; in religious, doctrinal and moral conceptions; in various interpretations of the same historic persons and events, and in their plans and methods of composition; differences which are no less striking than those which characterize the four Gospels.

VII.

THE ANALYSIS OF THE HEXATEUCH.

WE shall pause at this stage of the historical development of the Higher Criticism of the Hexateuch, in order to present some of the arguments for the differences of documents. We would refer to the valuable work of Prof. Kautzsch, of Halle, who presents all these documents and the work of the several editors, so far as they can be determined, by differences of type throughout the Hexateuch.*

I.—*The Argument from Language.*

The argument from language may be found in the detailed examination of the whole Hexateuch in the commentaries of Professor Dillmann of the University of Berlin;† and in the *Introduction to the Literature of the Old Testament*, recently published by Canon Driver, Regius Professor of Hebrew at Oxford, in the *International Theological Library*. Canon Driver gives a list of 41 characteristic phrases of D; 50 characteristic phrases of P; and 20 characteristic phrases of H, the code of holi-

---

* *Die Heilige Schrift des Alten Testaments.* Erster Halbband, Freiburg, 1892.

† *Kurzgefasstes exegetisches Handbuch zum Alten Testament, Die Genesis,* 5te Aufl., 1886. *Die Bücher Exodus und Leviticus,* 2te Aufl., 1880, *Die Bücher Numeri, Deuteronomium und Josua,* 2te Aufl., 1886.

ness which was eventually taken up into P, but for the most part remaining apart in the middle chapters of Leviticus. In the exhaustive word-study, necessary to the preparation of the new Hebrew Lexicon, evidence of this kind is constantly disclosing itself. It is impracticable to use such a vast amount of evidence in this volume. It will suffice to give a number of specimens of the usage of J E, and a few of the usage of the other documents. In the Appendix the word lists of Driver may be seen, showing the characteristics of D, H, and P.*

(1). The month *Abib* is used in J E D, Ex. xiii. 4, xxiii. 15, xxxiv. 18, 18; Dt. xvi. 1, 1;—but not in P, which uses instead "*the first month*," Ex. xii. 2, 18, xl. 2, 17; Lev. xxiii. 5; Nu. ix. 1, xxviii. 16, xxxiii. 3; for which *Nisan* in Ne. ii. 1, Est. iii. 7.

(2). אֲדָמָה is a characteristic word of J, used very often for the ground as tilled and yielding sustenance, as landed property, as material substance out of which things are made; as territory, and of the earth as inhabited. In these senses it is used less frequently by E D; but never by P, who uses אֶרֶץ instead. P uses אֲדָמָה only four times, and in these passages of the earth's visible surface, Gn. i. 25, vi. 20; Lev. xx. 25; Nu. xvi. 30.

(3). אֹכֶל *food* is used by J E D, and by P in Lev. xi. 34, xxv. 37, but אׇכְלָה is used only by P and Ezekiel.

(4). אָמָה *handmaid* is used in E 16 t, H 3 t, D 8 t, for which שִׁפְחָה is used by J and P.

(5). אׇמְנָה and אׇמְנָם *verily* are used by J E, for which D and P use אָמֵן.

(6). *Amorite*, as the general name of the ancient pop-

---
* See Appendix II.

ulation of both West and East Palestine, is used by E, Gn. xv. 16, xlviii. 22; Nu. xxi. 21, 31 f., Jos. xxiv. 8, 12, 15, 18, for which J prefers Canaanite, Gn. xii. 6, xiii. 7, xxiv. 3, 37, xxxiv. 30.

(7). The first personal pronoun אָנֹכִי is used in D, except twice; in J E by preference (אָנֹכִי 81 times, אֲנִי 48 times), due in large measure to E, which prefers it. But the shorter form אֲנִי is used in H and P about 130 times (always except Gn. xxiii. 4). This corresponds with Ezekiel, who uses it 138 times and אָנֹכִי only xxxvi. 28; the Chronicler, who uses it 30 times and אָנֹכִי only 1 Ch. xvii. 1; and Daniel, who uses it 23 times and אָנֹכִי only in x. 11. These exceptions are doubtless due to scribal error.

(8). בְּלִי with finite verb only in Gn. xxxi. 20 (E).

(9). בַּעַל *owner, husband, lord*, and as noun of relation, and *Baal*, the Canaanitish god, is often used by E and D, but never used by J H P.

(10). בָּעַר *to be brutish*, twice in E and בַּעִיר *brute*, 5 times in E, not elsewhere in Hexateuch.

(11). בָּשָׂר in the meaning of *body*, is used only in P of the Hexateuch, elsewhere in Ecclesiastes, and in Poetry.

(12). גֵּרֵשׁ *to drive out*, in J E not elsewhere in the Hexateuch.

(13). דִּבֶּר אֶת *speak with*, in P 19 times, E 5 times, D once, in J never used. J uses instead דִּבֶּר עִם, so in J E 11 times, D twice, but P never uses it.

(14). דְּמוּת *likeness, similitude*, is used in P and Ezekiel, elsewhere in the Bible only in the exilic Isaiah, xiii. 4, xl. 18; 2 K. xvi. 10; 2 Ch. iv. 3; Ps. lviii. 5; Dan. x. 16.

(15). דְּרוֹר *a flowing, liberty*, only in P of the Hexateuch, Ex. xxx. 23; Lv. xxv. 10; elsewhere Jer. xxxiv. 8, 15, 17; Is. lxi. 1; Ez. xlvi. 17.

(16). חָזָה *behold*, is only in E in the Hexateuch; elsewhere chiefly in Job, Psalms, and Isaiah.

(17). חֲטָאָה *sin*, Gn. xx. 9 (E); Ex. xxxii. 21, 30, 31 (J); elsewhere only 2 Kings xvii. 21; Pss. xxxii. 1; xl. 7, cix. 7.

(18). עוֹד חַי Gn. xxv. 6, xliii. 7, 27, 28, xlv. 28, xlvi. 30 (J); Gn. xlv. 3, 26; Ex. iv. 18 (E); Dt. xxxi. 27;—but not in H or P; elsewhere only 1 Sam. xx. 14; 2 Sam. xii. 22, xviii. 14; 1 K. xx. 32.

(19). יָרָה *cast, throw, shoot*, only in JE of Hexateuch, Gn. xxxi. 51; Ex. xv. 4, xix. 13; Nu. xxi. 30; Jos. xviii. 6; but as Hiphil, *to teach*, in all the documents.

(20.) The shorter form לֵב is always used in J and P, the longer form לֵבָב is always used in the law codes of D and H. In E the usage is mixed.

(21). מַרְאָה in the meaning, *vision*, in the Hexateuch only in E, Gn. xlvi. 2; Nu. xii. 6; elsewhere 1 Sam. iii. 15; Ez. i. 1, viii. 3, xl. 2, xliii. 3, Dn. x. 7–16.

(22). The phrases יְפַת מַרְאֶה, Gn. xii. 11, xxix. 17 (J); 2 Sam. xiv. 27; יְפֵה מַרְאֶה, יְפוֹת (הַ)מַרְאֶה, Gn. xli. 2, 4; Gn. xxxix. 6, 1 Sam. xvii. 42; טוֹבַת מַרְאֶה, Gn. xxiv. 16, xxvi. 7 (J); 2 Sam. xi. 2, Est. i. 11, ii. 2, 3, 7; טוֹבֵי מַרְאֶה, Dn. i. 4; נֶחְמָד לְמַרְאֶה, Gn. ii. 9 (J), not found elsewhere.

(23). מְלָאכָה in the meaning, *business, occupation*, is used in Gn. xxxix. 11 (J); in the meaning *property*, Ex. xxii. 7, 10 (E), Gn. xxxiii. 14 (J); but in the sense of

THE ANALYSIS OF THE HEXATEUCH

work, it is frequent in P and the Chronicler; elsewhere in the Hexateuch only in the reason of the Fourth Commandment, Ex. xx. 9, 10, =Dt. v. 13, 14, and Dt. xvi. 8.

(24). נְשָׁמָה *breath*, Gn. ii. 7, vii. 22 (J) and כָּל־(ה)נְשָׁמָה *every breathing thing*, Dt. xx. 16; Jos. x. 40, xi. 11, 14 (all D); neither elsewhere in the Hexateuch.

(25). צָבָא *serve*, 3 times in P, not elsewhere in Hexateuch.

צָבָא *war*, 13 times in P, יצא צבא 15 times in P, 5 times in Chronicles; *service*, P, 8 times; elsewhere in Hexateuch only Dt. xxiv. 5, Jos. iv. 13 (D); in the meaning *army, host*, 47 times in P, 23 times in Chronicler; elsewhere in Hexateuch, Gn. xxi. 22, 32 (E), xxvi. 26 (J), Jos. v. 14, 15; of heavenly bodies, twice in P; of the entire creation, Gn. ii. 1 (P).

(26). מַטֶּה *tribe*, is used by P about 100 times: J uses שֵׁבֶט instead.

(27). J uses the Qal ילד *beget*; but P uses instead the Hiphil הוליד 60 times.

(28). The Mount of the Lawgiving is called *Horeb* in E and D, but *Sinai* in J and P.

(29). E uses a large number of archaic words such as נְתֹן Nu. xx. 21 for תֵּת; עֲשֹׂר Gn. xxxi. 28, עָשֹׂה Gn. l. 20, עֲשֹׂהוּ Ex. xviii. 18 for עֲשֹׂתוֹ, עֲשׂוֹת; הֲלֹךְ Ex. iii. 19, Nu. xxii. 13, 16, for לֶכֶת; רָדָה Gn. xlvi. 3 for רֶדֶת; דֵּעָה Ex. ii. 4 for דַּעַת.

These are only specimens of a vast array of words. Many others will appear when we come to the argument from Religion and Doctrine.*

---

* See pp. 101 *seq.*, 149 *seq.*

Each of the four writers has his favorite words and phrases. They all use essentially the same vocabulary, because they use the same language and the same dialect, with the exception of E, who shows traces of an occasional use of the Ephraimitic dialect; but there are certain terms and phrases which are characteristic of each. Dr. Green, in his recent book on the *Hebrew Feasts*, misrepresents this line of argument. He thinks that he has disproved the difference of style between the several authors compacted in Ex. xii.–xiii., by pointing to an occasional use of the favorite words of one author by another author. But this is an avoidance of the question at issue. Those who are in the habit of using the methods of the Higher Criticism, whether in the study of the classics, of the Vedas, of the ecclesiastical writers, or of Shakespeare, know very well that there is an ascending scale in the use of words and phrases when we compare author with author in any language. (1). The great majority of words and phrases are the common stock of the language used by all. (2). The same theme leads to the use of similar words and phrases. (3). Differences begin in the percentage of use of certain words and phrases. That which is occasional with one writer is common with another, and the reverse. (4). There are a few words and expressions which are peculiar to certain authors, used by one author and avoided by other authors.

II.—*Difference of Style.*

It is agreed among critics that E is brief, terse, and archaic in his style. J is poetic and descriptive—as Wellhausen says, "the best narrator in the Bible." His imagination and fancy are ever active. P is annalistic and diffuse—fond of names and dates. He aims at

precision and completeness. The logical faculty prevails.
There is little color. D is rhetorical and hortatory,
practical and earnest. His aim is instruction and guidance. This difference of style was noted by Simon, and
has been carefully traced by criticism in our day. There
are those who try to explain away this difference as occasioned by the difference of theme, but this does not
account for the difference of style in the parallel treatment of the same theme. And then the differences of
style are alongside of the differences in the use of words
and phrases and the divine names. There is as great
a difference in style between the different documents of
the Hexateuch as there is between the four Gospels.
Kautzsch and Socin have recently presented the different documents of Genesis in different kinds of type.*
Bacon has exhibited them apart by themselves.†

III.—*Parallel Narratives.*

Another line of evidence is the very large number of
doublets and triplets. (1). There are two accounts of
the creation which have recently been discovered to be
two ancient poems. In the Pentameter poem, Gen. i.,
God creates by speaking. He is conceived as a commander of an army, summoning his troops into the field,
line upon line, until they all stand before him for review,
an organized host. In the Trimeter poem, Gn. ii., there
is a rapid change of image. God uses His hands in creation. He plants the garden in Eden as a gardener.
He moulds the forms of men and animals out of the soil
of the ground like a sculptor. He builds the form of Eve
from a piece of the body of man like a builder.

In the Pentameter poem the divine Spirit is conceived

---

* *Die Genesis mit äusserer Unterscheidung der Quellenschriften*, 1888.
† *The Genesis of Genesis*, 1891.

as a bird hovering over the original chaos with creative energy. In the Trimeter poem God's breath, proceeding from the divine nostrils into the nostrils of the creatures, imparts the breath of life.

In the Pentameter poem a waste, an empty abyss, is conceived as prior to the first creative word, and light appears as the first of God's creations to fill this abyss with illumination. In the Trimeter poem a rainless ground without vegetable and animal life is conceived as prior to the first divine activity which was forming a single man, Adam. The order of creation is different. In the Pentameter poem six orders of creation appear instantaneously in obedience to the creative word on the mornings of six creative days: (1). Light, (2). Expanse, (3). Dry land and vegetables, (4). The great luminaries, (5). Animals of water and air, (6). Land animals and mankind.

In the Trimeter poem, the ground is conceived as already existing, the great luminaries are left out of consideration, and the order is (1), Adam; (2), trees; (3), animals; and (4), Eve. The result of the divine inspection differs greatly in the two poems. In the Pentameter poem, as each order appears, it is recognized as "good" and is then assigned its service. The review concludes with the approbation, "very excellent." In the Trimeter poem, which proposes to give the origin and development of sin, we notice a striking antithesis to the "good" and "very good" of the six days' work. Thus it was not good to eat of the prohibited tree of knowledge of good and evil. "It was not good that the man should be alone." And the animals were not good for man. "But for man there was not found an helpmeet for him." The time of the Pentameter poem was six creative days. The time of the Trimeter was a day, unless we conceive that "day" has the more general sense of the time when. In the Pentameter, mankind was created male and female, a species alongside of the species of animals. In the Trimeter, first a man, then after the trees and animals a woman, and a plurality of men and women only after two great tragedies of sin. When God reviews His organized host, according to the Pentameter poem, He looks approvingly on mankind, male and female, a race whom He had just created, and pronounces them at the head and crown of all His creations, "very excellent." But according to the Trimeter poem, God looks upon mankind, male and female, as a race, only as very evil, after Adam and Eve have sinned, after Cain has killed his brother Abel, after mankind has become a race in the Sethite line of redemption and in the accursed line of Cain. Add to these material facts, this additional one that the verb *bārā*, in the Pentameter poem, is a word seldom used except in P, and the second Isaiah in the Qal species. The Trimeter poem uses *āsah* for it in accordance with the usage of J elsewhere, and of all the earlier writers. To these evidences we might add the evidences from vocabulary and style which may be found in the critical commentaries. How any one can look these facts in the face and say that these two accounts of the creation came from one and the same writer, Moses, it is difficult to understand.

(2). There are two narratives of the Deluge, also two poems of different movements skilfully compacted by the redactor from J and P, so that both pieces are preserved almost complete. These give variant accounts of the deluge and differ in style, poetical structure and their descriptions; and they agree in general in vocabulary and style with the corresponding poems of J and P relating to the creation.

(3). There are two versions of the Ten Words, the one in Deuteronomy, the other in Exodus, with important differences. The version in Exodus may be analyzed and the reasons distributed among E, J and P. The version in Exodus also bears traces of the use of the Deuteronomic version, showing that it is the latest and fullest version, made by the redactor of J, E, D, and P, from the versions in the four documents. E calls these tables, tables of stone; J, tables of stone; D, tables of the covenant; P, tables of the testimony.*

(4). E and J give three stories of the peril of the wives of the patriarchs at the courts of Pharaoh and Abimelek: Gen. xii. 10-20 (J); xx. 1-13 (E); xxvi. 6-11 (J). These stories, apart from persons and places, are so alike that they may be, two of them, parallel accounts of what transpired at the court of Abimelek, the one story referring to Isaac, the other to Abraham. And it may be that the story of Abraham at the court of Pharaoh is only a third variation of the same story. With similarity of theme, there are characteristic differences in the language and style of the different narrators.

(5). Among the Egyptian plagues J reports a murrain, a cattle-pest (Ex. ix. 1-7). This seems to be a parallel plague to the "boils breaking forth with blains" of P (Ex. ix. 8-12), which come upon man and beast. These narratives exhibit the characteristic differences of these two narrators.†

(6). There are three accounts of the insect pest. The narratives of J and E are mingled in Ex. viii. 16-28. P stands by itself in Ex. viii. 11*b*-15. In J E this pest is ערב, a swarm of insects. In P it is כנם, lice. Psalm lxxviii. gives the insect swarm of J, but omits the lice of P, but Psalm cv. uses both of these terms.

---
* See Appendix III. † See Appendix IV.

(7). There are several versions of the call and blessing of Abraham in Gen. xii. 1-3 (J); xv. 4-5 (E); xvii. 1-8 (P); xxii. 15-18 (R), which show the distinctive characteristics of the narrators.

(8). According to E, Joshua set up twelve stones in the bed of the Jordan as a memorial of the crossing. (Jos. iv. 7*b*, 9). According to J, the stones from the bed of the Jordan were set up at Gilgal. (Jos. iv. 20.)

(9). The rebellion of Dathan and Abiram, the Reubenites, is referred to in Dt. xi. 6. But no mention is made of the rebellion of the Levitical Korahites. These two rebellions are combined in the narrative Num. xvi. Critical analysis, however, shows that the redactor has here combined a narrative of J E, which gives the rebellion of the Reubenites and is the basis of the story of D, with a narrative of P, which gives the story of the Korahites, which is unknown to J E, and therefore to D.

(10). There are two reports of the bringing of the water from the rock. The one, Ex. xvii., is in the wilderness of Sin, early in the wanderings; the other, Num. xx., is in the wilderness of Zin, forty years after. The former is in the narrative of J E, the latter in the narrative of P. The question thus arises whether these are not variant accounts of the same miracle, occasioned by an unconscious mistake of Sin for Zin. This is a case very much like the two stories of the cleansing of the temple by Jesus, the one in the synoptists at the last passover of Jesus, the other in the Gospel of John at the first passover. There is room for difference of opinion regarding both of these events; but whether they are different events or not, the stories being about the same essential thing, the differences between J E and P, in the report of the water from the rock, are just as great as those between John and the synoptists in the story of the cleansing of the temple.

Many other instances might be given, but so many are reserved for the discussion of the development of the legislation and for the argument as to the date of the documents, that these may suffice for the present.

VIII.

THE DATE OF DEUTERONOMY.

HAVING given some of the evidences for the Analysis of the Documents we shall now consider the question of the date of Deuteronomy. The supplementary hypothesis tried to determine the order and fix the time of the genesis or production of these various documents. The pivot of the whole is the theory of De Wette, that Deuteronomy was composed shortly before the reform of Josiah. This theory is based on the statements of 2 Kings xxii. 3 f.,* as to discovery of the lost law book. The arguments in support of this theory, as stated by the late Prof. Riehm, of Halle, are as follows:

He argues (1) that Deuteronomy was not written until some time after the conquest, by the expression "within thy gates"; the statement, ii. 12, "as Israel did unto the land of his possession, which Yahweh gave unto them"; and the ancient landmarks, xix. 14. The first and last are often explained from the prophetic point of view of the Deuteronomic code which looks forward to the prolonged occupation of the Holy Land and shapes the legislation accordingly. The middle one is explained as a redactor's note of explanation. But while these

---

* See p. 15 *seq.*

explanations might satisfy if there were no other reasons against Mosaic authorship, they more naturally indicate a long occupation of the land when the code was framed in its present form. (2). The book is pushed down to the reign of Solomon by the law of the king (xxviii. 36; compare xvii. 14–20), and its prohibition of horses and chariots and many wives. We cannot deny to Moses the conception of a future kingdom in Israel. In view of the fact that the Israelites had just come out of bondage to the king of Egypt, and that they were surrounded by nations having kings; it was natural to think of kings for Israel likewise. The subsequent provision of temporary judges or rulers called by God and endued with His Spirit, is not contemplated in the Deuteronomic code. A king would be the likely thing in the subsequent times after the conquest. If the Deuteronomic code had this ideal, such a law in the code might be regarded as appropriate. The reproof by Samuel of a subsequent desire for a king might be in view of the altered circumstances. The nation was not ripe for the kingdom, as the history of Saul clearly indicates. It was premature on the part of the people, presumptuous, and overriding the divine provision of the temporary judges or saviors. And yet while all this speculation may be true, it is not so natural an interpretation as that the law was made in view of the historic occasions for it which were first in Solomon's time, and that the law of the king was given when Israel had ripened into a kingdom.

(3). Riehm presses the composition of Deuteronomy down to the time of Jehoshaphat, by the law of the supreme judiciary at one place, Deut. xvii. 8 *seq.*, which did not exist till the time of Jehoshaphat, 2 Chron. xix. 8–11. (4). He presses it down to the time of Hezekiah on account of the one only central altar which was not realized till the time of Hezekiah, 2 Kings xviii. 4; 2 Chron. xxxi. 1; Isaiah xxxvi. 7. The facts are that the one place of judgment and the one exclusive altar were not realized until the times mentioned, as the ideal of the king was not realized until the Davidic dynasty; but do these facts disprove the promulgation of the Deuteronomic code in the land of Moab? These facts prove the non-observance of the code, the disregard of it, and possibly also ignorance of it; they favor its non-existence, but do not entirely prove it. If we could present good and sufficient reasons for the opinion that the Deuteronomic code is a prophetic ideal code, given before the conquest in view of a long sojourn of the nation in Palestine, these facts might be explained. But the difficulty is to find such reasons. Who can prove it?

(5). Riehm fixes the composition in the time of Manasseh and the reign of Psammeticus on account of the going down to Egypt in ships, Deut. xxviii. 68. The author of *Deuteronomy, the People's Book*, (London, 1877), has referred to *The Records of the Past*, (vi., p. 37,) for a statement from the time of Rameses III., which shows the equipment of fleets on the Mediterranean at that time. This was therefore quite possible for Moses to conceive of. But if the other reasons for a late date are valid this helps to give the date more closely.

Canon Driver gives additional reasons as follows:

(6). "The forms of idolatry alluded to, especially the worship of the " host of heaven " (iv. 19; xvii. 3), seem to point to the middle period of the monarchy. It is true, the worship of the sun and moon is ancient, as is attested even by the names of places in Canaan; but in the notices (which are frequent) of idolatrous practices in Judges to Kings, no mention occurs of "the host of heaven" till the period of the later kings. That the cult is *presupposed* in Dt. and not merely anticipated prophetically, seems clear from the terms in which it is referred to. While we are not in a position to affirm positively that the danger was not felt earlier, the law, as formulated in Dt., seems designed to meet the form which the cult assumed at a later age."

(7). "The influence of Dt. upon subsequent writers is clear and indisputable. It is remarkable, now, that the early prophets, Amos, Hosea, and the undisputed portions of Isaiah, show no certain traces of this influence; Jeremiah exhibits marks of it on nearly every page; Zephaniah and Ezekiel are also evidently influenced by it. If Dt. were composed in the period between Isaiah and Jeremiah, these facts would be exactly accounted for."

(8). "The *prophetic teaching* of Dt., the point of view from which the laws are presented, the principles by which conduct is estimated, presuppose a relatively advanced stage of theological reflection, as they also approximate to what is found in Jeremiah and Ezekiel."

(9). "In Dt. xvi. 22, we read, 'Thou shalt not set thee up a *mazzébah* (obelisk or pillar), which the Lord thy God hateth.' Had Isaiah known of this law he would hardly have adopted the *mazzébah* (xix. 19) as a symbol of the conversion of Egypt to the true faith. the supposition that *heathen* pillars are meant in Dt. is not favored by the context (v. 21b); the use of these has, moreover, been proscribed before (vii. 5; xii. 3)." *

Riehm † represents the Deuteronomic code as a liter-

---
* *Introduction to the Literature of the Old Testament*, pp. 82, 83.
† In *l. c.*, p. 112.

THE DATE OF DEUTERONOMY

ary fiction. The author lets Moses appear as a prophetic, popular orator, and as the first priestly reader of the law. It is a literary fiction as Ecclesiastes is a literary fiction. The latter uses the person of Solomon as the master of wisdom to set forth the lesson of wisdom. The former uses Moses as the great lawgiver, to promulgate divine laws.

We shall now adduce on the other side what seem to be the chief obstacles to the composition of Deuteronomy in the age of Josiah. (1). The statement of 2 Kings xxii. 3 f. is to the effect that a law book was discovered which had for a long period been neglected, and whose commands had been so long disobeyed that the nation was rejected by Yahweh on that account. The Deuteronomic code had been lost sight of by kings and princes and the priesthood, the entire official class of the nation. This neglect was a national and a terrible sin that involved the extreme penalty of the exile of the nation. Under these circumstances a law book issued as a legal fiction would be most extraordinary. How could the nation incur such a penalty for trangressing laws which were now promulgated for the first time? A long series of violations is presupposed. The laws cannot, therefore, date from a period shortly before this Reform. The code was presented as an ancient and long-neglected law book. This argumentation makes it evident that an ancient law book was discovered, but it does not prove that that code is the same as the present rhetorical Deuteronomy. If an ancient law book of Moses had been found and its legislation was put in a rhetorical form in the time of Josiah, this reasoning would be satisfied. As Canon Driver says:

"The new element in Dt. is thus not the laws, but their *parenetic setting*. Deuteronomy may be described as the *prophetic re-formulation, and adaptation to new needs, of an older legislation.* Judging from the manner in which the legislation of JE is dealt with in Dt., it is highly probable that there existed the tradition—perhaps even in a written form—of a final address delivered by Moses in the plains of Moab, to which some of the laws peculiar to Dt. were attached, as those common to it and JE are attached to the legislation at Horeb. There would be a more obvious motive for the plan followed by the author if it could be supposed that he worked thus upon a traditional basis. But be that as it may, the bulk of the laws contained in Dt. is undoubtedly far more ancient than the time of the author himself: and in dealing with them as he has done, in combining them into a manual for the guidance of the people, and providing them with hortatory introductions and comments, he cannot, in the light of the parallels that have been referred to, be held to be guilty of dishonesty or literary fraud. There is nothing in Dt. implying an interested or dishonest motive on the part of the (post-Mosaic) author: and this being so, its moral and spiritual greatness remains unimpaired, its inspired authority is in no respect less than that of any other part of the O. T. Scriptures which happens to be anonymous."*

(2). There are several laws in the Deuteronomic code which are inappropriate to the time of Josiah, and which can only be explained in connection with the circumstances of Israel in the earliest history. The commands to exterminate the Canaanites and the Amalekites, with their circumstances of detail (Deut. vii. 22; xx. 19; xxv. 17); the general laws of war (Deut. xx. 1–15; xxi. 10–14), and others, are appropriate only in connection with the first occupation of the holy land and not in the time when Israel was threatened only by foreign enemies. But these laws may be ancient laws from the ancient code taken up into the Deuteronomic code in its present rhetorical form. They do not prove that the code in its present rhetorical form is ancient.

---

* *Liter. of the O. T.*, p. 85.

(3). The circumstances of the reign of Josiah were unfavorable to the promulgation and enforcement of a new code of the character of the Deuteronomic legislation, and Jeremiah was the last man to be the most zealous champion of such a code. The opposition to such a code coming down from the previous times of Manasseh and breaking out immediately on the death of Josiah, supported by the customs and prejudices of the nation, would have been too great to be overcome save by a code claiming and gaining recognition as of ancient and divine authority; and Jeremiah and the author of the Books of Kings, who are full of the spirit and ideas of Deuteronomy, could not have been deceived in such matters and would not have joined hands to deceive the people even with the pious end in view of serving Yahweh and saving the nation. This is valid as against a new code, but not against a new codification of an ancient code.

(4). The language of Jeremiah and of the Books of Kings is no longer the old classic Hebrew, but intermediate in the historic development of the language, showing a breaking off from classic usage, as, for instance, in the occasional neglect of the *waw* consec. of the imperfect, and the use of *waw* conj. with the perfect instead. But the Book of Deuteronomy is classic in its language throughout. In view of the fact of the resemblance of Jeremiah and the Books of Kings to Deuteronomy in other respects, this difference of language is the more striking, showing that Jeremiah and the author of Kings were imbued with the spirit of Deuteronomy as an ancient law book of divine authority, but that it must be placed in an earlier period of the language. But the time of Josiah was not after all late for Hebrew literature. We must take account of the fact that the author was recodifying an ancient code, and so would be influenced to use an archaic style and preserve as far as possible the flavor of the original, just as do the compilers of the Books of Samuel and Kings. And Deuteronomy has its peculiarities of language, many of which correspond with the editorial framework of the books of Kings. As Canon Driver says: "The language and style of Dt., clear and flowing, free from archaisms, but purer than that of Jeremiah, would suit the same period. It is difficult in this connexion not to feel the force of Dillmann's remark (p. 611), that 'the style of Dt. implies a long development of the art of public oratory, and is not of a character to belong to the first age of Iraelitish literature.'"*

(5). The Mosaic prophecy, Deut. xviii. 15 *sq.*, predicts another prophet like Moses, who will fulfil and complete his legislation with divine authority. It does not recognize an order of prophets. *Nabi*, in our opinion, is never used as a collective. If this passage came from the period of the kings and prophets there could hardly fail to be allusions to the prophetic order, or to other prophets of Yahweh. We find in Jeremiah and in Isaiah liii., where the Messianic prophet again comes into prominence in the Messianic idea, such references, and we would expect them in Deuteronomy under the same circumstances. This prophecy is Mosaic in essence,† but that does not prove that the term *Nabi* was used in the time of Moses, and this prophecy does not carry with it the whole code in which it is placed.

(6). Looking now at Deuteronomy itself, we note its language as to the authorship of its code (xxxi. 9–11, 24–26).

"And Moses wrote *this law* and gave it unto the priests, the

---

* *l. c.* p. 83. † See Briggs' *Messianic Prophecy*.

sons of Levi, who bare the ark of the covenant of Yahweh, and unto all the elders of Israel, and Moses enjoined them saying, At the end of seven years, in the festival of the year of release, in the feast of tabernacles, when all Israel shall come to appear before the face of Yahweh thy God, in the place which He will choose, thou shalt read this law before all Israel in their ears." "And it came to pass when Moses had finished writing *the words of this law in a book* to their end, Moses enjoined the Levites, the bearers of the ark of the covenant of Yahweh, saying: 'Take *this book of the law* and put it by the side of the ark of the covenant of Yahweh your God, and let it be there for a witness against thee.'"

This seems to imply the Mosaic authorship and composition of a code of law, but was that code the Deuteronomic code in its present form? The view of Delitzsch can hardly be regarded as doing violence to the text when he represents that Deuteronomy is in the same relation to Moses as the fourth gospel to Jesus, in that as the apostle John reproduces the discourses of Jesus, so the Deuteronomist reproduces the discourses of Moses, giving more attention to the internal spirit than the written form, and thus presents the discourses of Moses in a free rhetorical manner. All that is said may be true if we suppose that an ancient Mosaic code was discovered in Josiah's time and that this code was put in a popular rhetorical form as a people's law book for practical purposes under the authority of the king, prophet and priest. Would it be any the less inspired on that account? Were not Josiah, Hilkiah and Jeremiah capable of giving authority to such a law book as a code of divine law essentially Mosaic in origin?

IX.

THE DEVELOPMENT HYPOTHESIS.*

EDWARD REUSS is the chief who has given direction and character to this stadium of the Higher Criticism. As early as 1833 † he maintained that the priest-code of the middle books of the Pentateuch was subsequent to the Deuteronomic code. This came to him, he says, as an *intuition* in his Biblical studies, and he presented it to his students in his University lectures from 1834 onward. In 1835 George took independently a similar position.‡ Vatke also, in 1835, reached the same results from the point of view of the Hegelian philosophy, taking the ground that the religion of Israel has three stages of development, and that the simple religion of the feeling in the Prophets and Deuteronomy precedes the more external and reflective religion of the mass of

---

* For the history of this Stadium see Wellhausen in Bleek's *Einleitung*, 4th Aufl., p. 152 *sq.*; Merx in Tuch's *Com. ü. d. Genesis*, p. lxxviii. *sq.*; Duff, *History of Research concerning the Structure of the Old Testament Books* in the *Bibliotheca Sacra*, 1880, Oct., and 1882, July; Kayser, *Der gegenwärtige Stand der Pentateuchfrage* in the *Jahrbücher* f. *Prot. Theologie*, 1881, ii., iii., and iv.; Gast, *Pentateuch-Criticism, its History and Present State*, in the *Reformed Quarterly Review*, July, 1882.

† Article *Judenthum* in Ersch and Gruber's *Encyclop.*, ii. Bd. 27, p. 334. *Hall. Literaturzeitung*, 1838.

‡ *Die älteren judisch. Feste mit einer Kritik der Gesetzgebung des Pent.*, 1835.

the Pentateuch; and that Prophetism and Mosaism must, for the most part, be transposed.*

These writers did not receive much attention. Their positions were too *theoretical* and without a sufficient support in the details of practical exegesis to gain acceptance.

In 1862 J. Popper† took the position that the description of the erection of the tabernacle, Ex. xxxv.–xl., and the consecration of the priests, Lev. vii.–ix., were later than the directions respecting them both in Ex. xxv.–xxxi., and contended that they received their present form some time after the Babylonian captivity.

Reuss continued to work at his theory in his University lectures, and it was through his pupils that in recent times it has won its way to so wide an acceptance. The first of these was Heinrich Graf, who, in 1866,‡ presented strong arguments for the priority of Deuteronomy to the priest-code of Lev. xviii.–xxiii., xxv., xxvi., Ex. xxxi., holding that the latter was from the prophet Ezekiel, and that in the time of Ezra other legislation was was added, *e.g.* Ex. xii. 1–28, 43–51, xxv.–xxxi., xxxv.–xl.; Lev. i.–xvi., xxiv. 10–23; Num. i. 48–x. 28, xv.–xix., xxviii.–xxxi., xxxv. 16–xxxvi. 13, and that the last additions were made soon after Ezra. Graf still held to the priority of the Elohistic narrative. This inconsistency was exposed by Riehm and Nöldeke, so that Graf was forced to make the Elohistic narrative post-exilic also.§

Meanwhile the English world had been stirred by the

---

* *Biblische Theologie*, 1835, i. 1, p. 641 *sq.*

† *Biblische Bericht über die Stiftshütte.*

‡ Merx, *Archiv*, i., pp. 68–106, 208–236; *Die geschichtliche Bücher des Alt. Test.*

§ *Studien & Krit.*, 1868, p. 372; Merx, *Archiv*, i., 466–477. Reuss also at this time held the same position.

attacks of Bishop Colenso on the *historical* character of the Pentateuch and book of Joshua, and in the Essays and Reviews by a number of scholars representing free thought.* These writers fell back on the older deistic objections to the *Pentateuch* as *history*, and as containing a *supernatural* religion, and mingled therewith a reproduction of German thought, chiefly through Bunsen. They magnified the discrepancies in the narratives and legislation, and attacked the supernatural element, but added nothing to the Higher Criticism of the Scriptures. So far as they took position on this subject they fell into line with the more radical element of the school of De Wette. They called the attention of British and American scholars away from the literary study of the Bible and the true work of the Higher Criticism, to a defence of the supernatural and the inspiration of the Bible. They were attacked by various divines in Great Britain and America, and their influence overcome for the time.†

The work of Colenso, however, made a great impression upon the Dutch scholar Kuenen, who had already been advancing under the influence chiefly of Popper and Graf, to the most radical positions.‡ He

---

* *The Pentateuch and Book of Joshua critically examined*, Part i.-vii., 1862-79; *Recent Inquiries in Theology by eminent English Churchmen, being Essays and Reviews*, 4th Am. edition from 2d London, 1862.

† Among these we may mention the authors of *Aids to Faith*, being a reply to "Essays and Reviews," American edition 1862; W. H. Green, *The Pentateuch vindicated from the Aspersions of Bishop Colenso*, N. Y., 1863.

‡ In his *Historisch-kritisch Onderzoek*, Leiden, 1861-5, p. 165 f., 194 f., he had taken a similar position to Graf, that the legislation in the Elohistic document was composed of laws of various dates arising out of the priestly circle, the last editing of them being later than the Deuteronomist, so that the Redactor of the Pentateuch was a priest. But subsequent investigations led him further. His later positions are represented in his *Godsdienst van Israel*, 1869-70, the English edition, *Religion of Israel*, 1874; *De vijf Boeken van Mozes*, 1872; *De Profeten en de profetie onder Israel*, 1875, translated into English, *The*

THE DEVELOPMENT HYPOTHESIS

took the ground that the religion of Israel was a purely natural religion, developing like all other religions in various stages from the grossest polytheism and idolatry to the exalted spiritual conceptions of the prophets. He rejects the historical character of the Hexateuch, and regards it as composed of ancient but unreliable legends and myths, the legislation representing various stages, the earliest in the period of the kings. The Deuteronomic code is a programme of the Mosaic party in the reign of Josiah, the priest-code the programme of the hierarchy at the restoration under Ezra. He is unwilling to ascribe to Moses more than a fragment of the decalogue. He finds three forms of worship, that of the people, of the prophets, and of the law, the later developing out the earlier.

Meanwhile the new theory found a supporter in England in Dr. Kalisch, in 1867, who, influenced in part by Vatke and Kuenen, but chiefly by George, in a series of valuable excursus, traces the development of the various forms of legislation, and reaches the conclusion that the priestly requirements of Leviticus are post-exilic.*

The views of Reuss, in 1869, were advocated by Duhm,† and especially in 1874, by Kayser,‡ who undertook a most careful analysis of the Pentateuch with

---

Prophets and Prophecy in Israel, 1877, and numerous articles in *Theologisch Tijdschrift*, since that time, and last of all Hibbert Lectures, *National Religions and Universal Religions*, 1882. Kuenen's views are presented by Oort in a popular form in the *Bible for Learners*, 3 vols., 1880. His final opinion is given in his *Historisch-kritisch Onderzoek*, 2de Uitgave, 1887–1889.

* In his Commentary on Exodus, 1855, Dr. Kalisch is inclined to defend the traditional view of the authorship of the Pentateuch. In his Com. on Genesis, 1858, he is concerned only with the geographical and other scientific and historical difficulties. But in his Com. on Leviticus, Part i., 1867, Part ii., 1872, he advances to the most radical positions.

† *Theologie der Propheten.*

‡ *Vorexilische Buch der Urgeschichte.*

reference to the theory, and gave it much needed support from the literary side. Still later, Wellhausen,* in 1876–7, gave a masterly analysis of the literary features of the entire Hexateuch, which commanded the attention of all Old Testament scholars, and then, in 1878, carried the same method of analysis into the entire legislation, combining the philosophical method of Vatke with the exegetical of Reuss. These works at once won over a large number of prominent scholars to his position, such as Hermann Schultz, Kautzsch, Smend, Stade, König, Giesebrecht, Siegfried, and others in Germany; Lenormant and Vernes, in France; W. Robertson Smith, Samuel Sharp, C. H. Toy, and others in Great Britain and America.† Wellhausen, like Kuenen, attacks the historical character of the Pentateuch, denies the supernatural element, and reconstructs in the most arbitrary manner—but these features are personal, and have no necessary connection with his critical analysis of the literary documents and legislation of the Pentateuch, so that men of every shade of opinion with regard to the supernatural and to evangelical religion may be found among the advocates of the theory.

---

* *Jahr. f. Deutsche Theologie*, 1876, pp. 392–450, 531–602, 1877, p. 407–409; *Geschichte Israels*, i., 1878.

† Schultz, *Alttestamentliche Theologie*, ii. Auf., 1878; Kautzsch, *Theo. Literatur Zeitung*, 1879 (2); Stade, *Geschichte des Volkes Israel;* Smend, *Der Prophet Ezekiel*, 1880; König, *Der Offenbarungsbegriff des Alt. Test.*, 1882; Siegfried in Pünjer's *Theo. Jahresbericht*, 1882; Giesebrecht, *Der Sprachgebrauch des Hexateuchischen Elohisten in Zeit. f. d. Alt-test. Wissenschaft*, 1881–2; Lenormant, *Beginnings of History*, edited by Prof. Brown, 1882; Maurice Vernes in Lichtenberger's *Encyclopedia*, art. *Pentateuque*, x., p. 447; W. Robertson Smith, *The Old Testament in the Jewish Church*, 1881; *The Prophets of Israel*, 1882; Sam. Sharp, *History of the Hebrew Nation*, 4th Edit., 1882; C. H. Toy, *Babylonian Element in Ezekiel*, in *Journal of the Society of Biblical Literature and Exegesis*, 1882, and numerous others.

THE DEVELOPMENT HYPOTHESIS

At last the veteran scholar, Edward Reuss himself, sums up the results of his pupils' work as well as his own further studies in 1879 and 1881.* Reuss ascribes to Moses the Decalogue stript of its present paraphrase. The poetic pieces Gen. xlix.; Ex. xv.; Num. xxiii.–iv., the book of the wars of Jehovah, and the book of *Jasher*, belong to the northern kingdom after their separation from Judah. The book of the Covenant was written in the reign of Jehoshaphat. The Jehovist wrote the second integral part of our Pentateuch in the second half of the ninth century, and this was followed by Deut. xxxiii., and sundry legends as to the origin of the race preserved in our Genesis. Deut. xxxii. next appeared. Under Josiah the Deuteronomist composed the third great section of our Pentateuch, and was followed by the author of the book of Joshua. After the Restoration, the law book Lev. xvii.–xxvi. was issued, and the priest-code with the fourth great section of our Pentateuch.

It is evident that the school of Reuss propose a *revolutionary* theory of the Literature and Religion of Israel. How shall we meet it but on the same evangelical principles with which all other theories have been met, without fear and without prejudice, in the honest search for the real truth and facts of the case? In a critical examination of this theory, it is important to distinguish the essential features from the accidental. We must distinguish between the Rationalism and unbelief that characterize Kuenen, Wellhausen, and Reuss, which are not essential to the theory itself, and such supporters of the theory as König in Germany, Lenormant in

---

* *L'Histoire Sainte et la Loi*, 1879; *Geschichte der Heiligen Schriften Alten Testaments*, 1881.

France, Robertson Smith in Scotland, and C. H. Toy in this country.* We have still further here, as throughout our previous investigation, to distinguish between the theory and the new facts which have been brought to light for which this theory proposes to account better than any previous ones.

The facts are these: (1). Our Pentateuchal legislation is composed of several codes, which show throughout variation from one another. (2). If we take the Pentateuchal legislation as a unit at the basis of the history of Israel, we find a discrepancy between it and the History and the Literature of the nation prior to the exile in these two particulars: (*a*). A silence in the historical, prophetical, poetical, and ethical writings as to many of its chief institutions; (*b*). The infraction of this legislation by the leaders of the nation, throughout the history in unconscious innocence, and unrebuked. (3). We can trace a development in the religion of Israel from the conquest to the exile in four stages corresponding in a most remarkable manner to the variations between the codes. (4). The books of Kings and Chronicles in their representation of the history of Israel regard it, the former from the point of view of the Deuteronomic code, the latter from the point of view of the priest-code. (5). The prophet Ezekiel presents us a detailed representation of institutions which seem intermediate between the Deuteronomic code and the priest-code.

The theory of the school of Reuss attempts to account (1) for the variation of the codes by three different legislations at widely different periods of time, *e.g.*, in the

---

* König, *Der Offenbarungsbegriff*, ii., p. 333 *sq.*; Lenormant, *Beginnings of History*, p. x. *sq.*; W. Robertson Smith, *The Old Testament in the Jewish Church*, Chap. I.; C. H. Toy, in *The Journal of the Society of Biblical Literature and Exegesis*, 1882, p. 66; *Judaism and Christianity*, p. 70, 1890.

reign of Jehoshaphat, of Josiah, and at the Restoration; (2) for the silence and the infraction, the discrepancy between the Pentateuchal legislation, and the history and the literature, by the *non-existence* of the legislation in those times of silence and infraction; (3) for the development of the religion of Israel in accordance with these codes by the representation that the *origin* of these codes corresponds with that development; (4) for the difference in point of view of the authors of Kings and Chronicles, on the ground that the author of Kings knew *only* of Deuteronomy, while the author of Chronicles was filled with the spirit of the new priest-code; (5) for the peculiar position of Ezekiel's legislation by the statement, that his legislation was in fact an *advance* beyond the Deuteronomic code, and a *preparation* for the priest-code, which was post-exilic. No one can examine this *theory* in view of the facts which it seeks to explain without admitting at once its simplicity; its correspondence with the law of the development of other religions; its apparent harmony with these facts, and its removal of not a few difficulties. Hence its attractiveness and power over against the prevalent theory which was not constructed to account for these facts, and which has been too often defended by special pleading.

There are various ways of dealing with this radical and revolutionary theory. We might attempt to deny these facts or explain them away. Such a course is but kicking against the pricks. It does not satisfy inquirers, but rather destroys the confidence of all earnest seekers after the *truth*. We might yield to the attractiveness of the theory, and go with the tide of Biblical scholarship which has set so strongly in that direction. We might shut our eyes to the whole matter, go to work in other fields, attend to the practical duties of life, and leave these Pentateuchal studies to others. Any one of these three ways would be easier than to look the facts in the face, and inquire whether the theory of the school of Reuss accounts for them in whole or in part or at all.

X.

THE DEVELOPMENT OF THE CODES.

THE variation in the several codes, Ex. xx.-xxiv. Ex. xxxiv., Deut. xii.-xxvi., and the scattered legislation of the middle books, is so constant that it is impossible to explain it away. These variations were already noted in part by Calvin, who wrote a Harmony of the Legislation, but he was not followed by later writers. These variations were more closely scrutinized by Eichhorn, and he explained them on the ground that the Deuteronomic code was a *people's* code, the Legislation of the middle books a *priests'* code.*

Another important difference to which Riehm calls attention is that the priest-code seems designed for a people still wandering in the wilderness, the other for a people already dwelling in the land of Canaan. Moreover, the Deuteronomic code is connected with a covenant in the land of Moab, the covenant code with a covenant at Horeb (Deut. xxix. 9-14). The priest-code

---

* This is acknowledged by Riehm : " For all the Deuteronomic laws prescribe to the people who know not the law, what to do and leave undone, none of them define the duties of the priests and Levites who knew the law. . . . The first distinction between the ancient (Levitical) and Deuteronomic legislation is accordingly *this :* that the one will give a complete law-book designed for all, those knowing the law and those ignorant of it, the other designed only for the people who knew not the law." *Gesetzgebung Mosis,* 1854, p. 11 *sq.*

is given as the words of Yahweh revealed to Moses. In the Deuteronomic code Moses comes forward as a popular orator to urge the people to the observance of the laws which he makes known as the prophet of Yahweh.

Thus according to Eichhorn and Riehm we have a difference of *point of view* which determines the structure and the character of these codes and necessarily produced a variation throughout. To this discrimination of the Deuteronomic and priests' codes we may add that the two codes, Ex. xx.–xxiii. and xxxiv. differ no less strikingly from them both. They contain brief, terse, pregnant sentences of command. They resemble the decalogue itself. It is generally agreed among Biblical scholars, that the little book of the Covenant is also a decalogue (Ex. xxxiv.), and not a few find that the larger book of the Covenant is also composed of a series of decalogues.* To this opinion we subscribe without hesitation, and find in it an evidence that this legislation is the nearest to the fundamental Mosaic legislation, in accordance with the explicit statement that Moses wrote it in a book of the Covenant. We thus have a third and fourth earlier points of view. These four codes therefore present us the judicial, the prophetical, and the priestly points of view, which determine the variation in aim, form, structure, and character of the three codes. This has been entirely neglected by the advocates of the traditional theory. This has also been ignored to a great extent by the advocates of the theories of De Wette and Reuss, who have sought to explain these variations by a development extending over a wide period of time.

---

* Bertheau, *Die sieben Gruppen Mosaischer Gesetze*, 1840, even finds such decalogues in the middle books, but does not make it evident save in the two books of the Covenant.

THE DEVELOPMENT OF THE CODES

The evangelical men of our time naturally feel the force of the philosophical theory of development, and other things being equal, will accept it to account for the phenomena, if they can do it without peril to their faith. We shall look at the differences and inquire how they may be harmonized.

(1). When we compare the decalogue of the covenant code of J, with the corresponding parts of the covenant code of E, and then the laws corresponding to this decalogue in the codes of D, H, and P; the development of this decalogue in intension and extension is so clear in the constant order J, D, H, P, that it seems impossible to dispute it.*

(2). When now we take the decalogues of the covenant code of E, so far as they have not yet been used in the previous study, and trace them in their corresponding laws through the codes D, H, P, it becomes clear that the laws in the covenant code of E "form the foundation of the Deuteronomic legislation."†

(3). There is also an apparent development between the codes of D and H, which may be seen in the laws common to these codes.‡

(4). There is an evident development in the laws respecting altars.

JE narrate that altars were built by Noah after leaving the ark Gn. viii. 20; by Abraham at Shechem Gn. xii. 7, Bethel Gn. xii. 8, Hebron Gn. xiii. 18, Mt. Moriah Gn. xxii. 9; by Isaac at Beersheba Gn. xxvi. 25; by Jacob at Shechem Gn. xxxiii. 20,§ at Bethel Gn. xxxv. 7; by Moses at Rephidim Ex. xvii. 15, Horeb Ex. xxiv. 4; by

---

* See Appendix V.   † Driver *l. c* p. 70. See Appendix VI.
‡ See Appendix VII.
§ Yet this perhaps a mistake for מַצֵּבָה, being obj. of וַיַּצֶּב־שָׁם, not elsewhere with מזבח, cf. also Dillmann.

Balak at Bamoth Baal, Pisgah & Peor Nu. xxiii. 1, 14, 29; by Joshua on Mt. Ebal Jos. viii. 30; the prophetic histories narrate that altars were built by Gideon at Ophra Ju. vi. 24; by a man of God at Bethel Ju. xxi. 4; by Samuel at Ramah 1 S. vii. 17; by Saul after Michmash 1 S. xiv. 35; by David on the threshing floor of Ornan 2 S. xxiv. 25=1 Ch. xxi. 18, xxii. 1; that Solomon sacrificed on the altar at Gibeon 1 K. iii. 4 and built altars in the temple at Jerusalem 1 K. vi. 20, viii. 64; that Jeroboam built an altar at Bethel 1 K. xii. 32 (which was destroyed by Josiah 2 K. xxiii. 15); and that Elijah repaired an ancient altar on Carmel 1 K. xviii. 30. An altar in Egypt is predicted Is. xix. 19. All this accords with the law of the Covenant code Ex. xx. 24–26 which recognizes a plurality of altars and prescribes that they shall be built of soil or unhewn stones, and without steps; so of *stones* Dt. xxvii. 6, of *whole stones* Jos. viii. 31 and of *twelve stones* 1 K. xviii. 30, 32, cf. Is. xxvii. 9. The altar was also a place of refuge Ex. xxi. 14 (JE) 1 K. i. 50, 51, ii. 28. (2). D prescribes one central altar Dt. xii. 27, but no attempt to enforce this law appears until Josiah who destroys all other altars besides the one in Jerusalem 2 K. xxiii. 8–20. (3). P limits sacrifices to the altars of the tabernacle. A great altar was built East of the Jordan, but it was according to P only as an עֵד after the pattern of the altar before the Tabernacle Jos. xxii. 10–34. P describes two altars: *a.* the altar of burnt offering Ex. xxx. 28, xxxi. 9, xxxv. 16, xxxviii. 1, xl. 6, 10, 29, Lv. iv. 7, 10, 25, 25, 30, 34= *brazen altar* Ex. xxxviii. 30, xxxix. 39, made of acacia wood plated with brass $5 \times 5 \times 3$ cubits having four horns and a network of brass, upon which all sacrifices by fire were made Ex. xxvii. 1–8, xxxviii. 1–7; *b.* altar for the burning of incense, made of acacia wood plated with gold 1 × 1 × 2 cubits, with four horns and a crown of gold, Ex. xxx. 1–6=the altar of incense Ex. xxx. 27, xxxi. 8, xxxv. 15, xxxvii. 25=the altar of gold Ex. xxxix. 38, xl. 5, 26, Nu. iv. 11=the altar of sweet incense Lv. iv. 7; these altars are known elsewhere only in Chr.; 1 Ch. vi. 34, xvi. 40, xxi. 29; 2 Ch. i. 5, 6.

(5). There is also a development of the sacred tent. This is named, *The tent of meeting* of God with his people (tent of congregation or assembly Ges. M.V. al.). According to E, Moses so called the tent which he used to pitch without the camp, afar off, into which he used to enter, and where God spake with him face to face, Ex. xxxiii. 7–11, Nu. xii. 5, 10, Dt. xxxi. 14, 15. J seems to have some conception of a tent of meeting outside the camp, Nu. xi. 24, 26; D has no allusion to such a tent; P mentions it 131 t. as "the tent of meeting"; 19 t. as "the tent" (cf. Ez. xli. 1) and *tent of the testimony* Nu. ix. 15, xvii. 22, 23, xviii. 2 (as containing ark and tables of the testimony) cf. 2 Ch. xxiv. 6, this tent sometimes confounded with the tabernacle, but distinguished in "tabernacle of the tent of meeting" Ex. xxxix. 32, xl. 2, 6, 29, cf. 1 Ch. vi. 17; "the tabernacle and the tent" Nu. iii. 25; "the tabernacle and the tent" Ex. xxxv. 11. The tent was of three layers of skins, goatskins, ramskins, and *tachash* skins, each layer of eleven pieces stretched in the form of a tent, covering and protecting the tabernacle, which was in the form of a parallelopip. (Ex. xxvi.). A tent of meeting was at Shilo 1 Sam. ii. 22 (omitted in LXX., Vulg.) cf. Ps. lxxviii. 60, called "tent of Joseph" v. 67. The tent of meeting was later at Gibeon 2 Ch. i. 3, 6, 13; courses of ministry were arranged for service at the "tent of meeting" 1 Ch. vi. 17, xxiii. 32, cf. 1 Ch. ix. 19 (the tent) v. 21, 23 "house of the tent"; David erected a tent for ark on Mount

Zion 2 Sam. vi. 17, 1 Ch. xv. 1, xvi. 1, 2 Ch. i. 4; Joab fled for refuge to the tent of Yahweh 1 K. ii. 28-30; sacred oil was brought from the tent 1 K. i. 39; the tent of meeting was taken up into temple 1 K viii. 4=2 Ch. v. 5; Yahweh had not previously dwelt in a house, but had gone *from tent to tent*, from one to another, 1 Ch. xvii. 5, cf. 2 Sam. vii. 6.

(6). There is development in the conception of the priesthood. In the blessing of Moses the tribe of Levi was chosen to bear the Urim and Thummin, to teach Israel, to burn incense and sacrifice. (Dt. xxxiii. 8-11.) According to E, in the covenant of Horeb, Israel became a kingdom of priests. (Ex. xix. 5, 6.) At the covenant sacrifice Moses selected young men to assist him, showing that there were no official priests at that time. (Ex. xxiv. 5.) But priests bore the ark and the sacred trumpets at Jericho. (Josh. iv. 9; vi. 4.) According to J, priests draw near to Yahweh at Sinai (Ex. xix. 22), showing a priesthood at that date, an important difference of conception from E. At the conquest priests bear the ark. (Jos. iii. 6; iv. 3.) According to D, the tribe of Levi was separated to be the priestly tribe to bear the ark, to stand before Yahweh, to minister in his name, and to bless the people. (Dt. x. 8, 9; xxxi. 9; Jos. iii. 3; vi. 6; xiii. 33; xviii. 7.) P has an entirely different legislation respecting the priesthood. It gives an account of the consecration and ordination of the Levites as priests, in substitution for the first-born sons, and then of the consecration of an Aaronic priesthood; and of a high priesthood, each of the three grades with its distinguishing dress, and correspondingly discriminated duties.

(7). The sacrificial system shows a development in several stages. JE in their codes and histories frequently use the whole burnt-offering, and the peace-offering, the fundamental sacrifices, also the first fruits and firstlings. E gives an account of the national sacrifice at the ratification of the covenant at Horeb (Ex. xxiv.), and mentions the drink-offering of Jacob. (Gen. xxxv. 14.) J distinguishes between the clean and the unclean of animals as dating from the sacrifice of Noah, uses Minchah as a general name for both the sacrifice of sheep and fruit in the story of Cain and Abel, but in the covenant code as a name for the offering of unleavened bread. J also gives a law for the passover victim which seems unknown to E. D enlarges the scope of the offerings mentioned in J E. It uses the whole burnt-offering, peace-offerings and firstlings of J E and the passover victim of J. But in addition it uses the term " offerings of Yahweh made by fire," and gives the votive offerings, free-will offerings and heave-offerings. It also prohibits the offering of children in whole burnt-offering, a prohibition apparently unknown to J E and the earlier history.

P now gives an elaborate system of sacrifices and precise rules for their observance. All the terms of the offerings of JED appear, and many new ones. (1) קרבן is commonly employed for offerings of material things. (2). The sin-offering is in three stages as it purifies the three altars in its gradations of access to the divine presence. (3). The trespass-offering is in three varieties for the ordinary person, the Nazarite, and the leper. (4). The development of the peace-offerings into the votive offering, the free-will offering, the thank-offering, is evident as well as the ordinary peace-offering. (5). The special sacrifice of the ram of consecration at the installation of the priesthood is mentioned. These sacrifices, peculiar to the priest-code, involve an extensive list of phrases which are unknown to the other codes.*

---

* *c. g.* חטא is used in Gen. xxxi. 39 (E), in the primitive meaning of "bear

(8). According to the covenant code the men of Israel are holy and are not to eat of flesh torn off beasts in the field, they are to cast it to the dogs. (Ex. xxii. 31.) In D an animal that died of itself might be given to the stranger to eat, and sold to the foreigners. (Dt. xiv. 21.) In H these carcasses could not be eaten by home-born or stranger. (Lev. xvii. 15, 16.) In P the distinction between home-born and stranger has passed away, and the prohibition is universal. (Lev. xi. 39, 40.) Several generations are necessary to account for such a series of modifications of the same law. This is only an incident of the development of the legislation under the head of Purifications. The Deuteronomic code forbids to cut oneself, distinguishes the clean from the unclean animals (xiv. 3–21), and prescribes washing with water for uncleanness (xxiii. 10 *sq.*). The priest-code gives an extended series of purifications in the varied use of pure water, and by the use of ashes of the red heifer (Lev. xii., xv., Num. xix.), and of various ingredients in the healing of the leper (Lev. xiii.–xiv.).

(9). *The Feasts.* The Covenant-code ordains the Sabbath, feasts of unleavened bread, harvest and ingatherings, and the seventh year. (Ex. xxiii. 10–17.) The Deuteronomic code mentions the Passover, feast of unleavened bread, feast of weeks, feast of tabernacles, and year of release. (Deut. xv., xvi.) The priest-code gives a complete cycle of feasts (Lev. xxiii.; Num. xxviii.), new moons, Sabbaths, the seven great Sabbaths, Passover and unleavened bread, day of first fruits, feast of

---

loss," but in P it means only to make a sin-offering or to purify from sin or uncleanness. It is characteristic of H and P that שְׁלָמִים defines זבח in the construct singular or plural in a number of phrases used with great frequency. In P it is distinguished from נדבה and נדרים but not from תודה, and therefore probably is interchangeable with תודה.

trumpets, day of atonement, tabernacles, the seventh year's feast, the year of Jubilee,—a most artistic system.*

It will be observed that these variations are in the *chief* features of the ceremonial system. They present the appearance of development from the more simple to the complex, and in the order, Covenant codes, Deuteronomic code, code of Holiness, and priest-code. The traditional theory is certainly at fault here in regarding the Deuteronomic legislation as *secondary* over against the priest-code as *primary*. The Deuteronomic code is secondary to the Covenant codes, but not to the priest-code. This fault of the traditional theory had not been overcome by the theories of Eichhorn, Geddes or De Wette. Here is an advantage of Reuss' theory over all previous ones. We must admit the *order* of development. A code for the elders and judges of tribes or clans in their various localities, a code for the instruction of the nation as a whole in rhetorical and popular form, and a code for the priests from the holy place as a centre, in the nature of the case will show a progress from the simple to the more and more complex and elaborate in matters of ritualistic observance. The Covenant code of E is a series of decalogues for the elders in the administration of justice in various localities. It is based on the covenant at Horeb and lies at the root of the Pentateuchal legislation. It is claimed that Moses wrote such a book of the Covenant. The Deuteronomic code is a people's code in a prophetic form to instruct and stimulate the people of Yahweh as an organic whole. It is based on the experience of the wandering in the wilderness, it looks forward to a prolonged occupation of the promised

---

* See Appendix VI.

land, and is based on a new covenant in the plains of Moab. We would expect to find progress and development here especially on the practical side. It is claimed that Moses gives a law code at this time; and we can see no sufficient reasons for doubting it. The priest-code is from the priestly point of view in connection with the tabernacle and its institutions. It will necessarily exhibit progress and development on the technical side in the details of the ritual. This code is scattered in groups in the middle books, and broken up by insertions of historical incidents, but when put together exhibits an organic whole, a unity and symmetry which is wonderful in connection with the attention given to details. This code is represented as given by Yahweh to Moses or Aaron, or both, but it is not represented as written down by Moses as is the case with the two other codes. It claims to be Mosaic legislation, but if we should suppose that later priests gathered the detailed laws and groups of laws into codes at any times subsequent to the conquest, this claim would be satisfied. This collection of laws contains an earlier separate code called the code of Holiness. It may also contain other such codes yet to be determined by criticism, all constituent sources of the present priest-code and going back through several codifications to primitive times.

There are several obstacles which have been proposed to the composition of the priestly legislation in the post-exilic period: (1). The language of the Elohist and the priest-code is classic. The discussions respecting the language of the Elohist have proved marked differences from the other documents, but they have not proved any such deflection in the syntax of the *waw* consec., and the multiplication of nouns formed by affixes as characterize Ezekiel. And yet the word-lists show closer resemblance between the priestly code and Ezekiel than between that code and any earlier writer.

(2). The priest-code is a unit in its wonderful variety of detail. Given the ark of the covenant as the throne of Yahweh, the King of Israel, the holy God, and all the institutions, and the ritual, seem to be the most appropriate elaboration of that one idea. They are wrapt up in the idea itself as a germ. Why should it require centuries for the development of the germ into its legitimate flowers and fruit? An idea like that would be more than seed-corn to Israel in the wilderness. We would expect some such practical development as we do find in the priest's code at the time. Such a speculative development is possible. But is it so probable as a practical development, finding expression in appropriate legislation? The unity may come from the priestly compiler and express the unification of historic experience.

(3). The priest-code is realistic, and its realism is that of the wilderness, of the wanderings and the nomadic life. This is so inextricably involved with the ideal in all parts of the legislation, so simple, artless, and inartistic, that it seems unlikely that it should be pure invention, or the elaboration of an ideal which could not escape anachronisms in some particulars. But if the fundamental legislation is Mosaic, why might not the priestly compiler, taking his stand in the wilderness of the wanderings, have been true to his historic and ideal standpoint? And then there are apparently anachronisms as has been pointed out by several crities.*

---

* See Westphal, *Les Sources des Pentateuque*, ii. pp. 321 *seq.*

XI.

THE WITNESS OF THE HISTORY.

I.—*Discrepancy between the Codes and the History.*

It must be admitted by the candid investigator of the Scriptures that there is a discrepancy between the Pentateuchal legislation and the history and literature of Israel prior to the exile. It extends through the most important laws of the ritual. It is two-fold: that of silence on the one side, and that of unconscious and uncondemned violation on the other. In the period of the Judges there are many altars besides the altar at Shiloh, where the ark and the tent of meeting were situated. These altars were erected in places consecrated by Theophanies in accordance with the Covenant code and in violation of the Deuteronomic code and priests' code. The sacrifices were offered by laymen, such as Joshua and Gideon at Ebal (Jos. viii. 30); at Mispeh in Perea (Judges xi. 11); at Bochim (Judges ii. 5); at Ophra (vi. 24); at Mispeh in Benjamin (xxi. 8); and elsewhere (Judges xiii. 19). This is a violation of the Deuteronomic code and priest-code, but not of the covenant code.

Dr. Green explains these violations thus: "In every such instance sacrifices were offered on the spot by those to whom the Lord thus appeared; and in the absence of such a Theophany, sacrifices were never offered except at Shiloh or in the presence of the ark and by priests of the house of Aaron." This explanation does not satisfy us for these reasons: (1) These transactions are no more than the Covenant-code requires. (2) They indicate a practice identical with that of the patriarchs. The Deuteronomic code and priest-code required a change in the earlier practice. Why were these two great codes transgressed by the judges under the influence of the divine Spirit? (3) The ark of the Covenant, according to the priest-code, was the permanent place of divine Theophany. Why was this forsaken by Yahweh Himself in violation of His own law, and why did He encourage the chiefs of the nation to violate the law? Why did Yahweh Himself permit His one altar and sanctuary and the legitimate Aaronic priesthood to be so neglected and dishonored? (4) The statement that the sacrifices were never offered except at Shiloh or in the presence of the ark and by priests of the house of Aaron, except at the times specified, rests upon no other evidence than *silence*, which may count equally well on the other side; since that which is mentioned as having been done several times may be presumed, with no evidence to the contrary, to have been done at other times. Moreover, the *silence* of the history as to any national habitual worship at Shiloh as the one only legitimate altar in accordance with the Deuteronomic code and priest-code, seems rather to count against such a thing. For the neglect of the sanctuary at Shiloh does not seem from the narratives extraordinary or abnormal.

According to the history of this period the sacrifices are peace-offerings and burnt-offerings of the Covenant code, but no offerings peculiar to the Deuteronomic code, no sin and trespass offerings of the priests' code.

There are simple ceremonial washings, but none of the peculiar Levitical purifications. The Passover was once kept (Josh. v. 10) and an animal feast at Shiloh (Judges xxi. 19), but there is no mention of any of the feasts peculiar to the priests' code. The ark of the Covenant, the tent of meeting, and the Nazarite vow* are different from these things as presented in the priest-code.

In the time of Samuel a similar state of affairs is discovered. Sacrifices are offered by Samuel, tribal chiefs, and Saul at various places: at Mispeh (1 Sam. vii. 5), at Ramah (1 Sam. vii. 17), at Gilgal (1 Sam. x. 8, xi. 15, xv. 21–33), at Zuph (1 Sam. ix. 12 *sq.*), at Bethlehem (1 Sam. xvi. 4–5), at Michmash (1 Sam. xiv. 35). The sacrifices are burnt-offerings and peace-offerings. The purifications are by simple washing with water. The only feast mentioned is an annual one at Bethlehem (1 Sam. xx. 6). On the other hand, the ark of the Covenant comes into prominence as vindicating its sanctity wherever it was carried. It was captured by the Philistines and taken from Shiloh into their own country, but subsequently returned and placed under the charge of Levitical priests at Kirjath-Jearim, where it remained twenty years (1 Sam. v.–vii.). This hill is called the hill of God, and had its high place, whither pilgrimages were made (1 Sam. x. 5). Nob also was a holy place where the priests dwelt, having the tent of meeting, shew-bread, and ephod (1 Sam. xxi. 9). The Urim and Thummim was also consulted. These are sacred things of the

---

* The Nazarite Samson abstains from wine, and from eating unclean things, and from cutting the hair (Ju. xiii. 4-5), but he uses the jawbone of an ass as a weapon to destroy his enemies (Ju. xiv. 15-20), in violation of the law of the Nazarite in the priests' code, which forbids the Nazarite from coming in contact with a dead body. It is sufficient to read the law of Num. vi. to see that Samson was a very different kind of Nazarite from that contemplated in the priests code.

priest-code. They imply a use of these things at this time, but do not imply a use of the priest-code; for they are in a different form and of a different character from that in which they appear in the priest-code. Samuel and the nation as a whole neglected the ark of the Covenant, the tent of meeting, and the priesthood at Nob, in violation of the priest-code and Deuteronomic code.

Dr. Green thus explains these things: "During all this period of sad degeneracy and earnest labors for Israel's reformation, Samuel prayed for the people and pleaded with them and led their worship. He sacrificed at Mispeh, at Gilgal, at Ramah, at Bethel (possibly), and at Bethlehem, but never once at Kirjath-Jearim. He never assembled the people at or near the house of Abinidab. He never took measures to have the ark present at any assembly of the people or upon any occasion of sacrifice. The Lord had not indicated His will to establish another sanctuary where He might record His name in place of Shiloh, which he had forsaken."*

This explanation seems to us invalid for these reasons: (1) According to the priest-code the ark of the Covenant was the throne of Yahweh, and it alone gave the place where it rested sanctity. Shiloh was a holy place only so long as the ark was there. Wherever it went it made a holy place. So the hill Kirjath-Jearim became holy and the house of God so long as the ark was there. As we interpret 1 Sam. x., this place is called the hill of God and house of God, and pilgrimages were made thither for worship by bands of prophets. But if Dr. Green's interpretation of this passage be correct and Bethel is the hill of God, then, according to this passage, *it* is a place of pilgrimage and worship rather

---

* *Moses and the Prophets*, 1882, p. 150.

than the place of the ark, a still more flagrant violation of the priest-code. And if we do not find worship at Kirjath-Jearim here, what evidence is there save *silence*, that Samuel and the people did not resort thither for worship as well as to other places? (2) But why did Samuel, the fearless reformer, so neglect the priest-code and Deuteronomic code while the ark remained for twenty years within easy access at Kirjath-Jearim?

Advancing into the period of the Kings we find the worship at the high places continues. David brought up the ark of the Covenant to Zion and erected a new tent for it (2 Sam. vi. 1–17). He also erected an altar, and sacrificed on Mt. Moriah, the site of the temple. The offerings are whole burnt-offerings and peace-offerings. The purifications are not indicated; the feasts are the Sabbaths, new moons, and other festivals not specified. We note the presence of the brazen altar, the tabernacle of Yahweh, the tent of meeting and the shew-bread, of the priest-code, in the Chronicler (1 Chron. xv. 17, xvi. 39, 40, xxi. 29, xxiii. 29); but the other writers knew nothing of these things.

The erection of the temple of Solomon concentrated the worship of the people at Jerusalem, but did not do away with the worship on high places or bring about a general recognition of the Deuteronomic code. The offerings are confined to whole burnt-offerings and peace-offerings. The Levitical purifications are not mentioned. The Chronicler mentions the celebration of the Sabbath, new moons, and three great feasts, (unleavened bread, feast of weeks, and especially tabernacles 2 Chron. vii. 8–10; viii. 3.); and that the temple and its priesthood were organized in accordance with a *plan* given by God to David (1 Chron. xxviii. 19); but these things are unknown to the prophetic histories.

Taking our stand here by the temple of Solomon and looking back through the previous history to the conquest, we note a constant transgression of the Deuteronomic code and priests' code, or rather an apparent unconsciousness of their existence. And yet some of the most essential things of the priest-code are mentioned by the Chronicler. These cannot be explained by the theory of the school of Reuss. The way that Kuenen and Wellhausen meet the difficulty is hardly creditable to their fairness and good judgment. We cannot consent to the denial of the historical sense of the Chronicler for the sake of any theory. We might conceive that the tabernacle was an idealizing of the temple in accordance with the difference between the nomadic life and the settled life of the holy land, if there were any propriety in this idealization under the circumstances. We have a brilliant example of the power of the imagination of a prophet in such an artistic elaboration and detailed representation in Ezekiel xl.–xlviii. Ezekiel's imagination goes forth into the future and from the river Chebar to the Holy Land. We cannot therefore deny the possibility of such a prophet as Ezekiel constructing an ideal of legislation in the wilderness with all its details. And yet it seems arbitrary for the school of Reuss to make Ezekiel's legislation a programme and that of Exodus an idealization. There is propriety in the representation of Ezekiel in taking the Holy Land as the site of his temple and institution. But there is no propriety in the supposed post-exilic author of the middle books taking the wilderness and the nomadic life as the scene of his legislation. He would rather from the necessities of the case have followed the Deuteronomist and Ezekiel, and have legislated in his programme for the Holy Land. There must be some substantial basis in the history for his representation. This, however, does not force us to think of the antiquity of our present priests' code, but only of the antiquity of those laws and institutions in it which are ascribed to the earlier times. The Davidic legislation and the organization of the temple service point backward to the simpler Mosaic legislation of which it is an elaboration. The temple of Solomon is easier to explain on the basis of the tabernacle of Moses than the latter on the basis of the former.

But notwithstanding all this concentration of worship, the Deuteronomic code is not fulfilled by the doing away of high places and sacrifices thereon. The sacrifices of sin and trespass-offerings, the purifications and the feasts of the priest-code do not appear. The Davidic legislation is thus at an angle with the Pentateuchal; being on the one side an advance, and on the other a remarkable falling behind the requirements of the Deuteronomic code and priest-code, which cannot be accounted for if they were taken as the basis of the Davidic constitution, or if they had been in general observance since the conquest.

The rupture of the nation after the death of Solomon rendered the observance of the Davidic constitution as well as the priest-code and Deuteronomic code an impossibility for the northern kingdom. Ancestral worship on high places is conducted by Elijah on Carmel and by others at various altars. In Judah itself it continued as the prevailing mode of worship, save for the spasmodic efforts of Hezekiah and Josiah, until after the exile of the northern kingdom. This worship on high places even survives the destruction of the temple at Jerusalem, and we find a company of pilgrims resorting to the ancient sanctuary at Mispeh (Jer. xli. 5 *sq.*) after the overthrow of the nation. Dr. Green explains these things thus: "The worship on high places was irregular and illegal after the temple was built; but the fact that they were tolerated by pious princes, who contented themselves with abolishing the emblems and practice of idolatry found there, only shows that they did not do their whole duty—not that the law which had ruled ever since the days of Moses did not exist. They may very easily have persuaded themselves that the spirit of the law was maintained if only the abuses were rectified; that if God was sincerely and piously worshipped in these local sanctuaries, there could not be much harm in suffering them to remain." This explanation is not satisfactory. For (1) it is an unlikely supposition that these pious princes so neglected a well-known duty. (2) It assumes that the law ruled from the days of Moses, which is the reverse of the facts. (3) It assumes that these pious princes presumed to please God by neglecting the prescriptions of the law and recognizing true worship against the law.

Looking now at the testimony of Hebrew Literature with reference to the offerings, the purifications, and the feasts of the priest-code, these are conspicuous by their absence prior to the exile The sin-offering first and alone appears in the pre-exilic history in the reform of Hezekiah according to the Chronicler (2 Chron. xxix. 20–24). It is not found in the pre-exilic prophets, or in the entire Psalter save possibly the exilic Ps. xl.; or in the ethical writings. In pre-exilic writings the trespass-offering is not found. It first occurs in the exilic Isaiah liii.; the Levitical purifications are not mentioned; the feasts of the priest-code do not appear.*

---

*With reference to this sin-offering of Hezekiah, one can see no evidence that it was offered in accordance with the ritual of the sin-offering, Lev. iv. 13. *sq*,

What, then, are we to conclude from these facts? The traditional theory was not designed to account for them. The theory of Reuss was constructed in order to account for them on the ground that the codes did not come into existence until they are recognized in the literature and the history of Israel. The traditional theory is against the facts so far as it is claimed by Marsh, Horne, and others, that the Pentateuchal legislation was observed in Israel from the conquest to the exile, the infractions being only occasional. On the other hand the evidence is invincible from silence and repeated instances of infraction in unconscious innocence and uncondemned, that the Mosaic legislation was not so observed.

II.—*The witness of the Literature as to non-observance of the Law.*

There is also abundant evidence from positive statements in the literature of the Old Testament that the

---

where the blood must be sprinkled before Yahweh, and put some of it upon the horns of the altar of incense and all the rest poured out at the base of the altar of burnt-offering. The ritual seems rather to be similar to that of the burnt-offering (Lev. i.), where the blood is scattered upon the altar (comp 2 Chron. xxix. 22 and Lev. i. 5). We find in (2 Kings xii. 16) in the reign of Joash that sin and trespass *money* was given to the priests as a fine or compensation for neglected duties, which corresponds with the law of the sin-offering that the flesh goes to the priests, but there is no *victim* here, and hence no correspondence with the priest-code. The attempt of Delitzsch (*Pent. Krit. Studien*, p. 9), to find a sin-offering in Hos. iv. 8 (followed by Keil, *Com. Ezek.* 2d Auf., p. 21), is a novel explanation of the passage and against the context. The same is true of the passage, Micah vi. 7. They are properly rendered in the A. V.: "sin of my people," parallel with "iniquity," and "sin of my soul," parallel with "my transgression." The supposed sin-offering of the Psalm xl., is a mistaken rendering of a noun which here as everywhere else should be rendered "sin." The trespass-offering of Isaiah liii. 10 is the sacrifice of the Messianic servant consisting of himself. This undoubtedly presupposes a victim in the trespass-offering, but inasmuch as all critics agree that the second half of Isaiah is exilic, that passage cannot help us to prove it a pre-exilic trespass-offering.

Legislation of the Pentateuch was not observed in the historic life of the Hebrew people.

(1). The prophet Amos (v. 25) represents that during the forty years wanderings, Israel did not offer burnt-offerings and peace-offerings to Yahweh. This corresponds with the statement Josh. v. 5, that circumcision had been neglected so that an entire generation had to be circumcised at Gilgal, after the entrance into Palestine. Then the Passover was kept which had likewise been neglected. The neglect of those essential things carries with it the non-observance of the entire priests' code, for according to that code an uncircumcised man or one who did not keep the Passover was cut off from the congregation. The period of the Judges is characterized by the failure to exterminate the Canaanites and by a series of captivities under foreign oppressors, during which tribal chieftains and local judges assumed the place assigned to the Levitical priesthood and to the kings by the Deuteronomic code.

How could there be one sanctuary in the midst of independent, hostile, and warring tribes? The observance of the Deuteronomic code and priest-code was impossible even if they had been in existence. The rally of the nation under Phinehas against Benjamin (Judges xx.), to avenge the wrong of the Levite, was the last until the revival of Samuel, and this is narrated in one of the latest documents of the Book. Indeed, there was no nation as such under Samuel and Saul. It was not until David established his throne in Jerusalem and moved the ark of the Covenant thither that a political and religious unity became possible. Then again we see a great rally of the nation about the ark and the priesthood, but it would have been impossible to overcome the worship on high places and ancestral modes of worship, even if an attempt had been made to execute such legislation as is found in D, H, and P. That which could not be accomplished by David and Solomon became impossible when Jeroboam tore away the mass of Israel from the house of David. Nor could weakened Judah, under its most pious kings, such as Jehoshaphat and Joash, do more than overcome, in part, idolatry at the high places. It was not until the reforms of Hezekiah and especially of Josiah, that Israel for brief periods could be brought to the acceptance of the Deuteronomic code.

(2). And here we meet the statement that the Deuteronomic code, thrown aside and neglected in the temple, was providentially discovered and brought to light as the basis of the reform. If the Deuteronomic code could thus be lost sight of, how much more the elaborate and technical priests' code if such a code were in existence? We also meet the statement that the Passover had not been observed in accordance with the law from the time of the observance of the Passover by Joshua and Israel on their entrance into the holy land (Josh v.) If such an important institution as the Passover could have been so neglected from the conquest to the days of Josiah, how much more other institutions of Deuteronomy of less fundamental importance?

(3). After a brief period of reform under Josiah, Judah went into exile, and it was not until the return from exile under the more favorable circumstances of a small, compact and select population, that Ezra and Nehemiah could reform the nation on the basis of the priests' code. Here, again (Neh. viii. 17), we have the statement that the feast of tabernacles had not been observed according to the priest-code from the time of Joshua onward, until that occasion. If this be true of this great feast, how much more of other feasts and institutions of the priest-code?

(4). If we compare the statement of the Chronicler 2 Chron. xxxvi. 21 with Jer. xxv. 11, 12, and Lev. xxvi. 34 *seq.*, it is impossible to escape the conclusion that the non-observance of the Sabbatical year of the priest-code is assigned as one of the chief reasons of the exile, and that the seventy years of its duration have a certain proportion of retribution in relation to a long-continued series of non-observances. If now we compare the law of the seventh year in the three codes, we find a development from the more simple provisions of Ex. xxiii. 10, 11, through Deut. xv. 1–3, to Lev. xxv. In this latter passage the Sabbatical feasts reach their culmination in the year of Jubilee. The neglect of the seventh year carries with it the neglect of the Jubilee year. Indeed, this elaborate Sabbatical system required for its fulfilment a people and a land in an entirely different situation from that of Israel in the entire period from the conquest to the exile.

(5). The most sacred day of the Mosaic calendar was the Day of Atonement. On this day the sin-offering attained its culmination. The sin-offering of the ritual for the new moons and the double sin-offerings for the great feasts reached their climax in the goat for Azazel and the goat for Yahweh—expressing the two sides of expiation by blood and of forgiveness by entire removal. It is here a most singular fact that in the priest-code (Lev. xvi.) we have the institution of the Day of Atonement and its peculiar sacrifices, but nowhere in the Pentateuch or elsewhere in the Old Testament any account of the observance in fact. There is no allusion, direct or indirect, to its most solemn services in Hebrew history or prophecy, in sacred song or sentence of wisdom. It seems not to have formed a part of the *historic* life and experience of the people. The omission of the sin-offering in its simpler form shows very clearly that the people of Israel had not in their historical life attained the religious experience that was indispensable for an apprehension of the Day of Atonement and its deep religious lessons. The historical realization first appears in the first century before the advent of our Saviour.*

Thus comparing the codes with the history, we must regard them as ideals in an ascending series from the Covenant codes through the Deuteronomic code to the priests'-code, which could not be realized in the historical experience of the nation. If the Covenant code of E was based upon the idea that Israel was a kingdom of priests, a holy nation, and the Deuteronomic code was pervaded with deep spiritual conceptions of faith, love, and absolute devotion to God, and if, in the priests' code, the idea of holiness is wrought out from the holy throne of the ark into all the details of the national life,; then these were beyond the experience of the tribes who entered the Holy Land. In order to its execution, the priests' code required a holy land under the absolute control of a holy people, all the alien nations exterminated, and every impure influence banished. It required a united, homogeneous people, living in a land under the protection of the continued presence of God in the form of a theophany enthroned in the throne room of the Holy of

---

* Prof. Delitzsch discusses this subject in an admirable manner in *Zeitschrift f. Kirchliche Wissenschaft*, 1880, IV. We agree with him that the passages, 1 Kings viii. 27, *seq.*; Ezra iii. 1–6; Neh. viii. 13–17; Ezekiel xlv. 18–20; Zech. vii.–viii., do not necessarily exclude the Day of Atonement, but we must go further and conclude that the most natural explanation of this silence under the circumstances of these passages is that the Day of Atonement was not observed.

Holies on the cherubic throne above the ark. It required a strict attention to all the details of the life as to personal purity and ministry. The spirituality of the Deuteronomic code in its grand ideal was as far above Israel as a nation, as the discourses of Jesus in John's gospel are above the Church of Christ. The perfect sanctity of the priests' code was as far above the experience of Israel as a nation as our Saviour's Sermon on the Mount, and His parables of the kingdom of heaven are above the experience of our life as Christians to-day. This ideal and prophetic element of the Pentateuchal legislation has been buried under the traditional theories of the Pharisees, which have come down as a yoke of bondage and a dark cloud of superstition to the Christian Church. Stripping these off, we behold in the Pentateuch vastly more than it has been the custom to find there. We find not only the Deuteronomic prediction of a prophet like Moses fulfilled in Jesus Christ, but that the whole law is prophetic of the Gospel. To this the interpretation of the apostles, and especially the epistle to the Hebrews, pointed the Christian Church; but Christian exegetes have been halting on the threshold and have not entered into this grand tabernacle of prophecy.

Do these codes lie at the basis of the history of Israel as ideals to be realized in the experience of the nation, as the gospels lie at the basis of Christian History? This is the theory which was proposed in 1883. But a more thorough study shows that this theory does not account for all the facts of the case. There are evidences of the presence from time to time in the history and literature of certain laws of D before Josiah, and of certain laws of P before Ezra, but not of these codes and writings as such. In general there is silence as to these codes and there is unconscious infraction of them. The history knows nothing of the code of D before Josiah and of the code of P before Ezra. No attempt was made to enforce the codes of D or P until these dates. There is silence on the one hand, and there is infraction on the other. There seems no room for them in the times of Moses or Joshua or Samuel or David. The providential historical circumstances did not admit of obedience to such elaborate codes before we find them in the history of the times of Josiah and Ezra. A priestly code seems to require its historical origin in a dominant priesthood. A prophetic code seems best to originate in a period when prophets were in the pre-eminence. A theocratic code suits best a prosperous kingdom and a period when elders and judges were in authority. Is it the most natural supposition that the Deuteronomic code remained buried from Moses until Josiah and the priest-code from Moses until Ezra? Is it not more reasonable to suppose that the Deuteronomic code was a recodification of an ancient code discovered in the temple in Josiah's time, and that the priest-code is a recodification of older codes and priestly traditional customs and ritual for the purpose of Ezra's reform? Would God inspire holy men to codify these codes of legislation centuries before they could be used? The ideal prophetic character of these codes best explains itself when the law like the prophets and the wisdom literature and the psalmody springs out of the historic development of the kingdom of redemption.

III.—*The Religious Development of Israel.*

It is clear from the Literature that there is a development in the worship of Israel as well as in doctrines and morals. The traditional theory is at fault in interpreting the history chiefly as a series of apostasies. This pessimistic view of the religion of Israel is against the facts of the case. In morals and in faith there is manifest progress. There must have gone along with progress in these things religious progress also. Doctrinal and ethical progress is indeed impossible without a progress in the religion that underlies and shapes doctrines and morals. The ancient congregation of Israel no more went on declining until the exile than the Christian Church has been declining or will continue to decline till the Second Advent. There were temporary declensions, but in every case in order to a new advance. Rather as the Church in her historic life has been appropriating more and more the faith of the gospel, so did Israel in her experience appropriate more and more of the law of Moses. Thus we can trace in the history of Israel a religious progress in remarkable accordance with the codes. It is not surprising that the school of Reuss put the Covenant code in the reign of Jehoshaphat. It would be difficult to find it in all respects in the previous history, and there seems to have been a progress in the line of the Covenant code up to the reign of Jehoshaphat and beyond, with a realization of some features only of the laws of the other codes. It seems most probable that the greater code of the Covenant represents the Mosaic code, as it had been codified in the northern kingdom of Israel. The Deuteronomic code is certainly the basis of the reform of Josiah and enters into the literature of the time in the book of Jeremiah and the Books of Kings. The priests' code was certainly the basis of the reforms of Ezra and Nehemiah and enters into the literature of the Chronicler. These reforms show successive stages of appropriation of the Pentateuchal legislation. Was there not a development of that legislation in successive codifications in order to facilitate that appropriation?

IV.—*The Histories and the Codes.*

The fact that the author of Kings is familiar only with Deuteronomy and the author of Chronicles with the priest-code, does not of itself prove that the priest-code was not in existence at the time of the compiler of Kings, but only that it was not at hand; it was not known to him or used by him. But if it were in existence why was it not discovered and brought to light by the pious Josiah, Jeremiah and their associates? Did they not search the temple where if anywhere such a priest-code would be found? They certainly were anxious to obey God's law. The theory of the school of Reuss that the Chronicler so greatly colors the history from his point of view as to falsify it, cannot be justified. It was natural that each should examine the history from the point of view of the code most familiar to him; and that the author of Kings and the Chronicler should therefore occupy different planes of judgment. We could not reasonably demand that they should be colorless. These differences do not show any intentional misinterpretation on the part of either of them, or that the Chronicler undertook to invent the history. But it suggests the natural supposition that the priests' code was subsequent in origin to the Book of Kings.

V.—*Ezekiel and the Codes.*

The relation of the code of Ezekiel (xl.–xlviii.) to the priest's code is justly regarded as the key of the situation. The school of Reuss represents the code of Ezekiel as designed for the returned exiles; and that it was a preparation in development for the priests' code. The intermediate position of the code of Ezekiel between the Deuteronomic code and the priests' code is in dispute; but if it be intermediate it is no more necessary in this case, than in the others, to explain the fact by a historical development of the one into the other. But rather the changes are in the nature of an idealization. Ezekiel's construction of the temple, the division of the holy land among the tribes, the wonderful river of life, and tree of life, mingle, in a most magnificent prophetic ideal of the imagination, the representations of the garden of Eden, the temple of Solomon, the division of the land at the conquest, and the great works of architecture on the Euphrates,—in their combination, impossible of realization in fact. When the offerings and feasts of Ezekiel are considered from this point of view they seem to be intentionally diverse from those of the Mosaic legislation in Deuteronomy, and no less incapable of actual realization. It is not natural to think of them as a legal programme for the restoration. This whole legislation of Ezekiel is a symbol, tremendous in extent and in power; and it is to be compared with the symbols of the Resurrection (xxxvii. 1-14), the union of the two sticks (xxxvii. 15-28), the marvellous growth of the cedar twig (xvii. 22-24), and the battle with Gog and Magog (xxxviii.-ix.); for Ezekiel is the master of symbolical prophecy.

On the other hand it is worthy of note, that Ezekiel is in very close connection with the code of Holiness (Lev. xvii.-xxvi.). This section has certain features peculiar to itself, as we have seen. Graf, Kayser, and others ascribed it to the prophet Ezekiel himself. Horst regarded it as a codification of more ancient laws by Ezekiel prior to the composition of his own code. Klostermann calls it the "*Heiligkeitsgesetz.*" It is now agreed that it is a distinct code. We designate it by code of Holiness (H). Reuss, Wellhausen, and Kuenen make this code later than Ezekiel, but prior to the rest of the Priests' code. Questions of relative priority and dependence are among the most difficult in the field of Higher Criticism. Ezekiel's resemblance to it in many respects implies a knowledge of its legislation whether he knew it in its present form of codification or not. It is probable that Ezekiel knew of it, but it is difficult to prove the existence of the code prior to Ezekiel.

We have now gone over the arguments relied upon by the school of Reuss for their theory of the development of the Hexateuch. These sustain the theory so far as the codification of the legislation in its present literary forms is concerned; but not so far as to disprove earlier traditional Mosaic legislation and earlier Mosaic codes which have been used by holy men with historic reverence and under the influence of the divine Spirit in their codification of ancient laws and their composition of the historic documents into which the codes were taken up.

XIII.

THE MORE RECENT DISCUSSIONS.

THE development hypothesis of Reuss soon gained the mastery over the older theories of the composition of the Hexateuch and assumed various forms in the different schools of criticism. The discussion of the development hypothesis of the school of Reuss was opened in Great Britain by W. Robertson Smith in his article on the *Bible* in the *Encyclopædia Britannica*. Smith followed the school of Reuss with great boldness and thoroughness. He was opposed by Principal Douglas of Glasgow, who advocated the traditional theory. W. Robertson Smith, in defence, delivered his lectures on the *Old Testament in the Jewish Church*, and the *Prophets of Israel* which have exerted a vast influence in English-speaking lands. Charges of heresy were made against him before the Free Presbytery of Aberdeen and the case was carried by appeal to the General Assembly of the Free Presbyterian Church of Scotland which decided in his favor so far as his ministerial right, to hold such views under the Westminster Confession, was concerned; but deprived him of his professorial position at Aberdeen, in order to the peace and harmony of the Church. The contest in this case gained liberty of opinion in Great Britain. His teacher, Prof. A. B. Davidson of Edinburgh, who held essentially the same views, was undisturbed, and the General Assembly of the same Church, May, 1892, chose Dr. George Adam Smith, who holds similar views, to be the successor of Principal Douglas at Glasgow. The discussion was opened in America by an article by the author * in the *Presbyterian Review* in 1881, and it was continued in a series of articles in the same Review. He was sustained by Prof. Henry P. Smith of Cincinnati and by Prof. Francis Brown of New York. Prof. W. Henry Green of Princeton defended the traditional theory and was sustained by Drs. A. A. Hodge and F. L. Patton of Princeton. Prof. S. Ives Curtiss of Chicago and Prof. Willis J. Beecher of Auburn took a middle position. The discussion was closed by articles† by Prof. F. L. Patton and by the author‡ in 1883. Since the close of that discussion Profs. Bissell and Osgood have supported the traditional theory; but Profs. Gast, W. R. Harper, George F. Moore, J. P. Peters and many others have advanced to the support of the analysis of the Hexateuch. Pres. W. R. Harper has carried on a long discussion with Prof. W. Henry Green in the *Hebraica*, going over the greater part of the Hexateuch.

The school of Reuss has been strongly opposed by Dillmann, Baudissin, and Delitzsch in their more radical conclusions. These have been strengthened by younger scholars such as Strack and Kittel. These all make a very careful analysis of the documents, are agreed as to the order of development of EJ and D, but think that the legislation of P is in the main pre-exilic and that a considerable portion of it very ancient. They magnify the amount of ancient and original documents used by P.

---

* "*Right, Duty, and Limits of Biblical Criticism.*"
† *Critical Study of the History of the Higher Criticism.*
‡ *The Dogmatic Aspect of Pentateuchal Criticism.*

The school of Reuss agree with Dillmann as to the date of Deuteronomy, but differ from him as to the date of the priest's narrative. They hold it to be post-exilic, but Dillmann maintains that it was pre-exilic, and that it was written in the kingdom of Judah in the ninth century B.C. Dillmann in this has measurably advanced in the direction of the school of Reuss, but he stoutly resists their main thesis. Dillmann also differs from the school of Reuss as to the relation of JE. They make J the earlier document, but Dillmann holds that E was written in the northern kingdom in the first half of the ninth century B.C., and that J was written in the southern kingdom not earlier than the middle of the eighth century. There is also difference of opinion as to the work of editing the documents. Dillmann denies that E and J were first compacted and then D added to it and finally P. He holds that P, E and J were three independent documents, and that they were compacted at one editing just before the exile, and that during the exile they were attached to Deuteronomy.

One of the most important and successful parts of the analysis of Dillmann is his work upon that section of the priest-code, which he names the Sinai Code (S). This includes the code of Holiness in Leviticus, and other parts of the priestly legislation which share its peculiarities. Kuenen recognizes this as an earlier stage of P, and distinguishes it as P^1. But Dillmann holds that it is later than P, although it contains many laws of great antiquity. These had been handed down in the circle of priests and were codified shortly before the exile, possibly even before the composition of Deuteronomy. This code was, however, revised during the exile and enlarged. Other laws were also collected during the exile apart from this codex. These together with S were incorporated in JEDP by an editor of the priestly circle among the exiles. This view of Dillmann is also an approximation to the school of Reuss, for it makes a considerable portion of the priest-code later than the priestly narrative, and thus removes many of the objections to the older view of Ewald, De Wette, and others, that the priestly narrative was the fundamental writing of the Pentateuch. We think that Dillmann has done great service in the analysis of the Sinai code, but we cannot agree with him in his view of the date of it, and of its relation to the priests' narrative. Here is a field where, as Dillmann admits, the difficulties are very great. It is reserved for future investigators to solve this problem. It seems to us that Dillmann has shown that many of these laws of code S are in the very ancient form of the Pentade, and that the priest-code is really a complex of laws of different origin.

Baudissin* has rendered a real service to the Higher Criticism of the Hexateuch by his investigation of the genesis and the history of Priesthood in the Old Testament. He takes his stand with Dillmann, Delitzsch and Kittel over against the school of Reuss, and yet he is entirely independent in his methods, and has not a few opinions of his own. He holds that E was the most ancient of the documents. This was united with J by an editor who compacted them so tightly that it is often difficult to separate them. In the priestly document, he distinguishes P^1 and P^2 by differences in their views of the ministry of the Levites. He thinks that the legislation of P is the result of a long legislative development in priestly circles at Jerusalem. From time to time separate codes of priestly rules were written down. In

---

* *Die Geschichte des Alttestamentlichen Priesterthums.* Leipzig.

the first half of the seventh century, shortly before the reign of Josiah, a priest collected these, with the exception of the code of Holiness(Lev.xvii.–xxvi.), into a larger work with historical and genealogical frames. This document was a private code for the priesthood at Jerusalem. It elaborated the priestly legislation far beyond existing circumstances. The ideal in it is so prominent that many of its laws have never been realized in fact. The private priestly character of this document is the reason why it was unknown to the author of the Deuteronomic code, or disregarded by him. For the author of D wrote a people's book in view of the conditions and circumstances of his times. This code was composed shortly after P, and reflects the religion and doctrines of the times of Jeremiah. When discovered in the temple, it became the basis for the reform of Josiah. But the priests' code did not become a public code until after the exile, in the times of Ezra and Nehemiah. The code of Holiness remained as a document by itself until late in the exile, when it was incorporated in P. Ezekiel used it as his favorite law book, while it was a code by itself. Baudissin argues that the neglect to use P by D, together with the use of JE by D, implies, not the nonexistence of P, but only that at that time JE was a document by itself. He aims to prove the pre-exilic composition of P, by showing that the legislation of Ezekiel is an advance upon it in several particulars, such as the limitation of the priesthood to the line of Zadok; the slaying of sacrificial victims by Levites instead of by the offerers as in P; the partial substitution of the prince for the high priest and the ignoring of the latter; the enhanced sanctity of the priesthood, and the extreme precautions for guarding the approaches to the divine presence. He also shows an advance of the

Chronicler, who writes in the late Persian period or early Greek period with the use of older documents from the time of Ezra and Nehemiah, beyond P; and that the legislation of P does not suit the circumstances of the new community in Jerusalem at the Restoration in many important respects. He does not hesitate to regard P and D as written at about the same time. The documents were compacted during the last years of the exile by the Deuteronomist, who united P with JE and then used D as the closing legislation. Baudissin thinks that this order that was followed by the Deuteronomist who edited them, favors the priority of P to D. Baudissin agrees with all critics in the analysis of the Hexateuch, except that in a few cases he suggests improvements and modifications. The difference between him and other critics is in the date of the document P, and the time and method of compacting the four great documents. He adds to the investigation of Dillmann important materials for that work which is so greatly needed, the detailed analysis of the document P; for, after the separation of the code of Holiness, to which all critics are agreed, there still remain different layers of legislation which must be analyzed and arranged in historical order before the problem of the Hexateuch can be entirely solved.

Cornill, on the other hand, works in the lines of the school of Reuss. He goes into a detailed analysis of E, J, D and P, and throws fresh light upon their sources. He shows that D uses J E, but knows nothing of P. He regards E as an Ephraimitic writing, and places E^1 in the reign of Jeroboam II., about 750 B.C., and E^2 soon after the exile of the Northern Kingdom. J is a Judaic writing, originating in its different stages between the reign of Jehoshaphat, 850 B.C., and 625 B.C. P is an exilic law-book. A very important part of Cornill's work is the special consideration of a number of independent documents, which the great documents have taken up into themselves as older sources, and which have come in through the redactors, such as the ancient poems, the story of Balaam, Genesis xiv., the Covenant Code, the Code of Holiness, etc. The Covenant Code he regards as older than E, coming from the ninth century; the Code of Holiness, as a preparation for the Priest's Code. J and E were first combined by Rj; then these were combined with D by Rd. J E D were then compacted with P by Rp; but additions of various kinds were made to our Pentateuch even as late as the third century B.C.

A very important part of the work of Cornill is his effort to trace the documents of the Hexateuch, J E D, through the prophetic historians, Judges, Samuel, and Kings. Budde had already done valuable work in this department of investigation. If this theory can be worked out with any degree of certainty, then the date of the documents will speedily be determined within quite narrow limits. Here is a splendid field for Higher Criticism, in which the results will be of immense importance.

Canon S. R. Driver, in his invaluable work,* has massed the evidence for the analysis of the Hexateuch from language and style beyond any previous writer. He is not as strong in the historical and theological evidence, although he makes valuable contributions in these departments also. His analysis of J E from P, and of H from P, and D^2 from D, is masterly; but he halts in his separation of E from J. The date of Deuteronomy is not precisely determined, but it is said to be not later than the reign of Manasseh. "All things con-

---
* *The Literature of the Old Testament.*

sidered, a date in the early centuries of the monarchy would seem not to be unsuitable both for J and for E; but it must remain an open question whether both may not in reality be earlier." "The laws of H were arranged in their present parenetic frame-work by an author who was at once a priest and a prophet, probably towards the closing years of the monarchy."

"These arguments are cogent, and combine to make it probable that the *completed* Priests' Code is the work of the age subsequent to Ezekiel. When, however, this is said, it is very far from being implied that all the institutions of P are the *creation* of this age. The contradiction of the pre-exilic literature does not extend to the *whole* of the Priests' Code indiscriminately. The Priests' Code embodies some elements with which the earlier literature is in harmony, and which indeed it presupposes: it embodies other elements with which the same literature is in conflict, and the existence of which it even seems to preclude. This double aspect of the Priests' Code is reconciled by the supposition that the chief ceremonial institutions of Israel are *in their origin* of great antiquity; but that the laws respecting them were gradually developed and elaborated, and *in the shape in which they are formulated in the Priests' Code* that they belong to the exilic or early post-exilic period. In its main stock, the legislation of P was thus not (as the critical view of it is sometimes represented by its opponents as teaching) 'manufactured' by the priests during the exile: it is based upon *pre-existing Temple usage,* and exhibits the form which that finally assumed. Hebrew legislation took shape gradually; and the codes of JE (Ex. 20–23, 34, 10 ff.), Dt., and P represent three successive phases of it."*

---

* *Literature of the Old Testament*, p. 135.

These more recent investigations have greatly enriched our knowledge of the earlier strata in the documents. This is the field in which criticism will hereafter gain its greatest triumphs and reap its choicest fruits. It is delicate, intricate and difficult work, and yet it is necessary that it should be done. Only in this way can we now prove the antiquity of the legislation. It is clear that the present code is a complex of legislation, some parts of which have been taken from earlier codes, other parts being a codification of traditional liturgy and usage.

It is necessary not only to distinguish H from P, but also to distinguish P^1 and P^2. It is also necessary to distinguish D^1 and D^2, J^1 and J^2, E^1 and E^2, and thus the problem of Pentateuchal criticism becomes complex and extremely intricate. It is easy for anti-critics to make sport of such work. Dr. Bissell objects that this makes the Pentateuch a piece of patchwork, thus showing that he has not yet learned the difference between the fragmentary hypothesis of Geddes and Vater, which is open to that objection, and the documentary hypothesis, the supplementary hypothesis, and the development hypothesis, which have successively grown into one another as the study of the Hexateuch has advanced, and which no true scholar could possibly regard as making patchwork of the Pentateuch; for they all keep the unity of the Hexateuch in mind and endeavor to show how the unity springs out of the variety of documents. A nice piece of patchwork is to be seen in Prof. Osgood's recent tract of 35 pages on *A Reasonable Hypothesis of the Origin of the Pentateuch*, advocating the traditional theory. He objects to Wellhausen's extreme view of 20 or more writers and editors of the Hexateuch as an unreasonable hypothesis, and yet in the body of his tract, in 19 pages treating of Assyria, Egypt and Syria, he cites at length 25 different writers in 428 lines, and writes himself, counting introduction, conclusion and seams, 133 lines. If he had omitted quotation marks and marginal references, it would have been a tough piece of criticism to get at these 25 authors and one editor. We do not consider this method of Prof. Osgood an unreasonable method, although it is a little unusual. The unreasonableness of the Professor is in his doing himself in such a limited space so much more of the same work that he thinks it unreasonable that the editor of the Hexateuch should have done.

The climax of this opposition to the analysis of the Hexateuch has been reached by an ex-Hebrew professor, who prefers the pseudonym McRealsham under which to throw contempt upon criticism by applying what he thinks are its principles in a dissection of the Epistle to the Romans, in which he chiefly succeeds in showing the appropriateness of the name he selected for himself. It will be a task of some difficulty for him ever to get rid of it.

Prof. Geo. F. Moore of Andover has recently given a comparison of the methods of Tatian in his *Diatessaron*, or Harmony of the Gospels, with the methods of the redactor of our Hexateuch. He gives the following specimen from the Diatessaron, showing on the margin the Gospels from which the extracts were made:

[1] Matt. iii. 13.	*[1] Then cometh Jesus from Galilee to Jordan unto John, to be baptized of him. [2]And Jesus was about thirty years of age, and was sup-
[2] Luke iii. 23.	

---

* The No. indicates that the passage which follows belongs to the text of Scripture given with the number. This notation differs from that given by Moore.

[3] John i. 29–31.	posed to be the son of Joseph. [3]And John seeth Jesus coming unto him, and saith, Behold the Lamb of God which taketh away the sin of the world. 30. This is he of whom I said, After me cometh a man which is preferred before me, for he was before me. 31. And I knew him not; but that he should be made manifest to Israel, therefore am I come baptizing with water.
[4] Matt. iii. 14 f.	[4]And John forbade him, saying, I have need to be baptized of thee, and comest thou to me? 15. Jesus answering said unto him, Suffer it to be so now; for thus it becometh us to fulfil all righteousness. Then he suffered him.
[5] Luke iii. 21 a. [6] Matt. iii. 16 b.	[5]And when all the people were baptized, Jesus also was baptized. [6]And he went up straightway out of the water, and the heavens were opened unto him.
[7] Luke iii. 22 a.	[7]And the Holy Ghost descended upon him in the likeness of a dove;
[8] Matt. iii. 17.	[8]and lo, a voice from heaven, saying, This is my beloved Son, in whom I am well pleased.
[9] John i. 32–34.	[9]And John bare record, saying, I saw the Spirit descending from heaven, like a dove, and it abode upon him. 33. And I knew him not; but he that sent me to baptize with water, the same said unto me, Upon whom thou shalt see the Spirit descending and remaining on him, the same is he which baptizeth with the Holy Ghost. 34. And I saw and bare record that this is the Son of God.
[10] Luke iv. 1 a. [11] Mark i. 12. [12] Mark i. 13 b.	[10]And Jesus, being full of the Holy Ghost, returned from Jordan. [11]And immediately the Spirit driveth him into the wilderness [12]to be tempted of Satan; and he was with the wild beasts.
[13] Matt. iv. 2 a. [14] Luke iv. 2 b. [15] Matt. iv. 2 b–7.	[13]And he fasted forty days and forty nights, [14]and in those days he did eat nothing; [15]and he was afterward ahungered. 3. And the tempter came to him, and said, If thou be the Son of God, command that these stones be made bread. 4. But he answered and said, It is written, Man shall not live by

> bread alone, but by every word that proceedeth out of the mouth of God. 5. Then the devil taketh him up into the Holy City, and setteth him on a pinnacle of the temple, 6. and saith unto him, If thou be the Son of God, cast thyself down ; for it is written, He shall give his angels charge concerning thee, and in their hands they shall bear thee up, lest at any time thou dash thy foot against a stone. 7. Jesus said unto him, It is written again, Thou shalt not tempt the Lord thy God. [16]And the devil took him up into a high mountain, and showed unto him all the kingdoms of the world and the glory of them in a moment of time. 6. And the devil said unto him, All this power will I give thee, and the glory of it, for that is delivered unto me, and to whomsoever I will I give it. 7. If thou therefore wilt worship me, all shall be thine, etc.

[16] Luke iv. 5–7.

As Prof. Moore says :

"The most hair-splitting analysis of the Pentateuch seems sober in comparison with this Composite Gospel. It is, to use Prof. Mead's figure, a patchwork, crazier than the wildest dreams of the critics. And yet I think no one will read it, especially in a Semitic language, without feeling that the author has succeeded beyond what we should have thought possible in making a unity of it. It must be borne in mind, too, that this patchwork was made, not of indifferent historical writings, but of the sacred books of the Christian church; that it was meant to take the place of the Gospels; that it accomplished its end so successfully that it almost completely superseded the separate Gospels in the public use of a considerable part of the Syrian church; that it was apparently only under influences from without that it was banished from the use of these churches in the fifth century. Apharates and Ephraim are acquainted, indeed, with the separate Gospels; but it is certainly within the bounds of possibility that, if the Syrian church had been left to itself, without constant contact with the greater church to the West, the knowledge of the separate Gospels might in the end have been lost, even among the learned. The parallel to the history of the Pentateuch would then have been complete." *Journal of Biblical Literature*, 1890, ix., pp. 207 *seq*.

We have higher authority than Tatian for such compilations from different documents. No less an authority than the apostle Paul uses this method in Romans iii. 9–18, where he writes:

"What then? are we in worse case than they? No, in no wise: for we before laid to the charge both of Jews and Greeks, that they are all under sin; as it is written,
 There is none righteous, (Eccl. vii. 20.)
 No, not one; (Ps. xiv. 3).
 There is none that understandeth,
 There is none that seeketh after God;
 They have all turned aside,
 They are together become unprofitable;
 There is none that doeth good,
 No, not so much as one: (Ps. xiv. 2–3.)
 Their throat is an open sepulchre;
 With their tongues they have used deceit: (Ps. v. 9.)
 The poison of asps is under their lips: (Ps. cxl. 3.)
 Whose mouth is full of cursing and bitterness: (Ps. x. 7.)
 Their feet are swift to shed blood;
 Destruction and misery are in their ways;
 And the way of peace have they not known: (Is. lix. 7–8.)
 There is no fear of God before their eyes." (Ps. xxxvi. 1.)

On the basis of this compilation by the Apostle, a Greek scribe attached these passages to his manuscript of Ps. xiv., and from that resulted the following facts, summed up in the words of Bishop Perowne, as follows:

"But in some MSS. of the LXX., in the Vulg., and both Arab., Syro-Arab., and Copto-Arab., and strangest of all in the Syro-Hex., they are found in the Psalm, having evidently been transferred hither from the Epistle. So also in our Prayer Book version, which, it should be remembered, is, in fact, Coverdale's

(1535), and was made, not from the original, but mainly from the Latin and German, being based on the Zurich Bible."—(*The Psalms*, vol. i., p. 188.)

And thus for centuries this compilation has been sung all over Christendom as if it were a portion of a Psalm of David.

In view of such facts as these, is it not time that these American professors should have scholarship sufficient to deter them from calling the compiler's work in our Hexateuch a piece of patchwork?

As Eichhorn said at the beginning, the documentary hypothesis improves the evidence for the fidelity of the records. The editor of the Pentateuch, instead of writing a new narrative and making a new code, collects and compacts the several narratives and codes. He does it not by patchwork, but by the skilful use of the documents. Sometimes they are given side by side, sometimes they are interwoven, sometimes they are entirely worked over, and the pieces are skilfully seamed together. The work of the inspired editors is more important for us than the work of the original writers. The anti-critics find fault with the differences of the critics in certain verses and sections, and neglect to see the wonderful concord of the critics in the analysis as a whole. But the disagreements of the critics are where they must be from the nature of the case, namely, in the seams, where the material of the different narrators is wrought over in order to make the narrative harmonious. The differences do not exist to any extent elsewhere. This is rather an indirect evidence of the success of the analysis, and is not a valid argument against it.

Dr. Green's favorite method of argumentation is to throw the critics of the last two centuries into an indiscriminate mass, and then point to their discord as an evidence of the unsoundness of their conclusion. This is the method of an advocate, and not of a scholar. If the critics are ranged in their historic order, it will be manifest that the differences are chiefly between the critics of the several different stages of the work of criticism. As the work of criticism has advanced since the time of Astruc, the concord of critics has increased steadily, and differences have disappeared with every fresh effort. This is as it ought to be, from the very nature of the case. It is so in all science, in all search after truth. The truth-loving scholars advance step by step, one after another, and remove one difficulty after another as they advance.

The differences among the critics in the analysis of the Hexateuch are surprisingly few. We now have accessible to us the analyses of Dillmann, of Kuenen, of Wellhausen, and of Reuss, of Driver, and of Kautzsch, and they are essentially agreed.

These are some of the scholars who hold to the critical analysis of the Hexateuch. Dillmann, Kleinert, Schrader, and Strack of Berlin, Kittel of Breslau, Kautzsch and Meyer of Halle, Nöldeke, Budde and Nowack of Strassburg, Baudissin and Jülicher of Marburg, Stade of Giessen, König of Rostock, Bäthgen and Giesebrecht of Greifswald, Schultz, Wellhausen, Smend of Göttingen, Socin, Guthe, Fred. Delitzsch and Buhl of Leipzig, Merx and Lemme of Heidelberg, Cornill of Königsberg, Schürer, Klostermann and Bredenkamp of Kiel, Kamphausen of Bonn, Grill of Tübingen, Köhler of Erlangen, Hommel of Munich, Siegfried and Stickel of Jena, Orelli, Duhm and Marti of Basle, Oettli of Bern, Ryssel of Zurich, Montet of Geneva, Vuilleumier and Gautier of Lausanne, Volck of Dorpat, Bruston and Montet of Montaubon, Reville, Carriere,

Vernes, Darmstetter, of Paris; Castelli of Florence, Tiele and Oort of Leiden, Valeton of Utrecht, Wildeboer of Groningen, De La Saussaye and Knappert of Amsterdam, Lotz and Floigl of Vienna, Cheyne, Driver and Cooke of Oxford, Kirkpatrick, W. Robertson Smith, Ryle and Stanton of Cambridge, Drummond and Carpenter of the Manchester New College, Davison of Richmond, Whitehouse of Cheshunt, Duff of the Yorkshire Congregational College, Davidson of Edinburgh, Kennedy of Aberdeen, Adam Smith and Robertson of Glasgow, Wright and Spurrell of London, Harper and Addis of Melbourne. On what other subject can you find such agreement among specialists the world over? Where are the professors in the Old Testament department in the universities and colleges in Europe, who hold a different view? They cannot be found. Is it credible that all these specialists should be in error in their own departments, and that a few American Hebrew professors should have the right of it? Even in our country we may point to Toy and Lyon of Harvard, Ladd and Curtis of Yale, Peters and Jastrow of the University of Pennsylvania, W. R. Harper, Hirsch and S. Ives Curtiss of Chicago, Haupt of Johns Hopkins, George Moore of Andover, Gast of Lancaster, Henry P. Smith of Lane, Francis Brown of Union, Bartlett, Batten and Kellner of the Episcopal Divinity schools, Schmidt and Brown of the Baptist schools, and many others who agree with them, but who have not yet published their conclusions. Such men, sustained as they are by the unanimous voice of the Hebrew scholars of Europe, cannot be overcome by such appeals to popular prejudice as have thus far constituted the staple of all the arguments against them. In the field of scholarship the question is settled. It only remains for the ministry and people to accept it and adapt themselves to it.

The evidence sustaining the analysis of the Hexateuch and the late date of the composition of some of its documents, and the weight of scholarly authority which accepts it, are so great that it is difficult to see how any candid mind can resist them. That there are a few professorial Hebrew scholars who still resist them, is due, as it appears, solely and alone to *a priori* dogmatic considerations. They think it necessary to defend the traditional theory in order (1) to conserve their doctrine of the inerrancy of Holy Scripture, (2) to protect their doctrine that only a well-known prophet like Moses can write an inspired book, and (3) to secure their interpretation of the New Testament that Jesus Christ has decided this matter for us and that therefore the veracity and divinity of Jesus Christ are imperilled unless we recognize his testimony as decisive, that Moses wrote the Pentateuch. They, holding these dogmatic views, are incapable of being influenced by any arguments of criticism or by any weight of authority however great. The science of the Higher Criticism is resisted by speculative dogma and the supposed authority of Jesus, in precisely the same way that the other sciences have been resisted, each in its turn, by the same class of minds.

XIII.

THE ARGUMENT FROM BIBLICAL THEOLOGY.

THERE are a number of arguments from the field of Biblical theology which guide to the determination of the dates of the documents of the Hexateuch.

(1). Divine revelation in dreams is frequent in E (Gen. xxviii. 12–15; xxxvii. 5–10; xl. 5–8; xli. 1–15; xlii. 9.) It is mentioned in D, Deut. xiii. 2, 4, 6; but is not known to J. Revelation in the ecstatic state is mentioned by E and J, but P knows nothing of dreams or visions. He thinks of a direct communication by God to the soul of the prophet. Does not this indicate a later stage of reflection?

(2). There is a different conception of theophanies in these writers. E narrates frequent appearances of the theophanic angel of God. J reports appearances of the theophanic angel of *Yahweh*. These theophanic appearances are mentioned in the Ephraimitic and Judaic documents of the prophetic histories. But neither D nor P knows of such a theophanic angel. When God reveals Himself, in the Ephraimitic documents, He speaks to Moses face to face, and Moses sees the form of God in the pillar of God standing at the door of his tent. In the great theophany granted to Moses in the Judaic document Ex. xxxiii. 20–23, Moses is permitted only to see the departing form of God, and it is represented that it would be death to see God's face. In Deuteronomy it is said that the voice of God was heard, but His form was not seen. In the priestly document it is the light and fire of the glory of God which always constitutes the theophany. How was it possible for the same author to give four such different accounts of the methods of God's appearance to Moses and the people? *

(3). There is a different conception of miracles. The miracles of E were always wrought by means of some external instrument. The chief of these is the rod of God, which is used by Moses in working the plagues of Egypt (Ex. vii. 17; ix. 23*a*; x. 13; xiv. 16) and in the victory over Amalek (Ex. xvii. 8–13). A branch of a tree works a miracle at Mara (Ex. xv. 25), a brazen serpent was erected on a pole for healing (Num. xxi. 8–9), and the seven sacred trumpets were used at Jericho (Jos. vi. 5). The miracles of J were wrought without any instruments, by the wind (Ex. x. 13*b*, 19; xiv. 21*b*) by the hand of God (Ex. iii. 20; ix. 3, 15); by his strong hand (Ex. iii. 19; xiii. 3, 9, 14; xxxii. 11); by command (Ex. iv. 2–9); and without human mediation (Ex. iv. 1–9; viii. 17–19; xvi. 27–30; Num. xi. 18–33), and before the ark (Jos. iii. 15–17). The miracles of D were wrought by the strong hand and the outstretched arm of Jahveh without human mediation (Deut. iv. 34; Jos. iv. 24). They are gifts of Jahveh (Dt. viii. 3–4, 15–16; xxix. 1–4). The miracles of P were wrought by the finger of God (Ex. viii. 15), the hand of God (Ex. vii. 4–5). Aaron's rod takes the place of Moses' rod of E (Ex. vii. 9, 19–20; viii. 1–3, 12–13; Num. xvii. 21–25;

---

* See Appendix VIII.

xx. 8–17). A handful of ashes was once used (Ex. ix. 8–12).

The miracles of the narratives of the Hexateuch are referred to in such a way in the Psalter and the prophets as to give evidence of value as to their composition.

The Egyptian Plagues.

E.	J. (and *Psalm* lxxviii.)	P.	*Psalm* cv.
1. Bloody water.	1. Bloody water.	1. Bloody water.	2. Bloody water.
....	2. Frogs.	2. Frogs.	3. Frogs.
....	3. Swarms of insects.	3. Lice or gnats.	4. Swarm of insects and gnats.
....	4. Pestilence.	4. Ulcers.	....
2. Hail.	5. Hail.	....	5. Hail.
3. Locusts.	6. Locusts.	....	6. Locusts.
4. Darkness.	....	....	1. Darkness.
5. Death of First-born.	7. Death of First-born.	5. Death of First-born.	7. Death of First-born.

Psalm lxxviii. mentions the seven plagues of J, the manna and quails of J, and the miracles of cleaving the sea and the water from the rock of E; but none of the miracles of P. It seems evident that when this psalm was composed J and E had not been compacted, else why were the plagues of E omitted? P was apparently unknown, for why should all its miracles be ignored? On the other hand, Psalm cv. gives the plagues of Egypt from the combined narratives of E, J and P, the water from the rock of E, and the quails and manna

THE ARGUMENT FROM BIBLICAL THEOLOGY 149

of J, showing that when this psalm was written our present Pentateuch had been compacted. Ps. cvi. gives the water from the rock and the quails from the narrative of P, and the crossing of the sea from J, showing a preference for the story of P. Ps. lxxiv. mentions the cleaving of the sea and of the rock of E, and the drying of the Jordan of D, making it evident that the Psalm was written after the composition of D. The reference to the crossing of the Red Sea in the prophets Is. x. 26; xi. 15–16; the exilic Isaiah xliii. 16, l. 2, li. 10; the earlier, Zech. x. 11, are all based on JE, making it probable that P was unknown to them.

(4). There is a difference in the doctrine of the Covenants. E knows of two covenants, the one with Israel at Horeb (Ex. xxiv. 3–8), the other at Shechem (Jos. xxiv. 25). J reports a series of promises to our first parents and the patriarchs, but only two covenants, the one with Abraham (Gen. xv. 18), the other with Israel at Sinai (Ex. xxxiv. 10–27). D reports a covenant with Israel at Horeb, agreeing with E (Dt. iv. 13), and a second covenant in the land of Moab, unknown to the other writers (Dt. xxviii. 69, xxix. 20). P gives a series of great covenants: (1) the covenant with Noah and its sign the rainbow (Gen. ix. 1–17); (2) the covenant with Abraham and its sign circumcision (Gen. xvii.); (3) the covenant with Israel at Sinai and its sign the Sabbath (Ex. vi. 4, xxxi. 16–17); (4) the covenant with Phinehas (Num. xxv. 12–13).*

---

* The terms used on these documents are very different. כרת ברית is used 9 times in JED, but not in P, who uses הקים ברית [establish a covenant] 8 times, a phrase used elsewhere only in Ez. xvi. 60, 62, and in the sense of confirming a covenant Lev. xxvi. 9 (H) and Dt. viii. 18. So also "remember the covenant" is used only by P 4 and H Lev. xxvi. 42, 45, Ez. xvi. 60, 1 Chron. xvi. 15, and in the late Psalms cv. 8, cvi. 45, cxi. 5. The phrases "everlasting

(5). In 1 Sam. ix. 9, it is said: " Beforetime in Israel when a man went to inquire of God, thus he said, Come and let us go to the seer: for he that is now called a Prophet was before time called a Seer." This is an historical note by the editor of Samuel, stating that the Nabi of his time was anciently called a Roeh. This passage is an explanation of the fact that in this document Samuel was called a seer. The most natural interpretation of it is, that prior to the time of Samuel, and for some time afterwards, Nabi was not used. How then shall we explain the usage of Nabi with reference to Abraham and Moses in the Hexateuch? Are we justified in supposing that the writers of these documents, who use this term in the Hexateuch, wrote subsequent to Samuel and after the term Nabi had supplanted Roeh?

It is noteworthy that P does not use this term, doubtless because he was cognizant of this historical fact, writing with this note of Samuel before him. There appears to be a growth in the conception of a prophet. In ancient times the prophets were called "*seers*," from the ecstatic state in which they prophesied. The term "*man of God*" then came into use in the times of Elijah, and is commonly used in the Ephraimitic sources of Kings. At a later date "*Nabi*" was used to indicate prophets of a higher order who were the preachers or spokesmen of Yahweh. The fact that E J D use this term would indicate that these documents were not composed before the age of Elijah.

(6). The doctrine of the divine Spirit is not found in E. The Spirit of God in Gen. xli. 38 is the spiritual energy in man imparted by God to enable him to act. The

---

covenant" and "covenant of peace" are also confined to P in the Hexateuch. The former was not earlier than Jeremiah, except in the poetic passage 2 Sam. xxiii. 5 ; the latter, elsewhere only in Ezekiel and the exilic Isaiah.

divine Spirit in J rests upon Moses and the elders, endowing them with the power to prophesy in the ecstatic state (Num. xi. 25-29). The only other passage in which there is reference to the Spirit of God is Gen. vi. 3, where it refers to the spirit breathed into man by God, according to Gen. ii. 7. This doctrine of the Spirit, as coming upon men and endowing them with gifts of prophecy and government, is common in the earlier narratives of the prophetic historians and the earlier prophets. But P gives a doctrine of the divine Spirit which is vastly higher. In Ex. xxxi. 3 the divine Spirit fills the architect, who constructed the tabernacle and its furniture, with wisdom and understanding, and in Gen. i. 2, the divine Spirit hovers over the primeval abyss with creative energy. Such an exalted doctrine of the divine Spirit is found elsewhere in the literature no earlier than the second Isaiah. The poem which contains it must be of late date.

(7). The attributes of God are only indirectly taught in E, but in J they appear in several important passages, as Ex. xxxiv. 6-7, where the divine mercy is unfolded, and the song Deut. xxxii. 3-4, where the divine righteousness is set forth, each in a number of synonymous terms. It is worthy of mention that the phrase* "mercy and faithfulness" is only in the Judaic writer in the Hexateuch, both as applied to men and to God; elsewhere chiefly in the Psalter and Proverbs.

The doctrine of Holiness is characteristic of H and P. As Driver says of H: "The principle which determines most conspicuously the character of the entire section is that of *holiness*—partly ceremonial, partly moral—as a quality distinguishing Israel, demanded of Israel by

---

* חסד ואמת.

Jehovah (Lev. xix. 2; xx. 7, 8, 26; xxi. 6-8; xv. 23; xxii. 9, 16, 32), and regulating the Israelite's life. Holiness is, indeed, a duty laid upon Israel in other parts of the Pentateuch; but while elsewhere it appears merely as one injunction among many, it is here insisted on with an emphasis and frequency which constitute it the leading motive of the entire section. In consequence of this very prominent characteristic, the present group of chapters received from Klostermann in 1877, the happily chosen title of *Das Heiligkeitsgesetz*, or 'The Law of Holiness,' which it has since retained."*

The segholate noun *Qodesh* is used in the song of the Red Sea, Ex. xv. 11, of the holiness of God, where it is a synonym of majesty and exaltation, and of the place of the divine habitation Ex. xv. 13. J E uses it of the place of a theophany, Ex. iii. 5, Jos. v. 15, and of consecrated spoil, Jos. vi. 19. D uses it of the heavenly abode of Yahweh, Dt. xxvi. 15, and of consecrated things, Dt. xii. 26, xxvi. 13. But H and P use it about 217 times, and especially in a large number of phrases peculiar to them.

The adjective† "Holy" is used in E of Israel as a holy nation, Ex. xix. 6; and of God as a holy God, Jos. xxiv. 19; by D also of Israel as a holy people 6 times; of the camp of Israel as holy, Dt. xxiii. 15. But H and P use it of the holy place 8 times, of the holy people 7 times, of the holy priesthood 5 times, of holy water once, of the Nazarite twice, and above all of Yahweh's words, "I am holy," 5 times.

Glory‡ is used in J E of the honor and glory of men, Gen. xxxi. 1; xlv. 13; xlix. 6; Num. xxiv. 11; and of the glory of God in the theophany, Ex. xxxiii. 18, 22 (J), Dt. v. 21;

---

* *Literature of the O. T.*, p. 44. † "Holy," קדוש.
‡ "Glory," כבוד.

and of the glory or honor due to Yahweh, the God of Israel, Jos. vii. 19. In the mixed narrative Num. xiv. 21–22 (ascribed by Dillmann to R), the manifested glory of God is presented in an oath of God which reappears in Ps. lxxii. But in P this word becomes characteristic. It is used twice of the glory of the high priest's garments, Ex. xxviii. 2, 40; and 13 times of the theophanic glory in some form of light and fire. It is noteworthy that it is used in Ezekiel 17 times in the same sense, showing that a close relation exists between Ezekiel and P.

(8). There are striking differences in the doctrine of sin. Sin is mentioned in E only in general terms and in connection with special acts of evil-doing. J unfolds the doctrine of sin in a graphic manner from the point of view of personal relation to God. Evil is first presented to man in the divine prohibition of the tree of knowledge, then in the animal serpent, used by the evil intelligence who deceives the woman. The attractions of the sensuous good excites her desire, she partakes of the evil fruit, she tempts her husband and he sins with her. They both experience the blush of shame, they fear God and hide from His presence. When called to account they excuse themselves and blame others. Sin knocks as a wild beast at the door of Cain's heart; once admitted it rages in anger, revenge and murder. Sin develops in the race through the intercourse of evil spirits with the daughters of mankind, until mankind becomes totally corrupt. Sin unfolds in Babylon in a centralization of power and tyranny, and in Sodom and its sisters in sins of uncleanness until they become exceedingly wicked. Sin is a forsaking God, a violating his covenant, and a whoring after other gods.

D conceives of sin as turning away from God, rebelling against Him with a stiff neck, murmuring against Him and tempting Him.

P conceives of sin chiefly as a violation of the law; he does not attempt to describe its origin or develepment. He distinguishes technically between sin as an error, and as high-handed transgression. He represents sin in the use of a characteristic term,* both, noun and verb, to act treacherously, and treachery, 13 times, which term is unknown to the other narrators, is not found in the prophetic histories, but in Dan. ix. 7, Ezekiel 7 times and elsewhere chiefly in the Chronicler. This characteristic use of such a late word favors the exilic or post-exilic origin of P.

It should be noticed here that H has important phrases "to bear sin" or "his sin" or "their sin" or "iniquity" or "their iniquity" or "iniquity of another." These are used chiefly by H. Elsewhere in the Hexateuch only by P. Ezekiel frequently uses them. Elsewhere they are seldom found, but compare the exilic Isaiah liii. 12.

(9). The divine judgment of sin is commonly expressed in the Hexateuch by hardening the heart. But the documents have different expressions for it.†

(10). The doctrine of redemption in E is simply redemption from evil and not from sin. The only reference to the latter subject is in the warning at the close of the covenant code lest they should not be forgiven, Ex. xxiii. 21. In J it is the nature of God to forgive

---

*מעל.

† E uses the term חזק לב Ex. iv. 21, x. 20, 27; also D² in Jos. xi. 20; D uses הקשה רוח and אמץ לבב Dt. ii. 30; J uses the term הכביד לב Ex. viii. 11, 28, ix. 34, x. 1; כבד לב Ex. vii. 14, ix. 7; P uses הקשה לב Ex. vii. 3, and חזק לב Ex. vii. 13, 22, viii. 15, ix. 35; חזק לב Ex. ix. 12, xi. 10, xiv. 4, 8, 17.

sin, Ex. xxxiv. 6–9 and Num. xiv. 18–20; when Moses intercedes for the people then sin is covered over without sacrifice, Ex. xxxii. 30–34. In D Yahweh chooses Israel and enters into a relation of love with them. P conceives of redemption either as the removal of sin from the persons of the sinners or the sacred places, or as the covering it over at the divine altars by the blood of the sin-offerings. There is an interesting usage of terms in the documents.*

The relation of love between God and man is characteristic of D. God's love to His people is in Dt. iv. 37; vii. 8, 13; x. 15; xxiii. 6; not elsewhere in the Hexateuch, but first in Hosea the prophet. Love to God is in Dt. vi. 5; vii. 9; x. 12; xi. 1; xiii. 22; xiii. 4; xix. 9; xxx. 6, 16, 20; Jos. xxii. 5; xxiii. 11. Elsewhere in the Hexateuch only Ex. xx. 6=Dt. v. 10 [a Deuteronomic addition to the Ten Words].

These examples from the field of Biblical Theology are sufficient for our purpose at present. They might be increased to an indefinite extent. They show the same order of development that we have found in the legislation and in the language, and indicate that the documents were composed at such epochs as best explain this development.

---

* גאל is used in poetic passages of E of the redemption of Jacob, Gn. xlviii. 16, and of Israel's redemption by God, Ex. xv. 13 and Ex. vi. 6 (RP), but it is used by HP only in the lower sense of redemption of things by payment of a fine, Lv. xxvii. 13, 15, 19, 20, 31. It is used in the sense of acting as a kinsman chiefly in DHP and Ruth, not in JE. פדה is used for the redemption of Israel by D, but by JE and P only in the lower sense. נשא forgive is used in E; סלח in DP; both terms in J. נשא is used in Hos. xiv. 3; Mic. vii. 18; Is. ii. 9, xxxiii. 24; Jb. vii. 21; 1 Sam. xv. 25; but is unknown to Jeremiah, Kings the second Isaiah, Daniel, Lamentations, and the Chronicler, who use סלח. It is found only in the earlier and the latest Psalms.

XIV.

THE RESULT OF THE ARGUMENT.

We have gone over the several lines of argument usually employed in Higher Criticism in order to gain their witness to the composition of the Pentateuch. The several lines of evidence converge to the same results. These may be stated as follows: The document E is known to Hosea, it resembles the Ephraimitic prophet and also the Ephraimitic writers in the books of Samuel and Kings. It is the most archaic of the documents in language, style, and historical and doctrinal conceptions. It shows great interest in the sacred places of Northern Israel. It appears therefore that E was the narrative of the Northern kingdom of Israel, and that its law code, the greater book of the covenant, was the Mosaic law in its Ephraimitic codification.

It is possible that J was known to Hosea, but this is not certain. It was evidently known to the prophet Isaiah. Its interest in the sanctuaries in Judah and its resemblance with the Judaic writers of the histories of David and Solomon in the books of Samuel and Kings, make it altogether probable that we have in this writing the Judaic recension of the history. The only legislation it attributes to Moses is the moral law of the Ten Words, the decalogue of worship (the little book of the

Covenant) and a special law of the Passover. Its style is the very choicest and best. The author probably lived at the centre of Jewish affairs, in the holy city, Jerusalem, where he had access to the best sources of information and where he had acquired the best literary culture.

Deuteronomy cannot be traced earlier than the reign of Josiah. It then comes into full recognition and use in the work of the compiler of the Book of Kings and in the prophecy of Jeremiah. It was a recodification of the old covenant code of Moses in the Judaic recension, and thus the code shows parallelism with the covenant code of E. The prophetic codifier shows by his method and style that he had back of him a long history of prophetic oral and written discourses.

The code of Holiness comes into the historic field first in connection with Ezekiel. It is a codification of the immemorial practice of the priests of Jerusalem going back to Aaron and Moses.

The priest-code and the document which contains it cannot be proven till Ezra's time. It was a larger codification of the priestly ritual and customs coming down by tradition from Moses and Aaron in the priestly circles of Jerusalem, which had been carefully conserved as holy relics in the priestly families among the exiles, as bearing in them sacred memories and holy promises.

Driver makes this moderate and cautious statement:

"It cannot be doubted that Moses was the ultimate founder of both the national and the religious life of Israel; and that he provided his people not only with at least the nucleus of a system of civil ordinances (such as would, in fact, arise directly out of his judicial functions, as described in Ex. xviii.), but also (as the necessary correlative of the primary truth that *Jehovah was the God of Israel*) with some system of ceremonial observances, designed as the expression and concomitant of the religious and ethical duties involved in the people's relations to its national God. It is reasonable to suppose that the teaching of Moses on these subjects is preserved, in its least modified form, in the Decalogue and the " Book of the Covenant " (Ex. xx.–xxiii.) It is not, however, required by the view treated above as probable to conclude that the Mosaic legislation was *limited* to the subjects dealt with in Ex. xx.–xxiii.; amongst the enactments peculiar to Dt.—which tradition, as it seems, ascribed to a later period of the legislator's life—there are many which likewise may well have formed part of it. It is further in analogy with ancient custom to suppose that some form of *priesthood* would be established by Moses: that this priesthood would be hereditary; and that the priesthood would also inherit from their founder some traditional lore (beyond what is contained in Ex. xx.–xxiii.) on matters of ceremonial observance. And accordingly we find that JE both mentions repeatedly an Ark and " Tent of Meeting " as existing in the Mosaic age (Ex. xxxiii. 7–11, Nu. xi., 24ff, xii. 4ff, Dt. xxxi. 14ff), and assigns to Aaron a prominent and, indeed, an official position (Ex. iv. 14, " Aaron *the Levite;*" xviii. 12; xxiv. 1, 9); further, that in Dt. (x. 6b) a hereditary priesthood descended from him is expressly recognized; and also that there are early allusions to the " tribe of Levi " as enjoying priestly privileges and exercising priestly functions (Dt. xxxiii. 10; Mic. iii. 11; cf. Jud. xvii. 13). The principles by which the priesthood was to be guided were laid down, it may be supposed, in outline by Moses. In process of time, however, as national life grew more complex, and fresh cases requiring to be dealt with arose, these principles would be found no longer to suffice, and their extension would become a necessity. Especially in matters of ceremonial observance, which would remain naturally within the control of the priests, regulations such as those enjoined in Ex. xx. 24-26, xxii. 29-31, xxiii. 14-19, would not long continue in the same rudimentary state; fresh definitions and distinctions would be introduced, more precise rules would be prescribed for the method of sacrifice, the ritual to be observed by the priests, the dues which they were authorized to receive from the people, and other similar matters. After the priesthood had acquired, through the foundation of Solomon's temple, a permanent centre, it is probable that the process of development and systematization advanced more rapidly than before. And thus the allusions in Dt. imply the existence of usages beyond those which fall directly within the scope of the book, and belonging specially to the jurisdiction of the priests (*e. g.* xvii. 11, xxiv. 8): Ezekiel, being a priest himself, alludes to such usages more distinctly. Although, therefore, there are reasons for supposing that the priest-code assumed finally the shape in which we have it in the age subsequent to Ezekiel, it rests ultimately upon an ancient traditional basis; and many of the institutions prominent in it are recognized, in various stages of their growth, by the earlier pre-exilic literature, by Dt. and by Ezekiel. The laws of P, even when they included later elements, were still referred to Moses,—no doubt because in its basis and origin Hebrew legislation was actually derived from him, and was only modified gradually."*

The conclusions of our argument may be stated as follows:

---
* *Literature of the Old Testament*, pp. 145, 146.

(1). We have not one narrative, but a fourfold narrative of the origin of the old covenant religion, as we have a fourfold gospel giving the narrative of the origin of the new covenant religion. There is, indeed, a remarkable correspondence in these four types or points of view. The Ephraimitic writer may be compared with Mark, the Judaic writer with Matthew, the priestly writer with Luke, and the Deuteronomist with John. The difference between the Pentateuch and the Gospels is that the four narratives of the Pentateuch have been compacted by a series of inspired Redactors; whereas the Gospels have to be harmonized by uninspired teachers in the Church. This unity in variety strengthens the credibility of the Pentateuch. As the four Gospels contain the gospel of Christ, so the narratives of the Pentateuch contain the law of Moses. As our Saviour is set forth by the Evangelist as the mediator of the new covenant, Moses is set forth by the narratives of the Pentateuch as the mediator of the old covenant.

(2). The Pentateuch does not give us one Mosaic code, but several codes of Mosaic legislation, a decalogue of worship, a judicial code of several decalogues, a people's code, a code of holiness, and a priest-code, contained in the narratives, somewhat as the Gospels present us the discourses of Jesus in the varied types peculiar to Mark, Matthew, Luke, and John. As we harmonize the Gospels for a complete and symmetrical statement of the doctrine of Jesus, so we harmonize the codes of the Pentateuch for a complete and symmetrical exposition of the law of Moses. The law was given through Moses, grace and truth came through Jesus Christ.

(3). The Mosaic legislation was delivered through Moses, the great prophetic law-giver of Israel, and then unfolded in historical usage and interpretation in a series of codifications by inspired prophets and priests; but it was in several stages of advancement in the historical life and experience of Israel from the conquest to the exile. It was a divine ideal, a supernatural revealed instruction, to guide the people of Israel throughout their history, and lead them to the prophet greater than Moses, who was to fulfil and complete his legislation. The law was the true light of Israel until the first Advent, even as the Gospel is the light and guide of the Church until the Second Advent. Israel appropriated more and more the instruction of the law, as the Church has appropriated more and more the doctrine of the Gospel. The history of God's people under both covenants has been essentially the same—a grand march forward under the supernatural light of a divine revelation.

(4). Law and Prophecy are not two distinct and separate modes of revelation, but the same. The law of Moses was as truly prophetic as legal. Moses was even more a prophet than a law-giver. The prophets of God that followed him all give divine law as well as divine prophecy. As the apostles in the new covenant were not merely expositors of the Gospel, but came forth from the risen and glorified Christ with new revelations, enlarging and completing the Gospel; so the prophets were not *mere* expositors of the law, but came forth immediately from the presence of Jahweh as really as Moses did, with new revelations enlarging and completing the old. The distinction between law and prophecy in the Bible is a fluctuating one, so that the whole divine revelation may be called law, and also prophecy, according to the usage of the Bible itself.

(5). There is in the law, as in the Gospel, a divine transforming power which shaped the history of Israel, as the Gospel has shaped the history of the Church in successive stages of appropriation. Not without some reason have many recent Christian scholars after Neander divided the history of the Christian Church after the names of the chief apostles as indicating the various types of Christianity. With even more reason might we divide the history of Israel into stages of progress in accordance with the several law codes. The Christian Church may look forward to a time when the unity and variety of the gospel of Christ shall be fully manifested in her historic life. The people of Israel also reached a stage when in her historic life the several codes harmonized, and the whole bent of the nation was in the study of the law and a conscientious fulfilment of it, and then in the fulness of time Christ Jesus the Messiah came.

The deeper study of the unity and variety of the Hexateuchal narratives and laws, as we defend their historicity against Reuss, Kuenen, and Wellhausen, and advance in the apprehension of their sublime harmony, will fructify and enrich the theology of our day, just as the deeper study of the unity and variety of the gospels by the school of Neander, in the defence of them against Strauss, Renan, and Baur, has been an unspeakable blessing in the past generation. This having been accomplished, we may look forward to a time when our eyes shall be opened as never before to the magnificent unity of the whole Bible in the midst of its wondrous variety. Then the word of God, as one supernatural divine revelation, will rise into such a position of spiritual power and transcendent influence, as shall greatly advance the kingdom of our Lord and Saviour Jesus Christ, and hasten the realization of that most blessed hope of both the Old and New Testaments, the coming of the Messiah in glory.

APPENDIX.

I. THE TWO NARRATIVES OF THE REVELATION OF THE DIVINE NAME YAHWEH, p. 165.

II. THE CHARACTERISTIC WORDS AND PHRASES OF D, H, AND P ACCORDING TO CANON DRIVER, p. 168.

III. THE GENESIS OF THE TEN WORDS, p. 181.

IV. THE TWO NARRATIVES OF THE PESTILENCE IN EGYPT, p. 188.

V. THE DECALOGUE OF J AND ITS PARALLELS IN THE OTHER CODES, p. 189.

VI. THE GREATER BOOK OF THE COVENANT AND ITS PARALLELS IN THE LATER CODES, p. 211.

VII. VARIATIONS OF D AND H, p. 233.

VIII. THE SEVERAL REPRESENTATIONS OF THE THEOPHANY, p. 236.

I.

THE TWO NARRATIVES OF THE REVELATION OF THE DIVINE NAME YAHWEH.

Ex. iii. 12-15 (*E*).	*Ex.* vi. 2-7 (*P*).
And he said, Verily *I shall be with thee* (אהיה עמך) and this shall be the sign to thee that I (אנכי) have sent thee: when thou hast brought forth the people from Egypt, ye shall serve God (האלהים) upon this mountain. And Moses said unto God (האלהים), Behold I (אנכי) am going to come unto the children of Israel and say to them, the God of your fathers hath sent me unto you. If they say to me, what is his name, what shall I say unto them? And God said (אלהים) unto Moses, *I shall be the one who will be* (e. g. *with thee* אהיה אשר אהיה). And he said, Thus shalt thou say to the children of Israel, *I shall be* (e. g. *with thee* אהיה) hath sent me unto you. And God (אלהים) said again unto Moses, Thus shalt thou say unto the children of Israel *Jahveh* (יהוה *He who will be with thee*), the God of your fathers, the God of Abraham, the God of Isaac and the God of Jacob hath sent me unto you. This is my name for ever, and this is my memorial to all generations.	And God (אלהים) spake unto Moses and said unto him, *I am Yahweh* (אני יהוה). I appeared unto Abraham, unto Isaac and unto Jacob as '*El Shadday*, but as to my name *Jahveh* I was not known to them. And I have also established my covenant (הקמתי את בריתי) with them to give to them the land of Canaan, the land of their sojournings (מגריהם), in which they sojourned. And I (אני) have also heard the groaning (נאקה) of the children of Israel whom the Egyptians keep in bondage and have remembered my covenant (זכר ברית). Wherefore say to the children of Israel, *I am Yahweh* (אני יהוה), and I will bring you out from under the burdens of the Egyptians, and I will deliver you from their bondage and redeem you with a stretched-out arm and with great judgments; and take you to me for a people and be to you for a God (והיה לכם לאלהים), and ye shall know that I am Yahweh your God (ידעתם כי אני יהוה אלהיכם), who bringeth you forth from under the burdens of the Egyptians.

These parallel passages not only give different accounts of

the same revelation of the divine name, Jahveh, but they also exhibit the differences in style between E and P. I shall not mention all of these differences, but only some of the more striking ones.

(1). *establish a covenant* הקים ברית is used by P 8 times, and in Ez. xvi. 60, 62, in this sense; but by Lev. xxvi. 9 (H the Holiness code of P) and Deut. viii. 18 (D) in the sense *confirm a covenant*. It is not used elsewhere.

(2). *remember a covenant* זכר ברית is used by P 4 times and by H in Lev. xxvi. 42, 45; elsewhere, Ez. xvi. 60, 1 C. xvi. 15, Ps. cv. 8, cvi. 45, cxi. 5; Am. i 9. It is not used in J E D.

(3). *I am Jahveh* (אני יהוה) is used by J, Gen. xv. 7, xxviii. 13; Ex. vii. 17, viii. 18, x. 2; and xv. 26 (R); elsewhere in the Hexateuch in P 35 times and H 40 times, often in the emphatic sense *I Jahveh*. It is never used by E or D.

(4). אני is always used by P (130 times) for *I*, except possibly Gen. xxiii. 4; whereas אנכי, the longer form, is commonly used in E and D. The usage in J varies.

(5). האלהים is used as subject or object 33 times in E, and as an absolute defining a preceding construct 12 times in E. It is used by P only Gen. xvii. 18, Jos. xxii. 34 (?), and in his sources Gen. v. 22, 24, vi. 9, 11.

(6). *God of the fathers* אלהי אבות is a phrase used 12 times by E and 8 times in D; by J thrice, but never by P.

(7). היה לאלהים is used 10 times by P, 6 times by Jeremiah, 6 times by Ezekiel, by D in Deut. xxvi. 17, xxix. 12; elsewhere in 2 Sam. vii. 24, 1 C. xvii. 22, Zech. viii. 8, and in Gen. xxviii. 21, which is a redactor's insertion in the document E.

(8). מגור is used by P 7 times; elsewhere Job xviii. 19, Ez. xx. 38, Ps. lv. 16, cxix. 54, never in the other documents of the Hexateuch.

(9). נאקה is used by P here and Ex. ii. 24; elsewhere Judges ii. 18, Ez. xxx. 24.

(10). אל שדי is used in the blessing of Jacob, Gen. xlix. 25, according to LXX. Sam., Syriac, Arabic versions, and some Massoretic MSS. On this basis it is used by P 5 times and by the Redactor in Gen. xliii. 14, not elsewhere in the Hexateuch.

(11). The style of P in using suffixes with the sign of the definite accusative rather than with the verb appears 6 times in this passage, but not at all in the parallel passage of E.

(12). Notice also "And God spake unto Moses and said," the style of P, as compared with "And God said" of E.

II.

THE CHARACTERISTIC WORDS AND PHRASES OF THE DOCUMENTS.

In his invaluable work, *Introduction to the Literature of the Old Testament*, Canon Driver gives the following specimens of the characteristic words and phrases of D, H, and P.

(1). *The style of Deuteronomy.*

"The literary style of Dt. is very marked and individual. In vocabulary, indeed, it presents comparatively few exceptional words; but particular words and phrases, consisting sometimes of entire clauses, recur with extraordinary frequency, giving a *distinctive colouring* to every part of the work. In its predominant features the phraseology is strongly original, but in certain particulars it is based upon that of the parenetic sections of JE in the Book of Exodus (esp. 13, 3-16. 15, 26. 19, 3-8, parts of 20, 2-17. 23, 20 ff. 34, 10-26).

In the following select list of phrases characteristic of Dt., the first 10 appear to have been adopted by the author from these sections of JE; those which follow are original, or occur so rarely in JE, that there is no ground to suppose them to have been borrowed thence. For the convenience of the synopsis, the occurrences in the Deuteronomic sections of *Joshua* are annexed in brackets.

1. אהב *to love*, with God as object: 6, 5. 7, 9. 10, 12. 11, 1. 13. 22. 13, 3 [Heb. 4]. 19, 9. 30, 6. 16. 20. [Josh. 22, 5. 23, 11.] So Ex. 20, 6 (= Dt. 5, 10). A characteristic principle of Dt. Of God's love to His people: 4, 37. 7, 8. 13. 10, 15. 23, 5 [Heb. 6]. Not so before. Otherwise first in Hos. 3, 1. 9, 15. 11, 1, cf. 4. 14, 4 [Heb. 5].

CHARACTERISTIC WORDS AND PHRASES

2. אֱלֹהִים אֲחֵרִים *other gods*: 6, 14. 7, 4. 8, 19. 11, 16. 28. 13, 2. 6. 13 [Heb. 3. 7. 14]. 17, 3. 18, 20. 28, 14. 36. 64. 29, 26 [Heb. 25]. 30, 17. 31, 18. 20. [Josh. 23, 16. 24, 2 16.] So Ex. 20, 3 (= Dt. 5, 7). 23, 13; cf. 34, 14 (אֵל אַחֵר). Always in Dt. (except 5, 7. 18, 20. 31, 18. 20) with *to serve* or *go after*. Often in Kings and Jeremiah, but (as Kleinert remarks) usually with other verbs.

3. *That your* (*thy*) *days may be long* [or *to prolong days*]: 4, 26. 40. 5, 33 [Heb. 30]. 6, 2ʰ. 11, 9. 17, 20. 22, 7. 25, 15. 30, 18. 32, 47. So Ex. 20, 12 (= Dt. 5, 16). Elsewhere, only Is. 53, 10. Prov. 28, 16. Eccl. 8, 13; and rather differently, Josh. 24, 31 = Jud. 2, 7.†

4. *The land* (הָאָרֶץ: less frequently *the ground*, הָאֲדָמָה) *which Jehovah thy God is giving thee* (also *us, you, them* 1, 20 etc.): 4, 40. 15, 7, and constantly. So Ex. 20, 12 (= Dt. 5, 16) הָאֲדָמָה.

5. בֵּית עֲבָדִים *house of bondage* (lit. *of slaves*): 6, 12. 7, 8. 8, 14. 13, 5. 10 [Heb. 6. 11]. [Josh. 24, 17.] So Jud. 6, 8. Mic. 6, 4. Jer. 34, 13. From Ex. 13, 3. 14. 20, 2 (= Dt. 5, 6).†

6. *In thy gates* (of the cities of Israel): 12, 12. 15. 17. 18. 21. 14, 21. 27–29. 15, 7. 22. 16, 5. 11. 14. 18. 17, 2. 8. 18, 6. 23, 16 [Heb. 17]. 24, 14. 26, 12. 28, 52. 55. 57. 31, 12. So Ex. 20, 10 (= Dt. 5, 14). Nowhere else in this application: but cf. 1 Ki. 8, 37 = 2 Ch. 6, 28.

7a. עַם סְגֻלָּה *a people of special possession*: 7, 6. 14, 2. 26, 18.† Cf. Ex. 19, 5 וִהְיִיתֶם לִי סְגֻלָּה.

7b. עַם קָדוֹשׁ *a holy people*: 7, 6. 14, 2. 21. 26, 19. 28, 9.† Varied from Ex. 19, 6 גּוֹי קָדוֹשׁ *a holy nation*: cf. 22, 30 and *holy men shall ye be unto me*.

8. *Which I command thee this day*: 4, 40. 6, 6. 7, 11, and repeatedly. So Ex. 34, 11.

9. *Take heed to thyself* (*yourselves*) *lest*, etc.: 4, 9. 23. 6, 12. 8, 11. 11, 16. 12, 13. 19. 30. 15, 9 (cf. 24, 8); comp. 2, 4. 4, 15. [Josh. 23, 11.] So Ex. 34, 12; cf. 19, 12. (Also Ex. 10, 28. Gen. 24, 6. 31, 24, cf. 29; but with no special force.)

10. *A mighty hand and a stretched out arm*: 4, 34. 5, 15. 7, 19. 11, 2. 26, 8. The *combination* occurs first in Dt. *Mighty hand* alone: Dt. 3, 24. 6, 21. 7, 8. 9, 26. 34, 12 [cf. Josh. 4, 24]. So in JE Ex. 3, 19. 6, 1. 13, 9. 32, 11. (Nu. 20, 20 differently.) *Stretched out arm* alone: Dt. 9, 29 (varied from Ex. 32, 11). So Ex. 6, 6 P.

11. בָּחַר *to choose*: of Israel 4, 37. 7, 6. 7. 10, 15. 14, 2,—the priests 18, 5. 21, 5,—of the future king 17, 15,—and especially in the

phrase "the place which Jehovah shall choose to place (*or* set) His name there," 12, 5. 11. 14. 18. 21. 26. 14, 23–25. 15, 20. 16, 2. 6. 7. 11. 15. 16. 17, 8. 10. 26, 2, or "the place which Jehovah shall choose" 18, 6. 31, 11. [Josh. 9, 27.] Very characteristic of Dt.: not applied before to God's choice of Israel; often in Kings of Jerusalem (1 Ki. 8, 44. 11, 32 etc.); in Jeremiah once, 33, 24, of Israel. Also charact. of II. Isaiah (41, 8. 9. 43, 10. 44, 1. 2: cf. *chosen* 43, 20. 45, 4. Of the *future*, 14, 1. 65, 9. 15. 22: and applied to Jehovah's ideal Servant, 42, 1. 49, 7).

12. (ובערת הרע מקרבך מישראל) *and thou shalt extinguish the evil from thy midst* (or *from Israel*): 13, 5 [Heb. 6]. 17, 7. 12. 19, 19. 21, 21. 22, 21. 22. 24. 24, 7.† This phrase is peculiar to Dt.; but Jud. 20, 13 is similar.

13. *That the Lord thy God may* (or *Because He will*) *bless thee*: 14, 24. 29. 15, 4. 10. 16, 10. 15. 23, 20 [Heb. 21]. 24, 19: cf. 12, 7. 15, 6. 14.

14. *The stranger, the fatherless, and the widow*: 10, 18. 24, 17. 19. 20. 21. 27, 19. Cf. Ex. 22, 21 f. Hence Jer. 7, 6. 22, 3. Ezek. 22, 7. Together with *the Levite*: 14, 29. 16, 11. 14. 26, 12. 13.

15. דבק *to cleave*, of devotion to God: 10, 20. 11, 22. 13, 4 [Heb. 5]. 30, 20: the corresponding adjective, 4, 4. [Josh. 22, 5. 23, 8.] So 2 Ki. 18, 6: cf. 3, 3. 1 Ki. 11, 2.†

16. *And remember that thou wast a bondman in the land of Egypt*: 5, 15. 15, 15. 16, 12. 24, 18. 22.†

17. (עליו) לא תחום עינך *thine eye shall not spare* (*him*): 7, 16. 13, 8 [Heb. 9]. 19, 13. 21. 25, 12. Also Gen. 45, 20. Is. 13, 18, and frequently in Ezek.

18. והיה בך חטא *and it be sin in thee*: 15, 9. 23, 21 [Heb. 22]. 24, 15; cf. 23, 22: with *not*, 23, 22 [Heb. 23].

19. הארץ הטובה *the good land* (of Canaan): 1, 35. 3, 25. 4, 21. 22. 6, 18. 8, 10 (cf. 7). 9, 6. 11, 17. [Josh. 23, 16.] So 1 Ch. 28, 8.† Dt. 1, 25 (Nu. 14, 7) and Ex. 3, 8 are rather different.

20. *Which thou* (*ye*) *knowest* (or *knewest*) *not*: 8, 3. 16. 11, 28. 13, 2. 6. 13 [Heb. 3. 7. 14]. 28, 33. 36. 64. 29, 26 [Heb. 25]. Chiefly with reference to strange gods, or a foreign people. Cf. 32, 17.

21 *That it may be well with thee* (למען ייטב לך or אשר): 4. 40. 5, 16. 29 [Heb. 26]. 6, 3. 18. 12, 25. 28. 22, 7. Similarly (לכם) לך וטוב: 5, 33 [Heb. 30]. 19, 13, and למוב 6, 24. 10, 13.

22. היטיב, *inf. abs.*, used adverbially = *thoroughly*: 9, 21. 13, 14 [Heb. 15]. 17, 4. 19, 18. 27, 8. Elsewhere, as thus applied, only 2 Ki. 11, 18.†

CHARACTERISTIC WORDS AND PHRASES 171

23. *To fear God* (לִירְאָה): often with *that they may learn* prefixed): 4, 10. 5, 29 [Heb. 26]. 6, 24. 8, 6. 10, 12. 14, 23. 17, 19. 28, 58. 31, 13, cf. 12.

24. לֹא תוּכַל (יוּכַל), in the sense of *not to be allowed:* 7, 22. 12, 17. 16, 5. 17, 15. 21, 16. 22, 3. 19. 29. 24, 4. A very uncommon use; cf. Gen. 43, 32.

25. *To do that which is right* (הַיָּשָׁר) *in the eyes of Jehovah:* 12, 25. 13, 18 [Heb. 19]. 21, 9: with הַטּוֹב *that which is good* added, 6, 18. 12, 28. So Ex. 15, 26, then Jer. 34, 15, and several times in the framework of Kings and the parallel passages of Chronicles.

26. *To do that which is evil* (הָרַע) *in the eyes of Jehovah:* 4, 25. 9, 18. 17, 2. 31, 29. So Nu 32, ¦3 ; often in the framework of Judges and Kings, Jeremiah, and occasionally elsewhere. Both 25 and 26 gained currency through Dt., and are rare except in passages written under its influence

27. *The priests the Levites* (= the Levitical priests): 17, 9. 18, 1. 24, 8. 27, 9: *the priests the sons of Levi*, 21, 5. 31, 9. [Josh. 3, 3. 8, 33.] So Jer. 33, 18. Ez 43, 19. 44, 15. 2 Ch. 5, 5. 23, 18. 30, 27. P's expression "sons of Aaron" is never used in Dt.

28. *With all thy* (*your*) *heart and with all thy* (*your*) *soul:* 4, 29. 6, 5. 10, 12. 11, 13. 13, 3 [Heb. 4]. 26, 16. 30, 2. 6. 10. [Josh. 22, 5. 23, 14] A genuine expression of the spirit of the book (p. 73). Only besides (in the third person) 1 Ki. 2, 4. 8, 48 ǁ. 2 Ki. 23, 3. 25 ǁ. 2 Ch. 15, 12 ; and (in the first person, of God) Jer. 32, 41.

29. נָתַן לִפְנֵי, in the sense of *delivering up* to: 1, 8. 21. 2, 31. 33. 36. 7, 2. 23. 23, 14 [Heb. 15]. 28, 7 and 25 (with נָגַף). 31, 5. [Josh. 10, 12. 11, 6.] Also Jud. 11, 9. 1 Ki. 8, 46. Is. 41, 2.† The usual phrase in this sense is נָתַן בְּיַד.

30. *To turn* (סָר) *neither to the right hand nor to the left:* 2, 27 lit. (Nu. 20, 17 has נָטָה): so 1 Sa. 6, 12. *Metaph.* 5, 32 [Heb. 29]. 17, 11. 20. 28, 14. [Josh. 1, 7. 23, 6.] So 2 Ki. 22, 2 ǁ.†

31. מַעֲשֵׂה יָדַיִם *the work of the hands* (= enterprise): 2, 7. 14, 29, 16, 15. 24, 19. 28, 12. 30, 9 : in a bad sense, 31, 29.

32. פָּדָה, of the *redemption* from Egypt: 7, 8 (Mic. 6, 4). 9, 26. 13, 5 [Heb. 6]. 15, 15. 21, 8. 24, 18. Not so before: Ex. 15, 13 (the Song of Moses) uses גָּאַל (to *reclaim*).

33. קֶרֶב *midst*, in different connexions, especially מִקִּרְבְּךָ, בְּקִרְבְּךָ. A favourite word in Deut., though naturally occurring in JE, as also elsewhere. In P תּוֹךְ is preferred.

34. *To rejoice before Jehovah:* 12, 7. 12. 18, 14. 26, 16. 11. 14 (cf. Lev. 23, 40). 26, 11. 27, 7.

35. *To make His name dwell there* (לְשַׁכֵּן, שִׁכֵּן) : 12, 11. 14, 23. 16, 2. 6 11. 26, 2. Only besides Jer. 7, 12. Ezra 6, 12. Neh. 1, 9.† With לָשׂוּם (*to set*) : 12, 5. 21. 14, 24. This occurs also in Kings (together with להיות, יהיה, which are not in Dt.) : 1 Ki. 9, 3. 11, 36 *al.*

36. משלח ידך (ידיך, ידכם) *that to which thy* (*your*) *hand is put:* 12, 7. 18. 15, 10. 23, 20 [Heb. 21]. 28, 8. 20.†

37. *And . . . . shall hear and fear* (of the deterrent effect of punishment) : 13, 11 [Heb. 12]. 17, 13. 19, 20. 21, 21 †

38. *To observe to do* (שמר לעשות) : 5, 1. 32 [Heb. 29]. 6, 3 etc. (sixteen times : also four times with an object intervening). [Josh. 1, 7. 8. 22, 5.] Also a few times in Kings and Chronicles.

39. *To observe and do:* 4, 6. 7, 12. 16, 12. 23, 23 [Heb. 24]. 24, 8. 26, 16. 28, 13 ; cf. 29, 9 [Heb. 8]. [Josh. 23, 6.]

40. *The land whither ye go over* (or *enter in*) *to possess it:* 4, 5. 14 and repeatedly. Hence Ezra 9, 11. לרשתה *to possess it* follows also *which Jehovah is giving thee* (No. 4) : 12, 1. 19, 2. 14. 21, 1. [Josh. 1, 11ᵇ.] Cf. Gen. 15, 7. In P, with similar clauses, לאחזה is used : Lev. 14, 34. 25, 45. Nu 32, 29. Dt. 32, 49.

41. *a.* תועבת יהוה *Jehovah's abomination*, esp. as the final ground of a prohibition : 7, 25 (cf. 26). 12, 31. 17, 1. 18, 12ᵃ. 22, 5. 23, 18 [Heb. 19]. 24, 4. 25, 16. 27, 15 : *b.* תועבה alone, chiefly of heathen or idolatrous customs, 13, 14 [Heb. 15]. 14, 3. 17, 4. 18, 9. 12ᵇ. 20, 18. 32, 16. *a.* So often in Prov. ; comp. in H, Lev. 18, 22. 26 f. 29 f. 20, 13 (but *only* of sins of unchastity).*

(2). *The style of H.*

"H has points of contact with P, but lacks many of its most characteristic features. Ezekiel, the priestly prophet, has affinities with P, but his affinities with H are peculiarly striking and numerous : the laws comprised in H are frequently quoted by him, and the parenetic passages contain many expressions—sometimes remarkable ones—which otherwise occur in Ezekiel alone.[1]

1. אני יהוה *I am Jehovah*, esp. at the end of an injunction or series of injunctions (nearly fifty times) : 18, 2.[2] 4. 5.[2] 6. 21. 30.[2] 19, 3.[2] 4.[2] 10.[2] 12. 14. 16. 18. 25.[2] 28. 30. 31.[2] 32. 34.[2] 36.[2] 37. 20, 7.[2]

---

* *Literature of the Old Testament*, 91–95.
[1] *Literature of the Old Testament*, 45–46.
[2] Followed by *your* (*their*) *God.*

CHARACTERISTIC WORDS AND PHRASES

8.³ 24.⁴ 21, 12. 15.³ 23.³ 22, 2. 3. 8. 9.³ 16.² 30. 31. 32.³ 33. 23, 22.² 43.² 24, 22.² 25, 17.² 38.⁴ 55.² 26, 1.² 2. 13.⁴ 44.² 45. So Ex. 6, 2. 6. 8. 29. 12, 12ᵇ. 29, 46ᵃ.⁴ 46ᵇ.² 31, 13ᵇ.³ Nu. 3, 13 *end*. 41. 45. 10, 10.² 15, 41ᵃ.⁴ 41ᵇ.⁹

2. כי קדוש אני יהוה *For I Jehovah am holy*: 19, 2.² 20, 26. 21, 8.³ Cf. 11, 44. 45 (For I am holy).

3. *That sanctify you* (*them*, etc.): 20, 8. 21, 8. 15. 23. 22, 9. 16. 32. So Ex. 31, 13. Ez. 20, 12. 37, 28.†

4. איש איש for *whoever*: 17, 3. 8. 10. 13. 18, 6. 20, 2. 9. 22, 4. 18. 24, 15. So 15, 2. Nu. 5, 12. 9, 10. Ez. 14, 4. 7 (with מבית ישראל as ch. 17, 3. 8. 10).

5. *I will set* (ונתתי) *my face against* . . . : 17, 10. 20, 3. 5 (ושמתי אני). 6. 26, 17. So Ez. 14, 8. 15, 7ᵃ. 7ᵇ (שם). Jer. 21, 10 (שם). 44, 11 (שם).†

6. *I will cut off from the midst of his* (*its, their*) *people*: 17, 10. 20, 3. 5. 6.⁵ Cf. Ez. 14, 8 (. . . מתוך: in Lev. מקרב).

7. הלך בחקות *to walk in the statutes*: 18, 3. 20, 23. 26, 3. Also 1 Ki. 3, 3. 6, 12. 2 Ki. 17, 8. 19; but chiefly in Ez., viz, 5, 6. 7. 11, 20. 18, 9. 17. 20, 13. 19. 21. 33, 15: cf. Jer. 44, 10 בתורתי ובחקתי.†

8. חקותי ומשפטי *my statutes and my judgments*: 18, 4 (inverted). 5. 26. 19, 37. 20, 22. 22, 31. 25, 18. 26, 15. 43.

9. *To observe and do*: 18, 4. 19, 37. 20, 8. 22, 22, 31. 25, 18. 26, 3.

10. שאר *flesh = next-of-kin*: 18, 12. 13. 17 (שארה). 20, 19. 21, 2. Nu. 27, 11; שאר בשרו 18, 6. 25, 49. Not so elsewhere.

11. זמה *evil purpose* (of unchastity): 18, 17. 19, 29. 20, 14 *bis*. So Jud. 20, 6. Hos. 6, 9. Jer. 13, 27. Ez. 16, 27. 43. 58. 22, 9. 11. 23, 21. 27. 29. 35. 44. 48 *bis*. 49. 24, 13. (In RV. often *lewdness*.)

12. עמית *neighbor*: 18, 20. 19, 11. 15. 17. 24, 19. 25. 14 *bis*. 15. 17. 5, 21 *bis*. Zech. 13, 7.† A peculiar term; not the one in ordinary use.

---

³ Followed by the participial clause *that sanctify you* (*him*, etc.).

⁴ Followed by a relative clause.

† The dagger (both here and elsewhere) denotes that all instances of the word or phrase referred to that occur in the OT. have been cited. The *distinctive* character of an expression is evidently the more marked, and the agreement between two writers who use it is the more striking, in proportion to the rarity with which it occurs in the OT. generally.

⁵ In P always "*shall be* cut off" (see § 7). In general the Divine "I" appears here with a prominence which it never assumes in the laws of P.

13. *To profane—the name of Jehovah* 18, 21. 19, 12. 20, 3. 21, 6. 22, 2. 32 (Am. 2, 7. Isa. 48, 11): a *holy thing* or *sanctuary* 19, 8. 21, 12. 23. 22, 15 (so Nu. 18, 32): in other connexions 19, 29. 21, 9ᵇ. 15. 22, 9: comp. 21, 4. 9ᵃ. So Ex. 31, 14 (of the Sabbath). So often in Ezek.: of *Jehovah* 13, 19. 22, 26; *His name* 20, 9. 14. 22. 39. 36, 20–23. 39, 7; *His sabbaths* 20, 13. 16. 21. 24. 22, 8. 23, 38 (Isa. 56, 2. 6); *His holy things* or *sanctuary* 22, 26. 23, 39. 44, 7; cf. also 7, 21. 22. 24. 22, 16. 24, 21. 25, 3. 28, 7. 16. 18. Obviously the correlative of Nos. 2, 3.

14. *My sabbaths:* 19, 3. 30. 26, 2. Ex. 31, 13. Ez. 20, 12. 13. 16. 20. 21. 24. 22, 8. 26. 23, 38. 44, 24. Isa. 56, 4.†

15. אֱלִילִים *things of nought = vain gods:* 19, 4. 26, 1. Not elsewhere in Pent. Chiefly besides in Isaiah (9 times, and הָאֱלִיל once).

16. וְיָרֵאתָ מֵאֱלֹהֶיךָ *and thou shalt be afraid of thy God:* 19, 14. 32. 25, 17. 36. 43.†

17. דָּמָיו בּוֹ (דְּמֵיהֶם בָּם) *his (their) blood shall be upon him (them)*: 20, 9. 11. 12. 13. 16. 27. Ez. 18, 13 (דָּמָיו בּוֹ יִהְיֶה). 33, 5 (דָּמוֹ בוֹ). † (The ordinary phrase is דָּמוֹ עַל (ב) רֹאשׁוֹ (יִהְיֶה).

18. *The bread of (their) God:* 21, 6. 8. 17. 21. 22. 22, 25. Nu. 28, 2 (cf. 24. Lev. 3, 11. 16). Ez. 44, 7.† (Ez. 16, 19 differently.)

19ᵃ. נָשָׂא חֵטְא *to bear sin:* 19, 17. 22, 9. Nu. 18, 22. 32; cf. Ez. 23, 49.†

19ᵇ. נָשָׂא(וּ) חֲטָאוֹ(ם) *to bear his (their) sin:* 20, 20. 24, 15. Nu. 9, 13.†

20ᵃ. נָשָׂא(וּ) עֲוֹנוֹ(ם) *to bear his (their) iniquity:* 17, 16. 19, 8. 20, 17. 19. So 5, 1. 17. 7, 18. Nu. 5, 31. 14, 34 (cf. 15, 31 עֲוֹנָה בָהּ). Ez. 14, 10. 44, 10. 12.†

20ᵇ. נָשָׂא עָוֹן *to bear iniquity:* Ex. 28, 43; cf. Lev. 22, 16.†

20ᶜ. . . . נָשָׂא עֲוֹן *to bear the iniquity of* . . . (= *be responsible for*): Ex. 28, 38. Nu. 18, 1 *bis;* so *bear their iniquity, v.* 23 (see Dillm.; and comp. Wellh. *Comp.* p. 341).†

20ᵈ. . . . *to bear the iniquity of* another: Lev. 10, 17. 16, 22. Nu. 30, 15 [H. 16]. Ez. 4, 4. 5. 6 (not always in the same application). So נָשָׂא חֵטְא *to bear the sin of* many, Is. 53, 12.

(3). *The style of P.*

"The following is a select list of some of the most noticeable expressions characteristic of P; many occurring rarely or never besides, some only in Ezekiel. The list could readily be increased, especially if terms occurring *only* in the laws had been added;[1] these, however, have been excluded, as the object of the

---

[1] *E.g.* "savour of satisfaction," "fire-sacrifice," "statute for ever." But the

list is rather to show that the *historical* sections of P exhibit the same literary features as the *legal* ones, and that the same habits of thought and expression pervade both.[1] References to Lev. 17-26 have been included in the list. It will be recollected that these chapters do not consist wholly of excerpts from H, but comprise elements belonging to P (p. 44). H itself also, as was remarked, is related to P, representing likewise priestly usage, though in an earlier phase; so that it is but natural that its phraseology should exhibit points of contact with that of P.

1. *God*, not *Jehovah*: Gen. 1, 1 and uniformly, except Gen. 17, 1. 21, 1ᵇ, until Ex. 6, 2.
2. *Kind* (מִין): Gen. 1, 11. 12 *bis*. 21 *bis*. 24 *bis*. 25 *ter*. 6, 20 *ter*. 7, 14 *quater*. Lev. 11, 14. 15. 16. 19 [hence Dt. 14, 13. 14. 15. 18]. 22 *quater*. 29. Ez. 47, 10.†
3. *To swarm* (שָׁרַץ): Gen. 1, 20. 21. 7, 21. 8, 17. Ex. 7, 28 [hence Ps. 105, 30]. Lev. 11, 29. 41. 42. 43. 46. Ez. 47, 9. *Fig.* of men: Gen. 9, 7. Ex. 1, 7.†
4. *Swarming things* (שֶׁרֶץ): Gen. 1, 20. 7, 21. Lev. 5, 2. 11, 10. 20 [hence Dt. 14, 19]. 21. 23. 29. 31. 41. 42. 43. 44. 22, 5.†
5. *To be fruitful and multiply* (פרה ורבה): Gen. 1, 22. 28. 8, 17. 9, 1. 7. 17, 20 (cf. 2 and 6). 28, 3. 35, 11. 47, 27, 48, 4. Ex. 1, 7. Lev. 26, 9. Also Jer. 23, 3; and (inverted) 3, 16. Ez. 36, 11.†
6. *For food* (לְאָכְלָה): Gen. 1, 29. 30. 6, 21. 9, 3. Ex. 16, 15. Lev. 11, 39. 25, 6. Ez. 15, 4. 6. 21, 37. 23, 37. 29, 5. 34, 5. 8. 10. 12. 39, 4.† (In Jer. 12, 9 לְאָכְלָה is an infin.)
7. *Generations* (תּוֹלְדוֹת):
    (*a*) In the phrase *These are the generations of* . . . (see p. 5 f.).
    (*b*) Otherwise: Gen. 10, 32. 25, 13. Ex. 6, 16. 19. 28, 10. Nu. 1 (12 times). 1 Ch. 5, 7. 7, 2. 4. 9. 8, 28. 9, 9. 34. 26, 31.†

---

laws of P, it is worth remarking, are, as a rule, formulated differently from those of either JE or D (contrast *e.g.* the אשה כי, איש או נפש כי, אדם כי etc. of Lev. 1, 2. 4, 2. 5, 1. 15. 13, 2. 29. 38. Nu. 5, 6. 6, 2 *al.* with the וכי איש of Ex. 21, 7. 14. 20. 26, etc.), and show besides differences of terminology, which, however, the reader must be left to note for himself.

[1] Were these expressions *confined* to the legal sections, it might be argued that they were the work of the same hand as JE, who, with a change of subject, adopted naturally an altered phraseology; but they are found repeatedly in the *narrative* parts of the Hexateuch, where the peculiar phraseology cannot be attributed to the special character of the subject (*e.g.* Gen. 6-9. Ex. 6, 2-7, 13. c. 16. Nu. 13-14. 16-17. Josh. 22, 9 ff.).

8. מֵאֵת in the *st. c.*, in cases where ordinarily מֵאָה would be said: Gen. 5, 3. 6. 18. 25. 28. 7, 24. 8, 3. 11, 10. 25. 21, 5. 25, 7. 17. 35, 28. 47, 9. 28. Ex. 6, 16. 18. 20. 38, 25. 27 (thrice). Nu 2, 9. 16. 24. 31. 33, 39. So besides only Neh. 5, 11 (prob. corrupt). 2 Ch. 25, 9 Qri. Est. 1, 4.† (Peculiar. P uses מֵאָה in such cases only twice, Gen. 17, 17. 23, 1.)

9. *To expire* (גוע): Gen. 6, 17. 7, 21. 25, 8. 17. 35, 29. 49, 33. Nu. 17, 12. 13. 20, 3 *bis*. 29. Josh. 22, 20. (Only besides in poetry: Zech. 13, 8. Ps. 88, 16. 104, 29 Lam. 1, 19; and 8 times in Job.)†

10. *With thee* (*him*, etc.) appended to an enumeration: Gen. 6, 18. 7, 7. 13. 8, 16. 18. 9, 8. 28, 4. 46, 6. 7. Ex. 28, 1. 41. 29, 21 *bis*. Lev. 8, 2. 30. 10, 9. 14. 15 (25, 41. 54 עָם). Nu. 18, 1. 2. 7. 11. 19 *bis*. Similarly *after you* (*thee*, etc.) appended to "seed:" Gen. 9, 9. 17, 7 *bis*. 8. 9. 10. 19. 35, 12. 48, 4. Ex. 28, 43. Nu 25, 13.

11. *And Noah did* (*so*); *according to*, etc.: Gen. 6, 22: exactly the same form of sentence, Ex. 7, 6. 12, 28. 50 39, 32ᵇ. 40, 16. Nu. 1, 54. 2, 34. 8, 20. 17, 11 [Heb. 26]: cf. Ex. 39, 43. Nu. 5, 4. 9, 5.

12. *This selfsame day* (עֶצֶם הַיּוֹם הַזֶּה): Gen. 7, 13. 17, 23. 26. Ex. 12, 17. 41. 51. Lev. 23, 14. 21. 28. 29. 30. Dt. 32, 48. Josh. 5, 11. 10, 27 (not P: probably the compiler). Ez. 2, 3. 24, 2 *bis*. 40, 1.†

13. *After their families* (לְמִשְׁפְּחוֹתָם -יהם): Gen. 8, 19. 10, 5. 20. 31. 36. 40. Ex. 6, 17. 25. 12, 21.¹ Nu. 1 (13 times). 2, 34. 3–4 (15 times). 11, 10 (JE). 26 (16 times) 29, 12. 33, 54. Josh. 13, 15. 23. 24. 28. 29. 31. 15, 1. 12. 20. 16, 5. 8. 17, 2 *bis*. 18, 11. 20. 21. 28. 19 (12 times). 21, 7. 33. 40 (Heb. 38). 1 Sa. 10, 21. 1 Ch. 5, 7. 6, 62. 63 (Heb. 47. 48, from Josh. 21, 33. 38).†

14. לְכֹל *as regards all*, with a generalizing force = *namely*, *I mean* (Ewald, § 310ⁿ): Gen. 9, 10ᵇ. 23, 10ᵇ. Ex. 14, 28 (cf. 9 וְחֵילוֹ). 27, 3. 19 (si vera l). 28, 38. 36. 1ᵇ. Lev. 5, 3. 11, 26. 42. 16, 16. 21. 22, 18. Nu. 4, 27. 31. 32. 5, 9. 18, 4. 8. 9. Ez. 44, 9. (Prob. a juristic use. Occasionally elsewhere, esp. in Ch.)

15. *An everlasting covenant:* Gen. 9, 16. 17, 7. 13. 19. Ex. 31, 16. Lev. 24, 8; cf. Nu. 18, 19. 25, 13.*²

---

¹ The isolated occurrence of this expression in JE does not make it the less characteristic of P. Of course the writer of Ex. 12, 21 was acquainted with the word מִשְׁפָּחָה, and could use it, if he pleased, in combination with לְ. It is the *frequency* of the combination which causes it to be characteristic of a particular author. For the same reason εὐθὺς is characteristic of St. Mark's style, notwithstanding the fact that the other evangelists employ it occasionally. The same remark holds good of Nos. 12, 15, 17, 22, 38, 41, etc.

² The asterisk indicates that all passages of the Hexateuch in which the word or phrase quoted occurs are cited or referred to.

CHARACTERISTIC WORDS AND PHRASES 177

16. *Exceedingly* (במאד מאד, not the usual phrase): Gen. 17, 2. 6. 20. Ex 1, 7. Ez. 9, 9. 16, 13.†
17. *Substance* (רכוש): Gen. 12, 5. 13. 6. 31, 18. 36, 7. 46, 6. Nu. 16, 32 *end*. 35, 3. Elsewhere (not P): Gen. 14, 11. 12. 16 *bis*. 21. 15, 14; and in Ch. Ezr. Dan. (15 times).†
18. *To gather* (רכש—cognate with "substance"): Gen. 12, 5. 31, 18 *bis*. 36, 6 46, 6.†
19. *Soul* (נפש) in the sense of *person :* Gen. 12, 5. 36, 6. 46, 15. 18. 22. 25. 26. 27. Ex. 1, 5. 12, 4. 16 (RV. *man*). 19. 16, 16 (RV. *persons*). Lev. 2, 1 (RV. *one*). 4, 2. 27. 5, 1. 2; and often in the legal parts of Lev. Num. (as Lev. 17, 12. 22, 11. 27, 2) Nu. 31, 28. 35. 40. 46 (in the account of the war with Midian). Josh. 20, 3. 9 (from Nu. 35, 11. 15). See also below, No. 25ᵃ. A usage not confined to P, but much more frequent in P than elsewhere.
20. *Throughout your* (*their*) *generations* (לדרתם לדרתיכם): Gen. 17, 7. 9. 12. Ex. 12, 14. 17. 42. 16, 32. 33. 27, 21. 29, 42. 30, 8. 10. 21. 31. 31, 13. 16. 40, 15. Lev. 3, 17. 6, 11, 7, 36. 10, 9. 17, 7. 21, 17. 22, 3. 23, 14. 21. 31. 41. 24, 3. 25, 30 (*his*). Nu. 9, 10. 10, 8. 15, 14. 15. 21. 23. 38. 18, 23. 35, 29.†
21. *Sojournings* (מגורים), with *land :* Gen. 17, 8. 28, 4. 36, 7. 37, 1. Ex. 6, 4. Ez. 20, 38; with *days :* Gen. 47, 9 *bis*. Only besides Ps. 119, 54; and rather differently 55, 16. Job 18, 19.†
22. *Possession* (אחזה): Gen. 17, 8. 23, 4. 9. 20. 36, 43. 47, 11. 48, 4. 49, 30. 50, 13. Lev. 14, 34. 25, 10–46. 27, 16. 21. 22. 24. 28. Nu. 27, 4. 7. 32, 5. 22. 29. 32. 35, 2. 8. 28. Dt. 32, 49. Josh. 21, 12. 39. 22, 4 (D²). 9. 19 *bis*. Elsewhere only in Ezekiel (44, 28 *bis*. 45, 5. 6. 7 *bis*. 8. 46, 16. 18 *ter*. 48, 20. 21. 22 *bis*); Ps. 2, 8; 1 Ch. 7, 28. 9, 2 (= Neh. 11, 3). 2 Ch. 11, 14. 31, 1.†
23. The cognate verb *to get possessions* (נאחז), rather a peculiar word: Gen. 34, 10 47, 27. Nu. 32, 30. Josh. 22, 9. 19.†
24. *Purchase, purchased possession* (מקנה): Gen. 17, 12. 13. 23. 27. 23, 18. Ex. 12, 44. Lev. 25, 16 *bis*. 51. 27, 22. (Prob. a legal term. Only besides Jer. 22, 11. 12. 14. 16.)†
25. *Peoples* (עמים) in the sense of *kinsfolk* (peculiar):
    (*a*) *That soul* (or *that man*) *shall be cut off from his kinsfolk :* Gen. 17, 14. Ex. 30, 33. 38. 31, 14. Lev. 7, 20. 21. 25. 27. 17, 9. 19, 8. 23, 29. Nu. 9, 13†. (In Lev. 17, 4. 10. 18, 29, 20, 3. 5. 6. 18. 23, 30. Nu. 15, 30 the noun is *singular*.)
    (*b*) *To be gathered to one's kinsfolk :* Gen. 25, 8. 17. 35, 29. 49, 33. Nu. 20, 24. 27, 13. 31, 2. Dt. 32, 50 *bis*.†

(c) Lev. 19, 16. 21, 1. 4. 14. 15. Ez. 18, 18: perhaps Jud. 5, 14. Hos. 10. 14.†

26. *Settler* or *sojourner* (תושב): Gen. 23, 4 (hence Ps. 39, 13. 1 Ch. 29, 15). Ex. 12, 45. Lev. 22, 10. 25, 6. 23. 35. 40. 45. 47 *bis*. Nu. 35, 15. Also 1 Ki. 17, 1 (text doubtful).†

27. *Getting, acquisition* (קנין): Gen. 31, 18. 34, 23. 36, 6. Lev. 22, 11. Josh. 14, 4: cf. Ez. 38, 12 f.; also Pr. 4, 7. Ps. 104, 24. 105, 21.†

28. *Rigour* (פרך): Ex. 1, 13. 14. Lev. 25, 43. 46. 53. Ez. 34, 4.†

29. *Judgments* (שפטים [not the usual word]): Ex. 6, 6. 7, 4. 12. 12. Nu. 33, 4. Ez. 5, 10. 15. 11, 9. 14, 21. 16, 41. 25, 11. 28, 22. 26. 30, 14. 19. Pr. 19, 29. 2 Ch. 24, 24.†

30. *Fathers' houses* (= families: בית אבות, or sometimes אבות alone): Ex. 6, 14. 25. 12, 3. Nu. 1–4 (often). 17, 2. 3. 6. 26, 2. 31, 26. 32, 28. 34, 14. 36, 1. Josh. 14, 1. 19, 51. 21, 1. 22, 14.

31. *Hosts* (צבאות) of the Israelites: Ex. 6, 26. 7, 4. 12, 17. 41. 51. Nu. 1, 3. 52. 2, 3. 9. 10. 16. 18. 24. 25. 32. 10, 14. 18. 22. 25. 28. 33, 1.* (Dt. 20, 9 differently.)

32. *Congregation* (עדה) of the Israelites: Ex. 12, 3. 6. 19. 47. 16, 1. 2. 9. 10. 22. 17, 1. 34, 31. 35, 1. 4. 20. 38, 25. Lev. 4, 13. 15. 8, 3–5. 9, 5. 10, 6. 17. 16, 5. 19, 2. 24, 14. 16. Nu. 13, 26 *bis*. 14, 1. 2. 5. 7. 10. 27. 35. 36. 16, 2. 3. 9 *bis*. 19 *bis*. 21. 22 (Lev. 10, 6). 24. 26. 41. 42. 45. 46. [Heb. 17, 6. 7. 10. 11]. 20, 1 2. 8 *bis*. 11. 22. 27. 29. 25, 6. 7. 31, 12. 16. 26. 27. 43 (as well as often in the other chapters of Nu. assigned wholly to P). 32, 2. 4. Josh. 9, 15. 18 *bis*. 19. 21. 27. 18, 1. 20, 6. 9. 22, 12. 16. 17. 18 (Nu. 16, 22). 20. 30. (Cf. No. 39.) Never in JE or Dt., and rare in the other hist. books: Jud. 20, 1. 21, 10. 13. 16. 1 Ki. 8, 5 (= 2 Ch. 5, 6). 12, 20.

33. *Between the two evenings*: Ex. 12, 6. 16, 12. 29, 39. 41. 30, 8. Lev. 23, 5. Nu. 9, 3. 5. 11. 28, 4. 8.†

34. *In all your dwellings* (בכל מושבתיכם): Ex. 12, 20. 35, 3. Lev. 3, 17. 7, 26. 23, 3. 14. 21. 31. Nu. 35, 29 (cf. 15, 2. 31, 10). Ez. 6, 6. 14.

35. *This is the thing which Jehovah hath commanded*: Ex. 16, 16. 32. 35, 4. Lev. 8, 5. 9, 6. 17, 2. Nu. 30, 2. 36, 6.†

36. *A head* (גלגלת lit. *skull*) in enumerations: Ex. 16, 16. 38, 26. Nu 1, 2. 18. 20. 22. 3, 47. 1 Ch. 23, 3. 24.†

37. *To remain over* (עדף: not the usual word): Ex. 16, 18. 23. 26, 12 *bis*. 13. Lev. 25, 27. Nu. 3, 46. 48. 49.†

38. *Ruler* or *prince* (נשיא), among the Israelites: Ex. 16, 22. 35. 27. Lev. 4, 22. Nu. 1, 16. 44. cc. 2. 3. and 7 (repeatedly). 4, 46. 10,

CHARACTERISTIC WORDS AND PHRASES 179

4. 13, 2. 17, 2. 6 (Heb. 17. 21). 25, 14. 18. 34, 18–28. Josh. 22, 14. In JE once only, Ex. 22, 27: never in Dt. Jud. Sam.: in Kings only 1 Ki. 8, 1, and in a semi-poetical passage, 11, 34. Cf. Gen. 17, 20. 23, 6. 25, 16. 34, 2. Often in Ez., even of the king.

39. *Rulers* (*princes*) *of* (or *in*) *the congregation*: Ex. 16, 22. 34, 31. Nu. 4, 34. 16, 2. 31, 13. 32, 2. Josh. 9, 15. 18 (cf. 19. 21). 22, 30 (cf. 32): cf. Nu. 27, 2. 36, 1. Josh. 17, 4.†

40. *Deep rest* (שבתון): Ex. 16, 23. 31, 15. 35, 2. Lev. 16, 31. 23, 3. 24. 32. 39 *bis*. 25, 4. 5.†

41. *According to the command* (lit. *mouth*) *of Jehovah* (עַל פִּי יהוה): Ex. 17, 1. Lev. 24, 12. Nu. 3, 16. 39. 51. 4, 37. 41. 45. 49. 9, 18. 20. 23. 10, 13. 13, 3. 33, 2. 38. 36, 5. Josh. 15, 13 (אֶל). 17, 4 (אֶל). 19, 50. 21, 3 (אֶל). 22, 9. Very uncommon elsewhere: Dt. 34, 5ᵇ (probably from P: cf. Nu. 33, 38). 2 Ki. 24, 3.

42. *Half* (מחצית: not the usual word): Ex. 30, 13 *bis*. 15. 23. 38, 26. Lev. 6, 13 *bis*. Nu. 31, 29. 30. 42. 47. Josh. 21, 25 (= 1 Ch. 6, 55). Only besides 1 Ki. 16, 9. Neh. 8, 3. 1 Ch. 6, 46.†

43. מָעַל *to trespass* and מַעַל *trespass* (often combined, and then rendered in RV. *to commit* a *trespass*): Lev. 5, 15. 6, 2 [Heb. 5, 21]. 26, 40. Nu. 5, 6. 12. 27. 31, 16. Dt. 32, 51. Josh. 7, 1. 22, 16. 20. 22. 31.* Ez. 14, 13. 15, 8. 17, 20. 18, 24. 20, 27. 39, 23. 26. (A word belonging to the priestly terminology. Never in Jud., Sam., Kgs., or other prophets [except Dan. 9. 7]: and chiefly elsewhere in Ch.)

44. The methodical form of *subscription* and *superscription*: Gen. 10, [5]. 20. 30. 31. 25, 16. 36, 19. 20. 31. 40. 43. 46, 8. 15. 18. 22. 25. Ex. 1, 1. 6, 14. 16. 19ᵇ. 25ᵇ. 26. Nu. 1, 44. 4, 28. 33. 37. 41. 45. 7, 17ᵇ. 23ᵇ. 29ᵇ etc. 84. 33, 1. Josh. 13, 23ᵇ. 28. 32. 14, 1. 15, 12ᵇ. 20. 16, 8ᵇ. 18, 20. 28ᵇ. 19, 8ᵇ. 16. 23. 31. 39. 48. 51 [cf. Gen 10, 30. 31]. 21, 19. 26. 33. 40. 41–42. (Not a complete enumeration).

45. For *tribe* P has nearly always מטה, very rarely שבט; for *to beget* הוליד (Gen. 5, 3–32. 6, 10. 11, 11–27. 17, 20. 25, 19. 48, 6. Lev. 25, 45. Nu. 26, 29. 58), not ילד (as in the genealogies of J: Gen. 4, 18 *ter*. 10, 8. 13. 15. 24 *bis*. 26. 22, 23. 25, 3); for *to be hard* or *to harden* (of the heart) חזק, חזק lit. *to be* or *make strong* (Ex. 7, 13. 22, 8, 19 [Heb. 15]. 9, 12. 14, 4. 8. 17), not כבד, הכביד lit. *to be* or *make heavy* (Ex. 7, 14. 8, 15. 32 [Heb. 11. 28]. 9, 7. 34. 10, 1); for *to stone* רגם (Lev. 20, 2. 27. 24, 14. 16 *bis*. 23. Nu. 14, 10. 15, 35. 36: also Dt. 21, 21. Josh. 7, 25ᵃ [? P]*),

not סקל (Ex. 8, 26 [Heb. 22]. 17, 4. 19, 13 *bis*. 21, 28 *bis*. 29. 32. Dt. 13, 10 [Heb. 11]. 17, 5. 22, 21. 24. Josh 7, 25ᵇ *); for *to spy* תור (Nu. 13, 2. 16. 17. 21. 25. 32 *bis*. 14, 6. 7. 34. 36. 38. 15, 39: also 10, 33 JE. Dt. 1, 33 *), not רגּל (Nu. 21, 32. Dt. 1, 24. Josh. 2, 1. 6, 22. 23. 25. 7, 2 *bis*. 14, 7); and for the pron. of 1 ps. sing. אני (nearly 130 times; אנכי once only Gen. 23, 4: comp. in Ez. אני 138 times, אנכי once 36, 28).

III.

THE GENESIS OF THE TEN WORDS.

*The Ten Commandments.**

I. THOU SHALT HAVE NONE OTHER GODS BEFORE ME.

II. THOU SHALT NOT MAKE UNTO THEE A GRAVEN IMAGE [*nor*, E], any form that is in heaven above, or that is in the earth beneath, or that is in the water under the earth: thou shalt not bow down thyself unto them, nor be led to serve them: for I Yahweh thy God am a zealous God, visiting the iniquity of the fathers upon the children, [*and*, D] upon the third and upon the fourth generation of them that hate me; and shewing mercy unto thousands of them that love me and keep my commandments.

III. THOU SHALT NOT TAKE THE NAME OF YAHWEH THY GOD IN VAIN; for Yahweh will not hold him guiltless that taketh his name in vain.

IV. REMEMBER ["Observe," D] THE SABBATH DAY TO KEEP IT HOLY.

Exodus.	*Deuteronomy.*
Six days shalt thou labour, and do all thy work: but the seventh day is a sabbath unto Yahweh thy God: [*in it*] thou shalt not do any work, thou, nor thy son, nor thy daughter, thy man-	*as Yahweh thy God commanded thee.* Six days shalt thou labour, and do all thy work; but the seventh day is a sabbath unto Yahweh thy God: [in it] thou shalt not do any work,

[* The small capitals give the original words. Where the versions agree in specifications and reasons, they are not distinguished; but where they disagree, they appear in parallel columns, with the difference indicated by italics. In a few cases of minor difference, the variation is placed in brackets.]

servant, nor thy maid-servant, nor thy cattle, nor thy stranger that is within thy gates: for in six days Yahweh made heaven and earth, the sea, and all that in them is, and rested the seventh day: wherefore Yahweh blessed the sabbath day, and hallowed it.

thou, nor thy son, nor thy daughter, *nor* thy man-servant, nor thy maid-servant, nor *thine ox, nor thine ass, nor any of* thy cattle, nor thy stranger that is within thy gates: *in order that thy man-servant and thy maid-servant may rest as well as thou. And thou shalt remember that thou wast a servant in the land of Egypt, and Yahweh thy God brought thee out thence by a mighty hand, and by a stretched-out arm; therefore Yahweh thy God commanded thee to keep the sabbath day.*

V. HONOUR THY FATHER AND THY MOTHER:

that thy days may be long upon the land which Yahweh thy God giveth thee.

as Yahweh thy God commanded thee: that thy days may be long: *and that it may be well with thee* upon the land which *Yahweh* thy God giveth thee.

VI. THOU SHALT DO NO MURDER.

VII. ["And," D]. THOU SHALT NOT COMMIT ADULTERY.

VIII. ["And," D]. THOU SHALT NOT STEAL.

IX. ["And," D]. THOU SHALT NOT BEAR WITNESS AGAINST THY NEIGHBOUR TO A LIE ["to a vain thing," D].

X. ["And," D]. THOU SHALT NOT COVET THY NEIGHBOUR'S HOUSE [*wife*, D].

Thou shalt not covet thy neighbour's *wife*, nor his man-servant, nor his maid-servant, nor his ox, nor his ass, nor any thing that is thy neighbour's.

and thou shalt not *desire* thy neighbour's *house, his field*, or his man-servant, or his maid-servant, his ox, or his ass, or any thing that is thy neighbour's.

It will first be necessary to separate the work of the Deuteronomist. We have already seen that he has changed slightly the language of three of the Ten Words. We should expect, therefore, that in the reasons he would be freer still. His changes have been in commands four, five, and ten. In the specifications of the fourth command, he adds "nor thine ox, nor thine ass, nor any of [thy cattle]"; so, in the specification of the .enth command, he adds "his field." But the most striking difference is in the reason of the fourth command, which is totally different from the reason given in Exodus. The reason given in Deuteronomy is so characteristic of the author's style, and of his usage elsewhere, that no one can doubt that this reason is peculiar to him, and that he has added it to the fourth command. See the reason for the observance of the year of release (Deut. xv. 15), the Passover (xvi. 11, 12), and the regard for the poor (xxiv. 18, 22). Besides these additions, we observe the phrase "as Yahweh thy God commanded thee" appended immediately to the fourth and fifth words, and the additional reason, "and that it may be well with thee," added to the fifth command,—a reason which is a favorite one in Deuteronomy (v. 29; vi. 18; xii. 25). It would seem, therefore, quite evident, that all of these variations of Deuteronomy are additions in the way of enlargement, paraphrase, explanation, and enforcement of the Ten Words.

Looking now at the version of Exodus, we note that the reason for the observance of the sabbath is peculiar to it. It is not at all likely that the author of Deuteronomy would have taken the liberty of cutting off any portions of the commands as they were known to him, and substituting another and very different reason for the one previously given. It would seem, therefore, that this reason of Exodus is a later addition to the command, no less than the additions that we have found in Deuteronomy.

The writer or editor of Exodus xx. in its present form, clearly had before him the same command as the author of Deuteronomy, with the exception of the Deuteronomic additions and this reason of the fourth command. It is not difficult to trace the origin of this reason. We find it essentially in Genesis ii. 2, 3: "And on the seventh day God finished his work which he had made; and he rested on the seventh day from all his work which he had made. And God blessed the seventh day and hallowed it; because that in it he rested from all his work which God had created and made."

These passages are recognized as belonging to the priestly

narrative and the priests' code (P). It would seem, therefore, that this addition to the fourth command is due to him. The other parts of the commands are common to the versions, and we can find nothing more that can be ascribed to the priestly narrator except a single word in the fourth command, to be considered later.

We have now to explain the origin of the remaining specifications and reasons. We begin with the second command. The second part of the reason appended to this command, we find in essentially the same form in Exodus xxxiv. 6, 7, in the great revelation of the Divine grace by the theophanic voice to Moses: "Yahweh, Yahweh, a God full of compassion and gracious, slow to anger, and plenteous in mercy and faithfulness; keeping mercy for thousands, forgiving iniquity and transgression and sin: and that will by no means clear [the guilty]; visiting the iniquity of the fathers upon the children, and upon the children's children, upon the third and upon the fourth generation."

We find also, in the little Book of the Covenant, the first part of the reason, thus: "For Yahweh, whose name is Zealous, is a zealous God" (Exod. xxxiv. 14). Now, both of these passages belong to the writing of the Judaic narrator (J). It seems clear, therefore, that he must have appended this reason to the second command; and certainly nothing could be more appropriate. Moreover, in the specifications we have the same verb as in Exodus xxxiv. 14, although this fact is obscured by the Revised Version, which renders the verb in the second command "Thou shalt not bow down thyself," but in the little Book of the Covenant, "Thou shalt worship [no other god]." It seems probable, therefore, that the specifications, as well as the reason, of the second command, belong to J.

The reason appended to the third command reminds us of the phrase "will not hold [him] guiltless" of the theophanic words already referred to in connection with the reason of the previous command, where we find the same verb *naqah*, which is obscured by the Revised Version in its rendering "and that will by no means clear [the guilty]," which is a singularly bad translation in other respects (Exod. xxxiv. 7). This favors the opinion that this reason, like the previous one, was derived from J.

The specifications of the fourth command are more difficult. They seem to combine material from E as well as J. J gives us two sabbath laws. One of these is in the little Book of the Covenant (Exod. xxxiv. 21): "Six days shalt thou labour, and on the seventh day thou shalt keep sabbath. In ploughing and reaping, thou shalt keep sabbath." Here great stress is laid upon abstinence from labor, even in the busiest seasons of the year. The first clause, "Six days shalt thou labour," is the same in both commands, although here again the Revised Version has made a difference by rendering the one "labour" and the other "work."

Exodus xvi. gives an account of the sabbath in connection with the giving of the manna. Here the narratives of P and J are combined. In the parts belonging to J we find the following: "For to-day is a sabbath unto Yahweh: to-day ye shall not find it in the field. Six days ye shall gather it: but on the seventh day is the sabbath. In it there shall be none. . . . See, for that Yahweh hath given you the sabbath. . . . So the people rested on the seventh day" (Exod. xvi. 25–30). Here we notice the phrase "sabbath unto Yahweh," which recurs in the specification of the fourth command. It seems likely, therefore, that in these two phrases we have the version of J. But there remain some very striking features that cannot be found in J, and these we find in E. The greater Book of the Covenant gives the sabbath law of E thus: "Six days shalt thou do thy work, and on the seventh day thou shalt keep sabbath: that thine ox and thine ass may have rest, and the son of thy maid-servant and the stranger may be refreshed." We observe that this law lays stress upon the refreshment of the animal, servant, and stranger, rather than upon abstinence from labor. This striking feature of the command, not found in J, is characteristic of E elsewhere also in his code of legislation. We have seen that the first clause, "Six days thou shalt labour," belongs to J. To this is now added the phrase, "and do all thy work." This resembles E in the verb, but differs in the noun. The command here uses a noun, *melākhah*, which is peculiar to the style of P. We can ascribe this introduction of the word instead of the noun *ma'aseh* of E, only to the process of assimilation that was later than any of the versions, and which strongly tended in the direction of Genesis ii. 2, 3. Hence, in the clause "thou shalt not do any work," the same phrase is repeated, and then follow the specifications. E gives specifications of the ox and ass where the command uses "cattle," and son of thy maid-servant and stranger where the command gives "thy maid-servant and stranger." The command, however, adds "son and daughter and man-servant." It seems likely that these specifications all belong to E.

There is one difficulty remaining. E gives us simply "the stranger"; but the command, "thy stranger which is within thy gates." The phrase "within thy gates" is Deuteronomic. It seems likely that this has come into the text of Exodus by assimilation to the text of Deuteronomy at a late date, just as *melakhah* above is an assimilation to Genesis ii. 2. This is favored by the Septuagint Version, which uses instead of it "among thee," as if it read a different Hebrew word. We should not be surprised at so many changes in the fourth command; for it recurs so many times, and in so many different forms, in the several narratives and codes.

The reason appended to the fifth word is also Deuteronomic (see Deut. iv. 40; vi. 2; xi. 9). This must also be a late addition to the version of Exodus by assimilation to the version of Deuteronomy.

The specifications of the tenth command are like those of the fourth, and doubtless came from the same writer, E. We observe the ox and the ass and the maid-servant of E from Exodus xxiii. 12, and the man-servant of the fourth command. The wife is added here, for she could hardly be missing in any specifications here, whereas she would have been unsuitable in connection with the fourth command.

Thus we have, for the most part, traced the origin of the reasons and specifications that have been added to the Ten Words. We have found that each of the four writings that constitute our Pentateuch has a share in the work, and that their work has enriched the commands and enlarged their interpretation in many ways. It would be a serious loss if we were deprived of any of them.

The Divine voice gave the Ten Words with thunder tones from heaven, and the Divine finger wrote them upon the two tables; and then the Divine Spirit inspired the several writers of the Pentateuch, each in his own way, to illustrate and enforce them by specifications, reasons, and exhortations. In later times the prophets urged these Ten Words in other ways; and at last our Saviour, in the Sermon on the Mount, took them up, removed from them the rubbish of rabbinical speculation, and set them in the bright sunlight of the gospel, showing that they are the eternal words of God for all ages and for all men,—the guide of the tongue and the heart as well as the outward act and deportment; and summing them all up in the one blessed word "love," —love to God, and love to our neighbor.

IV.

THE PESTILENCE IN EGYPT.

J. Ex. ix. 1 7.

"And Yahweh said unto Moses, Come unto Pharaoh and speak unto him. Thus saith Yahweh, the God of the Hebrews, Let my people go that they may serve me. (1). For if thou refuse to let them go, and wilt hold them still (2). Behold the hand of Yahweh is going to be upon thy cattle, which is in the field, upon the horses, upon the asses, upon the camels, upon the herds, and upon the flocks, a very grievous murrain. (3). And Yahweh will sever between the cattle of Israel and the cattle of Egypt; and there shall nothing die of all that belongeth to the children of Israel. (4). And Yahweh set a time, saying, To-morrow Yahweh will do this thing in the land. (5). And Yahweh did this thing on the morrow, and all the cattle of Egypt died; but of the cattle of the children of Israel died not one. (6). And Pharaoh sent and behold not even one of the cattle of the Israelites had died. But the heart of Pharaoh was stubborn and he did not let the people go." (7).

P. Ex. ix. 8-12.

"And Yahweh said unto Moses and unto Aaron, Take to you handfuls of ashes of the furnace, and let Moses sprinkle it toward heaven in the sight of Pharaoh. (8). And it shall become small dust over all the land of Egypt, and shall be upon man and upon beast a boil breaking forth with blains throughout all the land of Egypt. (9). And they took ashes of the furnace and stood before Pharaoh; and Moses sprinkled it up toward heaven, and it became a boil breaking forth with blains upon man and upon beast. (10). And the magicians were not able to stand before Moses because of the boils; for the boils were upon the magicians and upon all the Egyptians. (11). And Yahweh hardened the heart of Pharaoh and he hearkened not unto them, as Yahweh had spoken unto Moses." (12).

V.

THE DECALOGUE OF J AND ITS PARALLELS IN THE OTHER CODES.

THE book which Moses was commanded to write as the basis of the Covenant according to J (Ex. xxxiv. 27), is called the little book of the Covenant, to distinguish it from the book which Moses wrote according to E as the basis of the Covenant at Horeb (Ex. xxiv. 4) which is called the greater book of the Covenant. This little book of the Covenant is scarcely larger than the tables of the Covenant (Ex. xx. 1–17). Indeed it is now the opinion of many critics that we have here another decalogue. It is true the critics differ in their arrangement of these commands, but as there have always been differences in the synagogue and the church as to the arrangement of the " Ten Commandments of the Tables," such differences of opinion as to the arrangement of this decalogue cannot destroy the consensus as to their number in either case. There are some critics who hold that this decalogue was written upon the Tables (Ex. xxxiv. 28), on account of "the words of the covenant," which seem to go back upon "write thou these words, for upon the basis of these words do I conclude a covenant with thee and with Israel " (v. 27); and also on account of the verb ויכתב which has no subject expressed and where the most natural interpretation finds the subject in Moses, the subject of the verbs which immediately precede. If the section Ex. xxxiv. 11-28 stood by itself we could not escape this conclusion; but if we go back to Ex. xxxiv. 1 we find the promise that Yahweh will write upon these tables the same commands that were upon the former tables destroyed by Moses, and these were certainly the ten words of Ex. xx. 2–17. This certainly was the opinion of the Redactor.

We shall take the decalogue of J as a basis for our comparison: We shall compare these laws of J and E with corresponding laws in the Deuteronomic code (D), the code of Holiness (H), and the Priests' code (P). We shall also bring into comparison the Ten Words of the Tables. There are two versions of these, the one in Ex. xx. (T *a*), the other in Deuteronomy v. (T *b*). The version in Ex. xx. embraces material from P, and, accordingly, has embedded in it the Tables of E and J. The Tables in D are called "Tables of the Covenant," Deut. ix. 9; in P

"Tables of the testimony," Ex. xxxi. 18a; in E "Tables of stone," Ex. xxxi. 18b; in J "Tables of stones," Ex. xxxiv. 1, 4.

I. Command.

J.—"*Surely ye shall not worship another God*" (Ex. xxxiv. 14 a).
E.—"*Ye shall not make with me gods of silver*" (Ex. xx. 23 a).
T.—"*Thou shalt have no other gods before me*" (Ex. xx. 3).
D.—"If there arise in the midst of thee a prophet, ... saying, *Let us go after other gods . . . . and let us serve, them*," thou shalt not hearken unto the words of that prophet." (Dt. xiii. 2).
H.—"*Turn ye not unto worthless gods*" (Lev. xix. 4).

This is the same command in five different codes (a) "other gods" (T and D), = "another god" (J), = "gods of silver" (E), = "worthless gods" (H); (b) "have" (T), = "go after and serve" (D), = "make" (E), = "turn unto" (H), = "worship" (J); (c) "with me" (E), = "before me" (T).

II. Command.

J.—"*Molten gods thou shalt not make thee*" (Ex. xxxiv. 17).
E.—"*And gods of gold ye shall not make you*" (Ex. xx. 23 b).
T.—"*Thou shalt not make thee any graven image*" (Ex. xx. 4).
H.—"*Molten gods ye shall not make you*" (Lev. xix. 4).
D.—"*Cursed be the man that maketh a graven or molten image*" (Dt. xxvii. 15).

"Molten gods" (J and H), = "gods of gold" (E), = "graven image" (T), = "graven or molten image" (D).

It is probable that the reasons attached to these commands were not original. In J the reasons are appended to the first command.

"For Yahweh, his name is jealous. The jealous God is He. (Take heed) lest thou conclude a covenant with the inhabitants of the land, and when they go whoring after their gods and sacrifice unto their gods, they invite thee and thou eat of their peace offerings, and then take some of their daughters for thy sons, and when their daughters go whoring after their gods they make thy sons go whoring after their gods" (Ex. xxxiv. 14 b, 16). These verses simply unfold the meaning of קנא. As Yahweh is the husband of Israel he demands the exclusive allegiance of his people. Any worship of other gods is as the neglect of her husband by a wife and her going after other lovers. Any participation in the sacrificial meals of these gods is committing whoredom with them. In both versions of the Tables a corresponding reason is appended to the second command.

"(*nor* T *a*) any form that is in heaven above, or that is in the earth beneath, or that is in the water under the earth; thou shalt not bow down thyself unto them, nor be led to serve them: for I Yahweh thy God am a jealous God, visiting the iniquity of the fathers upon the children (*and* T *b*) upon the third and upon the fourth generation of them that hate me; and shewing mercy unto thousands of them that love me and keep my commandments" (Ex. xx. 4-6; Dt. v. 8-10).

(*a*). This enlargement of the command has its parallel in Dt. iv. 15-19.

"Take ye, therefore, good heed unto yourselves; for ye saw no manner of form on the day that Yahweh spake unto you in Horeb out of the midst of the fire: lest ye corrupt yourselves, and make you a graven image in the form of any figure, the likeness of male or female, the likeness of any beast that is on the earth, the likeness of any winged fowl that flieth in the heaven, the likeness of any thing that creepeth on the ground, the likeness of any fish that is in the water under the earth: and lest thou lift up thine eyes unto heaven, and when thou seest the sun and the moon and the stars, even all the host of heaven, thou be drawn away and worship them and serve them."

It is evident that this is an expansion by D of the lesser specification given in connection with the Tables. The specification in the Tables is earlier than D, and not derived from D.

(*b*). The first part of the reason of the 2d command of the Tables is the same essentially as the first part of the reason of the decalogue of J.

J.—"For Yahweh, his name is jealous. The jealous God is He" (Ex. xxxiv. 14 *b*).

T.—"For I, Yahweh, thy God, am a jealous God" (Ex. xx. 5). This we may also compare with

D.—"For Yahweh, thy God, is a consuming fire, a jealous God" (Dt. iv. 24).

(*c*). The second part of the reason of the 2d command of the decalogue of the Tables we find in essentially the same form in the revelation of the divine grace by the theophanic voice, "Yahweh, Yahweh, a God full of compassion and gracious, slow to anger, and plenteous in mercy and faithfulness: keeping mercy for thousands, forgiving iniquity and transgression and sin: and that will by no means acquit; visiting the iniquity of the fathers upon the children, and upon the children's children, upon the third and upon the fourth generation" (Ex. xxxiv. 6, 7). This passage certainly belongs to J. It is probable, therefore, that the whole of the specification and reasons appended to the 2d command of the Tables belongs to the document J.

(*a*). The larger portion of the reason attached to the first command of the decalogue of worship in J is not found in T. We find this prohibition of making a covenant with the Canaanites in D.

"Thou shalt make no covenant with them, nor shew mercy unto them: neither shalt thou make marriages with them; thy daughter thou shalt not give unto his son, nor his daughter shalt thou take unto thy son. For he will turn away thy son from following me, that they may serve other gods; so will the anger of Jahveh be kindled against you, and he will destroy thee quickly" (Dt. vii. 2-4).

The conception of "whoring after other gods" is found in the Hexateuch elsewhere in Deut. xxxi. 16 (J); Lev. xvii. 7; xx. 5-6 (H), and Num. xiv. 33 (J?); xv. 39 (P). There seems to be little doubt that this conception also is original to J.

III. Command.

J.—*Six days shalt thou labor, but on the seventh day thou shalt rest* (Ex. xxxiv. 21).

E.—*Six days shalt thou do thy work, but on the seventh day thou shalt rest* (Ex. xxiii. 12).

T *a*.—*Remember the Sabbath day to sanctify it* (Ex. xx. 8).

T *b*.—*Observe the Sabbath day to sanctify it* (Dt. v. 12).

H.—*Ye shall observe my Sabbaths* (Lev. xix. 3, 30; xxvi. 2).

P.—*Verily ye shall observe my Sabbaths* (Ex. xxxi. 13).

In the decalogue of J the feast of unleavened bread precedes the Sabbath, but in the parallel passage in E, and in the catalogues of holy days in P, the Sabbath comes first. The reason for this strange transposition it is difficult to see.

J mentions the six days as days in which to "labor"—"do

thy work." (E). The seventh day is for "rest," שבת (J E). In the Tables "the seventh day" gives place to "the Sabbath," שבת. This is to be "sanctified," קדש. It is to be "remembered" (T *a*); but observed (T *b*, H, P). The Sabbath becomes Sabbaths in H, P.

J gives an additional specification.

E.—"In ploughing and reaping thou shalt rest" (Ex. xxxiv. 21), that is, in the busiest seasons of the year, when the temptation to labor would be strongest.

The Tables also give specifications.

T *a*.—"Six days shalt thou labor and do all thy work; but the seventh day is a Sabbath unto Jahveh thy God: thou shalt not do any work, thou, nor thy son, nor thy daughter, thy manservant, nor thy maidservant, nor thy cattle, nor thy stranger that is within thy gates" (Ex. xx. 9, 10).

T *b*.—"As Jahveh thy God commanded thee,—Six days shalt thou labor, and do all thy work; but the seventh day is a Sabbath unto Jahveh thy God: thou shalt not do any work, thou, nor thy son, nor thy daughter, nor thy manservant, nor thy maidservant, nor thine ox, nor thine ass, nor any of thy cattle, nor thy stranger that is within thy gates" (Dt. v. 12-14).

The Priest code contains two sets of specifications from different sources.

P *a*.—"Ye shall keep the Sabbath therefore; for it is holy unto you: every one that profaneth it shall be put to a violent death: for whosoever doth any work therein, that soul shall be cut off from among his people. Six days shall work be done; but on the seventh day is a Sabbath of solemn rest, holy to Jahveh: whosoever doeth any work on the Sabbath day, he shall be put to a violent death. Wherefore the children of Israel shall keep the Sabbath, to observe the Sabbath throughout their generations for an everlasting covenant" (Ex. xxxi. 14-16).

Compare also in the catalogue of מועדים of P.

P *b*.—"Six days shall work be done: but on the seventh day is a Sabbath of solemn rest, an holy convocation; ye shall do no manner of work: it is a sabbath unto Jahveh in all your dwellings" (Lev. xxiii. 3).

Compare also the catalogue of ritual offerings, Num. xxviii. 9-10, where the offerings for the Sabbath are presented.

The specifications are two-fold: (*a*) as to the method of observing the day, and (*b*) as to those who are to observe it.

(*a*). The first object is abstinence from labor, לא תעשה כל מלאכה T *a* and *b*. This takes the place of תעשה מעשיך of E. The second object is rest. To this fundamental conception contained in the שבת of J we have the ינוח, rest, ינפש, *take breath*, of E. The third object in view, religious observance, is peculiar to P in his phrases עשה שבת, שבת שבתון and מקרא קדש.

(*b*). Those who are to observe it are in J "thou," in E ox and ass, the son of the maidservant, and stranger; in T *a*, son, daughter, manservant, maidservant, cattle, and stranger; T *b*, ox and ass are added to those of T *a*; in P, it is every soul, or person, under penalty of a violent death.

(*c*). The reasons of the command are still more varied than the specifications. There are none in J.

E.—"that thine ox and thine ass may rest and that the son of thy maidservant and the stranger may take breath" (Ex. xxiii. 12).

T *b*.—"in order that thy manservant and thy maidservant may rest as well as thou. And thou shalt remember that thou wast a servant in the land of Egypt, and Jahveh thy God brought thee out thence by a mighty hand, and by a stretched-out arm; therefore Jahveh thy God commanded thee to keep the Sabbath day" (Dt. v. 14-15).

T *a*.—"For in six days Jahveh made heaven and earth, the sea, and all that in them is, and rested the seventh day; wherefore Jahveh blessed the Sabbath day, and hallowed it" (Ex. xx. 11).

P.—"For it is a sign between me and you throughout your generations: that ye may know that I am Jahveh which sanctify you. . . . . it is a sign between me and the children of Israel for ever: for in six days Jahveh made heaven and earth, and on the seventh day he rested and was refreshed" (Ex. xxxi. 13, 17.)

It is evident that the reason given in T *b* is only a Deuteronomic enlargement of E fortified by the reference to the deliverance from Egypt which is the Deuteronomic underlying motive of gratitude to keep all the commands. This reason is omitted in T *a*, and was without doubt absent from the Tables as given in the Versions of J and E. It is not difficult to trace the origin of the reason given in T *a*. We find it essentially in the appendix to the Poem of the Creation: "And on the seventh day God finished his work which he had made; and he rested on the seventh day from all his work which he had made. And God blessed the seventh day and sanctified it; because that in it he rested from all his work which God had created and made" (Gen. ii. 2-3). It is a characteristic of the priestly document.

It is also characteristic of P that he represents the Sabbath as a sign of the covenant, just as he has given the sign of the Abrahamic covenant, circumcision (Gen. xvii.), and the sign of the covenant with Noah, the rainbow (Gen. ix. 13 *seq.*), these three signs being peculiar to his document.

The three commands thus far given have their parallels in the Tables; the seven now to be considered have nothing to correspond with them in the Tables.

IV. Command.

J.—*The feast of unleavened bread thou shalt observe* (Ex. xxxiv. 18*a*).

E.—*The feast of unleavened broad thou shalt observe* (Ex. xxiii. 15*a*).

D.—*Observe the month Abib and keep Passover to Jahveh thy God* (Dt. xvi. 1*a*).

P.—*In the first month on the fourteenth day of the month, between the evenings, is passover to Jahveh. And on the fifteenth day of this month is the feast of unleavened bread to Jahveh* (Lev. xxiii. 5-6).

In the ritual of the holy days, Num. xxviii. 16-17, (P *b*), we have a section identical with Lev. xxiii. 5-6, save that "Mazzoth to Jahveh" has fallen out after "feast," probably by an ancient copyist's mistake, and "between the evenings" is omitted. H probably had a similar brief law, but it was left off when his law was appended to P in Lev. xxiii. The comparison of these parallel laws in the four codes shows that the feast of unleavened bread was the great feast of J E. There is no reference to the Passover in E. In J it is mentioned in his 8th command. Passover has become a proper name in D and has risen above the feast of unleavened bread. So also in P, the Passover comes first in importance. The simple command for the observance of the feast of unleavened bread is enlarged in all the laws. In D and P it is appended to the Passover. We shall reserve the Passover for discussion under the 8th Command of J and limit ourselves here to the feast of unleavened bread.

J.—"Seven days thou shalt eat unleavened bread according as I have commanded thee, at the season of the month Abib. For in the month Abib thou didst go out from Egypt" (Ex. xxxiv. 18).

E.—"Seven days thou shalt eat unleavened bread according as I have commanded thee, at the season of the month Abib. For in it thou didst go forth from Egypt" (Ex. xxiii. 15).

D.—"Seven days shalt thou eat unleavened bread therewith, even the bread of affliction; for thou camest forth out of the land of Egypt in haste: that thou mayest remember the day when thou camest forth out of the land of Egypt all the days of thy life. And there shall be no leaven seen with thee in all thy borders seven days. . . . . Six days thou shalt eat unleavened bread: and on the seventh day shall be a *Azereth* to Jahveh thy God; thou shalt do no work" (Dt. xvi. 3-4, 8).

P (*a*).—"Seven days ye shall eat unleavened bread. In the first day ye shall have an holy convocation: ye shall do no servile work. But ye shall offer an offering made by fire to Jahveh seven days: on the seventh day is an holy convocation; ye shall do no servile work" (Lev. xxiii. 6-8).

(*b*).—"Seven days shall unleavened bread be eaten. In the first day shall be an holy convocation; ye shall do no servile work; but ye shall offer an offering made by fire, etc." (Num. xxviii. 17-25).

The month Abib is the time of J E D, but P in accordance with his usage mentions the number of the month. The simple rule of J E as regards eating unleavened bread, in D is paraphrased and intensified, and the last day is made into a special day called עצרת.

In P the feast opens and concludes with great Sabbaths of holy convocation, and an elaborate scheme of sacrifices was prepared.

Attached to the feast of unleavened bread in J is the law of firstlings.

J.—"All firstlings of the womb are mine, and all male cattle, the firstlings of the ox and sheep. And the firstlings of the ass thou shalt redeem with a sheep. And if thou canst not redeem it thou shalt break its neck. All the firstborn of thy sons thou shalt redeem" (Ex. xxxiv. 19–20).

E.—"The firstborn of thy sons thou shalt give me. So shalt thou do to thy oxen, to thy sheep; seven days shall it be with its mother, on the eighth day thou shalt give it to me" (Ex. xxii. 28–29).

D.—"All the firstling males that are born of thy herd and of thy flock thou shalt sanctify unto Jahveh thy God: thou shalt do no work with the firstling of thine ox, nor shear the firstling of thy flock. Thou shalt eat it before Jahvah thy God year by year in the place which Jahveh shall choose, thou and thy household. And if it have any blemish (*as if it be*), lame or blind, any ill blemish whatsoever, thou shalt not sacrifice it unto Jahveh thy God. Thou shalt eat it within thy gates: the unclean and the clean (*shall eat it*) alike, as the gazelle, and as the hart" (Dt. xv. 19–22).

H.—"Only the firstling among beasts, which is made a firstling to Jahveh, no man shall sanctify it; whether it be ox or sheep. It is Jahveh's. And if it be an unclean beast, then he shall ransom it according to thine estimation, and shall add unto it the fifth part thereof: or if it be not redeemed, then it shall be sold according to thine estimation" (Lev. xxvii. 26–27).

P.—"Every thing that openeth the womb, of all flesh which they offer unto Jahveh, both of man and beast, shall be thine: nevertheless the firstborn of man shalt thou surely redeem, and the firstling of unclean beasts shalt thou redeem. And those that are to be redeemed of them from a month old shalt thou redeem, according to thine estimation, for the money of five shekels, after the shekel of the sanctuary (the same is twenty gerahs). But

> the firstling of an ox, or the firstling of a sheep, or the firstling of a goat, thou shalt not redeem: they are holy: thou shalt sprinkle their blood upon the altar, and shalt burn their fat for an offering made by fire for a sweet savour unto Jahveh. And the flesh of them shall be thine" (*e. g.* the priests), (Num. xviii. 15-18).

The law of the firstborn is associated with the feast of unleavened bread in the narrative of J, and there is a remarkable verbal correspondence between the law of J and the narrative of J. In the narrative we find the following:

> "Thou shalt cause to pass over to Jahveh all that openeth the womb, and every firstling which thou hast that cometh of a beast: the males shall be Jahveh's. And every firstling of an ass thou shalt redeem with a sheep; and if thou canst not redeem it thou shalt break its neck: and all the firstborn of man among thy sons shalt thou redeem" (Ex. xiii. 12-13).

The law of E is not in the decalogue of worship, but in a pentade (Ex. xxii. 28). In D nothing is said of redemption. Only the animals without blemish could go to the sacrifice. The others could be eaten at home. The firstborn suitable for sacrifice were to be eaten in the communion meal of the peace-offering in the central sanctuary of D. In H the beasts were to be ransomed according to an estimation and a fifth part added to their value. In P the firstborn of men and unclean beasts were to be redeemed. The שׁוֹר is common to the five codes; but there is a difference between the codes as to the terms for the animals of the flock. J and H agree in giving שֶׂה, a term comprehending sheep and goat. E and D use צֹאן, sheep. P uses the two words כֶּשֶׂב, sheep, and עֵז, goat. The estimation of the redemption price was five shekels of the sanctuary. The firstlings unredeemed went to the priests as well as the redemption money of the redeemed. The stages of legal development are clearly marked in these successive codes.

Attached to the law of the feast of the unleavened bread in J is the command.

J.—"And thou shalt not appear in my presence empty" (Ex. xxxiv. 20).

E.—"And they shall not appear in my presence empty" (Ex. xxiii. 15).

THE DECALOGUE OF J AND ITS PARALLELS. 199

D.—"And they shall not appear before Jahveh empty" (Dt. xvi. 16).

In J E this is attached to the feast of unleavened bread. In D it is extended to the three great feasts, and the command is enlarged, "every man according to the gift of his hand, according to the blessing of Jahveh thy God which he hath given thee" (Dt. xvi. 17). In H and P these become prescribed offerings of an elaborate ritual (Lev. xxiii.; Num. xxviii., xxix.).

V. Command.

J.—"*And the feast of weeks thou shalt keep* at the first fruits of the wheat harvest" (Ex. xxxiv. 22*a*).

E.—"*And the feast of harvest* (thou shalt observe) the first fruits of thy work which thou shalt sow in the field" (Ex. xxiii. 16).

D.—"Seven weeks shalt thou number unto thee: from the time thou beginnest to put the sickle to the standing grain shalt thou begin to number seven weeks. And *thou shalt keep the feast of weeks unto Jahveh thy God* with a tribute of a freewill offering of thine hand, which thou shalt give, according as Jahveh thy God blesseth thee: and thou shalt rejoice before Jahveh thy God, thou, and thy son, and thy daughter, and thy manservant, and thy maidservant, and the Levite that is within thy gates, and the stranger, and the fatherless, and the widow, that are in the midst of thee, in the place which Jahveh thy God shall choose to cause his name to dwell there. And thou shalt remember that thou wast a bondman in Egypt; and thou shalt observe and do these statutes" (Dt. xvi. 9–12).

H.—"And ye shall count unto you from the morrow after the sabbath, from the day that ye brought the sheaf of the wave offering; seven sabbaths shall there be complete: even unto the morrow after the seventh sabbath shall ye number fifty days; *and ye shall offer a new minchah unto Jahveh.* Ye shall bring out of your habitations two wave loaves of two tenth parts (*of an ephah*): they shall be of fine flour, they shall be baken with leaven, for first fruits unto Jahveh. And ye shall present with the bread seven lambs without blemish of the first year, and one young bullock, and two rams: they shall be a burnt offering unto Jahveh, with their minchah and their drink offerings, even an offering made by fire, of a sweet savour, unto Jahveh. And ye shall offer one he-goat for a sin-offering, and two he-lambs of the first year for a sacrifice of peace offerings. And the priest shall wave them with the bread of the first-fruits for a wave offering before Jahveh, with the two lambs: they shall be holy to Jahveh for the priest. And ye shall make proclamation on the self-same day; there shall be an holy convocation unto you: ye shall do no servile work: it is a statute forever in all your dwellings throughout your generations" (Lev. xxiii. 15–21).

P.—" Also in the day of the first-fruits, when ye offer a *new minchah unto Jahveh in your weeks,* ye shall have an holy convocation; ye shall do no servile work, but ye shall offer a burnt offering for a sweet savour unto Jahveh; two young bullocks, one ram, seven he-lambs of the first year; and their minchah, fine flour mingled with oil, three tenth parts for each bullock, two tenth parts for the one ram, a several tenth part for every lamb of the seven lambs; one he-goat, to make atonement for you. Beside the continual burnt offering, and the minchah thereof, ye shall offer them (they shall be unto you without blemish), and their drink offerings" (Num. xxviii. 26–31).

The name of this feast in J and D is feast of weeks, in E the feast of harvest, in P the day of the first-fruits. The time of observance of J is at the first-fruits of the wheat harvest. E is more general—the first-fruits of thy sowing. D counts seven weeks from the time of the first putting the sickle to the standing grain. H counts seven Sabbaths from the day of the *'omer* offering, on the morrow after the Sabbath of the feast of unleavened bread. According to D it was a joyful family feast, in which freewill offerings were offered at the central sanctuary. According to H, it was the time for the offering of the two fresh loaves of the new harvest, prior to which no portion of the harvest could be eaten by the people. It was also a great Sabbath with a ritual sin offering and peace offerings, burnt offerings and minchoth. P gives explicit directions as to these offerings.

VI. Command.

J.—"*And the feast of the ingathering* (thou shalt observe) at the circuit of the year" (Ex. xxxiv. 22*b*).

E.—"*And the feast of the ingathering* (thou shalt observe) in the going forth of the year when thou gatherest in thy work from the field" (Ex. xxiii. 16*b*).

D.—"*Thou shalt keep the feast of booths seven days*, after that thou hast gathered in from thy threshing-floor and from thy winepress: and thou shalt rejoice in thy feast, thou, and thy son, and thy daughter, and thy manservant, and thy maidservant, and the Levite, and the stranger, and the fatherless, and the widow, that are within thy gates. Seven days shalt thou keep a feast unto Jahveh thy God in the place which Jahveh shall choose: because Jahveh thy God shall bless thee in all thine increase, and in all the work of thine hands, and thou shalt be altogether joyful" (Dt. xvi. 13–15).

H.—"And ye shall take you on the first day the fruit of goodly trees, branches of palm trees, and boughs of thick trees, and willows of the brook; and ye shall rejoice before Jahveh your God seven days. And ye shall keep it a feast unto Jahveh seven days in the year: it is a statute forever in your generations: ye shall keep it in the seventh month. Ye shall dwell in booths seven days; all that are homeborn in Israel shall dwell in booths: that your generations may know that I made the children of Israel to dwell in booths, when I brought them out of the land of Egypt: I am Jahveh your God" (Lev. xxiii. 40–44).

P (*a*).—"Speak unto the children of Israel, saying, *On the fifteenth day of this seventh month is the feast of booths for seven days unto Jahveh*. On the first day shall be an holy convocation: ye shall do no servile work. Seven days ye shall offer an offering made by fire unto Jahveh: on the eighth day shall be an holy convocation unto you, and ye shall offer an offering made by fire unto Jahveh: it is a closing festival; ye shall do no servile work" (Lev. xxiii. 34–36).

(*b*).—"And on the fifteenth day of the seventh month ye shall have an holy convocation; ye shall do no servile work, and ye shall keep a feast unto Jahveh seven days: and ye shall offer a burnt offering, an offering made by fire, of a sweet savour unto Jahveh; thirteen young bullocks, two rams, fourteen he-lambs of the first year; they shall be without blemish: and their minchah, fine flour mingled with oil, three tenth parts for every bullock of the thirteen bullocks, two tenth parts for each ram of the two rams, and a several tenth part for every lamb of the fourteen lambs: and one he-goat for a sin offering; beside the continual burnt offering, the minchah thereof, and the drink offering thereof. And on the second day (*ye shall offer*) twelve young bullocks, two rams, fourteen he-lambs of the first year without blemish: and their minchah and their drink offerings for the bullocks, for the rams, and for the lambs, according to their number, after the ordinance: and one he-goat for a sin offering; beside the continual burnt offering, and the minchah thereof, and their drink offerings" .... (Each of the intervening days has its ritual).

"On the eighth day ye shall have a closing festival: ye shall do no servile work: but ye shall offer a burnt offering, an offering made by fire, of a sweet savour unto the Lord: one bullock, one ram, seven he-lambs of the first year without blemish: their minchah and their drink offerings for the bullock, for the ram, and for the lambs, shall be according to their number, after the ordinance: and one he-goat for a sin offering; beside the continual burnt offering, and the minchah thereof, and the drink offering thereof" (Num. xxix. 12–19, 35–38).

The third annual feast is called "the feast of the ingathering" אסיף in J E = feast of booths סכת in D and P, observed by dwelling in booths in H. The time in J is "at the circuit of the year," תקופת השנה = in the going forth of the year בצאת השנה E. In E the additional statement is made, "when thou gatherest in thy work from the field,"="after thou hast gathered in from thy threshing floor and from thy winepress," D. H puts the feast in the seventh month, and P on the fifteenth day of the seventh month. From J E we would suppose the feast was for a single day. But D H P mention seven days of observance. P mentions an עצרת on the eighth day, the seventh great Sabbath of the year. In D it is a joyful harvest feast at the central sanctuary. In H it is a celebration of their dwelling in booths when they came forth from Egypt. In P it is a feast in which the ritual prescribes a greater amount of whole burnt offerings expressing worship than at any other feast. It is the culmination of the worship of the year.

Appended to this command in J is the command, "Three times in the year shall all thy males appear before the Lord Jahveh, the God of Israel. For I will dispossess nations from thy presence, and I will make thy boundary broad in order that no one may desire thy land when thou goest up to appear before Jahveh thy God three times in the year" (Ex. xxxiv. 23, 24).

In the other codes we find similar prescriptions:

E *a*.—"Three times shalt thou keep feast to me in the year" (Ex. xxiii. 14).

E *b*.—"Three times in the year shall all thy males appear before the Lord Jahveh" (Ex. xxiii. 17).

D.—"Three times in the year shall all thy males appear before Jahveh thy God in the place which he shall choose" (Dt. xvi. 16).

Instead of the three times of J E D, we have the three harvest feasts of H, the offering of the first ripe sheaf, the offering of the first loaves of the harvest, and the dwelling in booths after all the harvests had been gathered in (Lev. xxiii.). P gives the ritual of the seven great Sabbaths of the year in Num. xxviii.-xxix.

D appends his law of the one central sanctuary as is usual with him. E gives the command as an introduction to the three feasts as well as a conclusion. But these differ in language to such an extent that one of them must have been taken from another source. It seems probable that E *b*, as less original, is a later addition. E *a* uses רגלים for פעמים in E *b*. J D; and חגג for "appear before" of E *b*. J D. E *b* uses אל for את of J and D. The encouragement of J is peculiar to him.

VII. Command.

J.—"*Thou shalt not offer the blood of my zebach with leavened bread*" (Ex. xxxiv. 25 *a*).

E.—"*Thou shalt not offer the blood of my zebach with leavened bread*" (Ex. xxiii. 18 a).

P a.—"*He shall bring with the zebach of the thank-offering perforated cakes, unleavened, mingled with oil* and wafers unleavened, anointed with oil, and cakes mingled with oil, of fine flour, soaked. With perforated cakes of leavened bread he may offer his oblation with the zebach of his peace-offering for thank-offering*" (Lev. vii. 12, 13).

P b.—"*No minchah which ye bring to Jahveh shall be offered leavened*" (Lev. ii. 11).

J E and P b use חמץ, leavened. P a uses מצות, unleavened, as well as חמץ. J uses for offer שחט = זבח E = הקריב P a, b. J E use זבח = זבח השלמים P a. P allows the use of leavened bread in the case specified to be eaten at the common meal of the peace-offering, and H mentions the offering of the two leavened loaves at the harvest feast (Lev. xxiii. 17).

VIII. Command.

J.—"*And the zebach of the feast of the Passover shall not be left unto the morning*" (Ex. xxxiv. 25 b).

E.—"*And the fat of my feast shall not remain all night until the morning*" (Ex. xxiii. 18 b).

D.—"And thou shalt sacrifice the passover unto Jahveh thy God, of the flock and the herd, in the place which Jahveh shall choose to cause his name to dwell there." . . . .

"*Neither shall any of the flesh, which thou sacrificest the first day at even, remain all night until the morning.* Thou mayest not sacrifice the passover within any of thy gates, which Jahveh thy God giveth thee: but at the place which Jahveh thy God shall choose to cause his name to dwell in, there thou shalt sacrifice the passover at even, at the going down of the sun, at the season that thou camest forth out of Egypt. And thou shalt roast and eat it in the place which Jahveh thy God shall choose: and thou shalt turn in the morning, and go unto thy tents" (Deut. xvi. 2, 4 b—7).

P (a).—"*They shall leave none of it until the morning*, nor break a bone thereof: according to all the statute of the passover, they shall keep it" (Num. ix. 12).

P (b).—"And in the first month, on the fourteenth day of the month, is Jahveh's passover" (Num. xxviii. 16).

The fuller law of the passover is given in connection with the mingled history of J and P in Ex. xii.

P.—"Speak ye unto all the congregation of Israel, saying, In the tenth (*day*) of this month they shall take to them every man a lamb, according to their fathers' houses, a lamb for an household: and if the household be too little for a lamb, then shall he and his neighbor next unto his house take one according to the number of the souls; according to every man's eating, ye shall make your count for the lamb. Your lamb shall be without blemish, a male of the first year: ye shall take it from the sheep, or from the goats: and ye shall keep it up until the fourteenth day of the same month: and the whole assembly of the congregation of Israel shall kill it at even. And they shall take of the blood, and put it on the two side posts and on the lintel, upon the houses wherein they shall eat it. And they shall eat the flesh in that night, roast with fire, and unleavened bread; with bitter herbs they shall eat it. Eat not of it raw, nor sodden at all with water, but roast with fire; its head with its legs and with the inwards thereof. *And ye shall let nothing of it remain until the morning;* but that which remaineth of it until the morning, ye shall burn with fire. And thus shall ye eat it; with your loins girded, your shoes on your feet, and your staff in your hand: and ye shall eat it in haste: it is Jahveh's passover." . . . .

"And Jahveh said unto Moses and Aaron, This is the ordinance of the passover: there shall no alien eat thereof: but every man's servant that is bought for money, when thou hast circumcised him, then shall he eat thereof. A sojourner and an hired servant shall not eat thereof. In one house shall it be eaten; thou shalt not carry forth aught of the flesh abroad out of the house: neither shall ye break a bone thereof" (Ex. xii. 3-11; 43-46).

J.—" Then Moses called for all the elders of Israel, and said unto them, Draw out, and take you lambs according to your families, and kill the passover. And ye shall take a bunch of hyssop, and dip it in the blood that is in the basin, and strike the lintel and the two side posts with the blood that is in the basin; and none of you shall go out of the door of his house until the morning. For Jahveh will pass through to smite the Egyptians; and when he seeth the blood upon the lintel, and on the two side posts, Jahveh will pass over the door, and will not suffer the destroyer to come in unto your houses to smite you. And ye shall observe this thing for an ordinance to thee and to thy sons for ever. And it shall come to pass, when ye be come to the land which Jahveh will give you, according as he hath promised, that ye shall keep this service. And it shall come to pass, when your children shall say unto you, What mean ye by this service? that ye shall say, It is the sacrifice of Jahveh's passover, who passed over the houses of the children of Israel in Egypt, when he smote the Egyptians, and delivered our houses" (Ex. xii. 21-27).

The passover feast of the eighth command of J, which is here incidentally referred to under the offering peculiar to the feast, is more fully mentioned in the narrative of J. The passover sacrifice is indeed a special kind of the zebach, or peace-offering, זבח פסח = זבח חג הפסח of Ex. xii. 27. E gives the command a more general reference to all the feasts. D uses the phrase "sacrifice the passover," שחט הפסח = זבח הפסח of J. In the narrative of J the victim is צאן, a lamb; in P, a שה, embracing כבש, lamb, and עז, kid. There is no specification in the codes of E and J. In J the zebach shall not be left until the morning, לא ילין מן הבשר לבקר of D = לא ילין עד בקר of E = לא ישאירו עד בקר of P (narrative) = לא תותירו עד בקר of P *a*. D emphasizes the celebration of the feast at the central sanctuary. P *a* gives the additional rule, " nor break a bone thereof," both in his code and in his narrative. If we had space we could point to a large number of features which distinguish the documents here and elsewhere, as illustrated by these extensive passages. Any one of our readers may do it for himself.

IX. *Command.*

J.—" *The first of the first-fruits of thy ground thou shalt bring to the house of Jahveh thy God*" (Ex. xxxiv. 26 a).

E.—" *The first of the first-fruits of thy ground thou shalt bring to the house of Jahveh thy God*" (Ex. xxiii. 19).

D.—"*That thou shalt take of the first of all the fruit of the ground*, which thou shalt bring in from thy land that Jahveh thy God giveth thee; and thou shalt put it in a basket, *and shalt go unto the place which Jahveh thy God shall choose* to cause his name to dwell there. And thou shalt come unto the priest that shall be in those days, and say unto him, I profess this day unto Jahveh thy God, that I am come unto the land which Jahveh sware unto our fathers for to give us. And the priest shall take the basket out of thine hand, and set it down before the altar of Jahveh thy God. And thou shalt answer and say before Jahveh thy God, A Syrian ready to perish was my father, and he went down into Egypt and sojourned there, few in number; and he became there a nation, great, mighty, and populous: and the Egyptians evil entreated us, and afflicted us, and laid upon us hard bondage: and we cried unto Jahveh the God of our fathers, and Jahveh heard our voice and saw our affliction, and our toil, and our oppression: and Jahveh brought us forth out of Egypt with a mighty hand, and with an outstretched arm, and with great terribleness, and with signs, and with wonders: and he hath brought us into this place, and hath given us this land, a land flowing with milk and honey. And now, behold, I have brought the first of the fruit of the ground, which thou, Jahveh, hast given me. And thou shalt set it down before Jahveh thy God, and worship before Jahveh thy God: and thou shalt rejoice in all the good which Jahveh thy God hath given unto thee, and unto thine house, thou, and the Levite, and the stranger that is in the midst of thee " (Deut. xxvi. 2–11).

H.—"Speak unto the children of Israel, and say unto them, When ye be come into the land which I give unto you, and shall reap the harvest thereof, then *ye shall bring the sheaf of the first-fruits of your harvest unto the priest: and he shall wave the sheaf before Jahveh* to be accepted for you: on the morrow after the sabbath the priest shall wave it. And in the day when ye wave the sheaf, ye shall offer a he-lamb without blemish of the first year for a burnt offering unto Jahveh. And the *minchah* thereof shall be two tenth parts (of an *ephah*) of fine flour mingled with oil, an offering made by fire unto Jahveh for a sweet savour: and the drink offering thereof shall be of wine, the fourth part of an hin. And ye shall eat neither bread, nor parched corn, nor fresh ears, until this self-same day, until ye have brought the oblation of your God. It is a statute for ever throughout your generations in all your dwellings" (Lev. xxiii. 10-14).

P.—"All the best of the oil, and all the best of the vintage, and of the corn, the first-fruits of them which they give unto Jahveh, to thee have I given them. The first ripe fruits of all that is in their land, which they bring unto Jahveh, shall be thine; every one that is clean in thy house shall eat thereof" (Num. xviii. 12-13).

The phrase of J E is ראשית בכורי אדמתך =
of D = ראשית כל פרי האדמה
of H = ראשית קצירכם
of P. כל חלב יצהר וכל חלב תירוש ודגן ראשיתם

The house of Jahveh seems to imply a temple. It may have been a change by insertion from an original command to bring the first fruits to Jahveh. In D it is brought to the priest of Jahveh. In H it is the offering of the first ripe sheaf. In P it is generalized so as to include oil and wine and grain, and these are to be given to the priests for food.

X. Command.

J.—" *Thou shalt not seethe a kid* (which is still) *with its mother's milk* " (Ex. xxxiv. 26*b*).

E.—" *Thou shalt not seethe a kid* (which is still) *with its mother's milk* " (Ex. xxiii. 19).

D.—"*Thou shalt not seethe a kid* (which is still) *with its mother's milk*" (Dt. xiv. 21).

This command is identical in these three codes. It is not clear in itself, and probably remained as an enigma after the law and usage had changed. The older Protestant interpreters, Luther, Calvin, Piscator, *et al.*, thought of a limitation of the age of the animal for purposes of sacrifice. This is most suited to the context, for we have had three laws of offerings prior to it. But the Rabbinical interpretation that it is a dietary law against eating a kid in the milk of its mother has been followed by most moderns. The Deuteronomic code (xiv. 21) is thought to favor the latter view from the fact that it is there preceded by the command not to eat anything that dies of itself. But on the other hand, it is followed by the laws of tithes and first-fruits, and it may rather go with these laws there, as it is associated with the law of first-fruits here. We do not hesitate to follow the former interpretation and class this law with the three preceding ones as laws of offerings. בשׁל is used for cooking the portions of the animal victim that were eaten by the offerers in the communion meal of the זבח (Ex. xxix. 31). This then would forbid the sacrifice of suckling animals. It is true that in the larger book of the Covenant (Ex. xxii. 29) first born of animals were to be given to Jahveh on the eighth day, notwithstanding the law in Ex. xxiii. 19, corresponding exactly with ours. It is also true that in Lev. xxii. 27, we have the more explicit statement, "From the eighth day and upward it shall be accepted for a *qorban* an offering by fire unto Jahveh," but notwithstanding the consensus of Rabbinical interpretation we are not sure that this amounts to any more than that as the male child was circumcised on the eighth day, so the animal on the eighth day was taken from its mother to the divine presence. It may then have been kept in the flocks and herds of the altar for subsequent use at the proper age. Indeed the "and upward," favors our view. But even if the ordinary view is taken as to the age of animals suitable for offerings, we have still to bear in mind that the various codes differ not infrequently in their prescriptions. The offerings are generally of animals a year old or more, in the specifiations of age that are not infrequently made.

We have gone over this decalogue of worship given in the narrative of J, and have compared its ten laws with similar laws in the other codes. We have found that the same fundamental commands underlie the several forms in which they appear in the different codes. These fundamental commands we may regard as Mosaic; but how is it possible to explain the variations in the codes on the traditional theory that all these variations were given by Moses to the same people before their entrance into the Holy Land, and ere it was possible to fulfil any of them in action? They appear in the codes in several stages of development representing different stages of codification, as changes were rendered necessary in the experience of God's people in the Holy Land. If any one can propose any more reasonable explanation, or one more in accord with the traditional theory that will take the facts of the case into account, we shall gladly follow him.

VI.

THE GREATER BOOK OF THE COVENANT AND ITS PARALLELS IN THE LATER CODES.

THE book written by Moses and called the book of the Covenant Ex. xxiv. 4-7, because the great Covenant at Sinai was made upon the basis of it (xxiv. 8), is also called the greater book of the Covenant in order to distinguish it from the little book of the Covenant, Ex. xxxiv. 27. This book contained all the words and judgments which had just been given to Moses in the mount (xxiv. 3). The words certainly embrace Ex. xx. 22-26, and Ex. xxiii. 20-33, the Introduction and Conclusion of the book. Some have maintained that the ten words of the tables, Ex. xx. 3-17, should likewise be included. The judgments embrace xxi.—xxiii. 19 in accordance with the title xxi. 1 : "These are the judgments which thou shalt set before them."

These judgments are regarded by many as a series of pentades or groups of five commands, and also decalogues. The first effort to arrange them in such groups was made by Bertheau in his *Sieben Gruppen Mosaischer Gesetze.*, Goettingen, 1840. He makes seven decalogues: xx. 3-7; xxi. 2-11, 12-27; xxi. 28—xxii. 16, 17-30; xxiii. 1-8; xxiii. 14-19. He regards xx. 22-26 as four commands introductory to the judgments; Ex. xxiii. 9-13 as an interpolation, and Ex. xxiii. 26-43 as a decalogue of promises. Great credit is due to Bertheau for breaking the way into this previously unexplored wilderness of commands. It is not surprising that he sometimes missed the proper arrangement. Ewald in his *Gesch. d. Volkes Israel*, II. p. 235, 1865, improves upon Bertheau's scheme and finds: xxi. 2-11, two pentades, xxi. 12-16, a pentade followed by v. 17 a fragment of another pentade relating to crimes other than murders with a death

(211)

penalty; xxi. 18–32, two pentades; xxi. 33—xxii. 5, a decalogue; xxii. 6–16, two pentades, xxii. 17–30, two pentades, xxiii. 1–9, two pentades; xxiii. 10–19, two pentades. Dillmann in his edition of Knobel's Com. on Exodus and Leviticus, 1880, improves upon Ewald by a more careful analysis. He thinks that the Redactor has only given a selection of commands of the original series in Ex. xx. 24-26 and xxii. 17–30; that Ex. xxiii. 4-5 is a later interpolation, and that xxiii. 10–19 has been rearranged and improved by the Redactor. On the basis of these efforts we propose what seems to us a still further improvemant.

I.—*The Pentade of Worship* xx. 23–26.

(1). Ye shall not make with me gods of silver.

(2). And gods of gold ye shall not make you.

(3). An altar of earth thou shalt make me, and sacrifice upon it thy whole burnt-offerings and thy peace-offerings, thy sheep and thy cattle. In all places where I record my name I will come unto thee and bless thee.

(4). And if an altar of stones thou wilt make me, thou shalt not build them hewn. And if thou hast swung thy tool over it thou hast defiled it.

(5). And thou shalt not ascend by steps upon my altar that thy nakedness may not be disclosed upon it.

1 and 2 have been studied in connection with their parallels in the code of *J*.

3. This command prescribes the material out of which the divine altar should be constructed, the earth, אֲדָמָה, the natural soil of the ground. It mentions the two kinds of sacrifices, both primitive and Pre-Mosaic, which might be made upon it: עוֹלוֹת = whole burnt-offerings, and שלמים = peace-offerings. Many different altars are contemplated in כל המקום, which, in accordance with the rule of כל with the article must be translated "all places." These places for the erection of altars were indicated by divine selection.

The law of the Deuteronomic Code (xii. 5–7, 12–14) is as follows:

"But unto the place which Yahweh your God shall choose out of all your tribes to put his name there, even unto his habitation shall ye seek, and thither thou shalt come: and thither ye shall bring your burnt-offerings, and your sacrifices, and your tithes, and the heave-offering of your hand, and your vows, and your free-will offerings, and the firstlings of your herd and of your flock; and there ye shall eat before Yahweh your God, and ye shall rejoice in all that ye put your hand unto, ye and your households, wherein Yahweh thy God hath blessed thee."

"And ye shall rejoice before Yahweh your God, ye, and your sons, and your daughters, and your menservants, and your maidservants, and the Levite that is within your gates, forasmuch as he hath no portion nor inheritance with you. Take heed to thyself that thou offer not thy burnt-offerings in every place that thou seest; but in the place which Yahweh shall choose in one of thy tribes, there thou shalt offer thy burnt-offerings, and there thou shalt do all that I command thee."

This law substitutes "the place which Yahweh your God shall choose out of all your tribes" for the "*all places*" of the covenant code, and prohibits offering burnt-offerings in "every place that thou seest" (בכל מקום), xii. 13, thus limiting sacrifices to *one* national altar. The Deuteronomic expressions for divine selection are "to put his name there" (לשום), xii. 5, and "cause his name to dwell there" (לשכן), xii. 11, instead of "record my name" (הזכיר) of the covenant code. The sacrifices are increased beyond the whole burnt-offerings and peace-offerings of the covenant code to the tithes, heave-offerings, votive-offerings, free-will offerings and firstlings (xii. 6).

The law of H is as follows (Lev. xvii. 3-9):

"What man soever there be of the house of Israel, that killeth an ox, or lamb, or goat, in the camp, or that killeth it without the camp, and hath not brought it unto the door of the tent of meeting, to offer it as an oblation unto Yahweh before the tabernacle of Yahweh: blood shall be imputed unto that man; he hath shed blood; and that man shall be cut off from among his people: to the end that the children of Israel may bring their sacrifices, which they sacrifice in the open field, even that they may bring them unto Yahweh, unto the door of the tent of meeting, unto the priest, and sacrifice them for sacrifices of peace-offerings unto Yahweh. And the priest shall sprinkle the blood upon the altar of Yahweh at the door of the tent of meeting, and burn the fat for a sweet savour unto Yahweh. And they shall no more sacrifice their sacrifices unto the he goats, after whom they go a whoring. This shall be a statute forever unto them throughout their generations. And thou shalt say unto them, Whatsoever man there be of the house of Israel, or of the strangers that sojourn among them, that offereth a burnt-offering or sacrifice, and bringeth it not unto the door of the tent of meeting, to sacrifice it unto Yahweh; even that man shall be cut off from his people."

This law is a still further advance. The sacrifices are limited under severe penalty to the altar at the door of the tent of meeting.

4. The native rock or natural stones were allowed for use in altar building as well as the natural soil of the ground, only these must remain in their natural condition. No tool could be used upon them. With this prohibition compare the law of P. (Exodus xxvii. 1–5.)

"And thou shalt make the altar of acacia wood, five cubits long, and five cubits broad; the altar shall be four-square: and the height thereof shall be three cubits. And thou shalt make the horns of it upon the four corners thereof: the horns thereof shall be of one piece with it: and thou shalt overlay it with brass, and thou shalt make its pots to take away its ashes, and its shovels, and its basons, and its fleshhooks, and its firepans: all the vessels thereof thou shalt make of brass. And thou shalt make for it a grating of network of brass; and upon the net shalt thou make four brasen rings in the four corners thereof. And thou shalt put it under the ledge round the altar beneath, that the net may reach halfway up the altar."

This law makes the use of tools necessary both in cutting the acacia wood and in overlaying with brass. The material of the covenant code is no longer thought of.

5. The sanctity of the altar was also maintained by the prohibition of any exposure of the person there, even such as might arise in the use of stairs. עָרְוַת has here the same sense as in Lev. xviii. 6 *sq*. These three commands form a group in the unfolding of the reverence of the divine name of the third Command of the tables.

There seems to be rather an abrupt transition from the pentade of Worship to the מִשְׁפָּטִים. We would expect other laws

THE GREATER BOOK OF THE COVENANT 215

of worship to follow. It may be that the Redactor has omitted one or more pentades and used them elsewhere. If the closing decalogue of our book xxiii. 10-19, immediately followed, it would seem more natural than the present order. We must leave these questions undecided for the present.

II.—*The Pentade of the Rights of the Hebrew Slave* (xxi. 2-6).

(1). If thou acquire a Hebrew slave, six years shall he serve, and in the seventh go forth to freedom without price.

(2). If by himself he came, by himself he shall go forth.

(3). If he were married, his wife shall go forth with him.

(4). If his lord give him a wife and she bear him sons and daughters, the wife and her children shall belong to her lord and he shall go forth alone.

(5). But if the slave earnestly say, I love my lord, my wife and my children, I will not go forth free, then his lord shall bring him unto God and bring him to the door or to the post, and bore his ear with his awl, and he shall become his slave forever.

The Deuteronomic code, (xv. 12-18), gives (1) and (5) in different language and greatly enlarged:

(1). The Deuteronomic code uses יִמָּכֵר for תִּקְנֶה and תְּשַׁלְּחֶנּוּ חָפְשִׁי for יֵצֵא לַחָפְשִׁי, thus:

"If thy brother, a Hebrew man or woman be sold unto thee, he shall serve thee six years and in the seventh year thou shalt dismiss him free from thee; and when thou dismissest him free from thee thou shalt not dismiss him empty."

(5). The Deuteronomic code, vs. 16-17, gives:

"And it shall come to pass if he say unto thee: I will not go out from thee. I love thee and thy house, because it is good for me to be with thee, then thou shalt take the awl and put it in his ear and in the door, and he shall become thy slave forever. So also shalt thou do to thy female slave."

הָאלהים is the divine name usual in the second Elohist. רצע is only here in the verbal form, the noun מרצע only here and Deut. xv. 17, both of them archaic terms. The Deuteronomic code embraces male and female slaves under the same laws. Here only the male slave is contemplated.

The law of P is given in Lev. xxv. 39-46;

"And if thy brother be waxen poor with thee, and sell himself unto thee; thou shalt not make him to serve as a bondservant. As an hired servant, and as a sojourner, he shall be with thee; he shall serve with thee unto the year of jubile: then shall he go out from thee, he and his children with him, and shall return unto his own family, and unto the possession of his fathers shall he return. For they are my servants, which I brought forth out of the land of Egypt: they shall not be sold as bondmen. Thou shalt not rule over him with rigour; but shalt fear thy God. And as for thy bondmen, and thy bondmaids, which thou shalt have; of the nations that are round about you, of them shall ye buy bondmen and bondmaids. Moreover of the children of the strangers that do sojourn among you, of them shall ye buy, and of their families that are with you, which they have begotten in your land; and they shall be your possession. And ye shall make them an inheritance for your children after you, to hold for a possession; of them shall ye take your bondmen for ever: but over your brethren the children of Israel ye shall not rule, one over another, with rigour."

In the Priests' Code (1) the verb נמכר is used as in D, and the year of jubile takes the place of the seventh year. The Hebrew slave was to be treated as a hired servant and a sojourner. (4). He and his children "shall go out from thee." (יצא מעמך) (5). There is a distinction between the Hebrew slave and the foreign slave: the latter could be enslaved forever, but not the Hebrew slave. This seems to reverse the law in E and D in this respect.

III.—*Pentade of Hebrew Slave Concubines* (xxi. 7-11).

(1). If a man shall sell his daughter for a slave woman she shall not go forth as the slaves go forth.

(2). If she be displeasing to her lord who has appointed her for himself, he shall let her be redeemed. To a foreign people he shall not have the power to sell her when he has acted treacheously with her.

(3). But if for his son he appointed her, according to the rights of daughters he shall do for her.

(4). If another he take to himself, her (provision of) flesh, her clothing and cohabiting with her he shall not withhold.

(5). And if these three things he will not do to her she shall go forth without price, without silver.

This series gives us not laws for dealing with a female slave who according to Deut. xv. 17, was to be treated exactly as a male slave; but for female slaves who were rather concubines. There are no parallels to this Pentade in the other codes.

2. בגד is used especially for treacherous dealing between the sexes, but only here in the Hexateuch.

4. שאר = flesh — that is the meat of animals as the chief provision of her support. It is only here and Ps. lxxviii. 20, 27, in this sense. It is used in Lev. xviii., xxi. 2, (H), xxv. 49, Num. xxvii. 11, (P), of near relatives. כסות is also archaic, found again xxii. 26, of our code and in Job. It is found elsewhere only in the brief law, Deut. xxii. 12, respecting the fringes, and in the narrative of the Ephraimitic writer, Gen. xx. 16, and Isaiah iv. 3. עֹנָה is only found here from עון = dwell, meaning cohabitation. This was her right, as well as food and clothing, and these things could not be withheld from her.

IV.—*Pentade of Acts of Violence* (xxi. 12–16).

(1). Whoso smiteth a man and he die, shall be put to a violent death.

(2). But as for the one who hath not hunted after him, but God has caused him to fall into his hands—I will appoint thee a place whither he may flee.

(3). But if a man act passionately against his neighbour, to slay him by craft, from my altar thou shalt take him to die.

(4). Whoso smiteth his father or his mother shall be put to a violent death.

(5). Whoso stealeth a man and selleth him, or he be found in his possession, he shall be put to a violent death.

1. This law is found in the priests' code in the form: "A man when he smiteth any human person shall be put to a violent death." Lev. xxiv. 17. נֶפֶשׁ אָדָם is used instead of אִישׁ. In Deut. xix. 4, it is in the form אֲשֶׁר יַכֶּה אֶת־רֵעֵהוּ.

2. This case in which the man did not hunt for him (צדה) is presented in the Deuteronomic code, xix. 4, thus: "without knowledge, he not hating him (שנא) yesterday and the day

before" with an illustration v. 5. In the priest's code Num. xxxv. 22, "If accidentally without enmity (אֵיבָה) he push him (הדף) or cast any vessel upon him without purpose" (צְדִיָּה). The appointed place is in accordance with the next command, the divine altar. In accordance with the priest's code and Deuteronomic code it is one of the cities of refuge. (Num. xxxv., Deut. xix.).

3. The case of intentional murder is here presented as an act of violent passion (זוּד) and of craft (עָרְמָה). In the Deuteronomic code xix. 11 it is expressed: "If there be a man hating (שנא) his neighbour and he lie in wait for him (ארב) and rise up against him and smite a person (נפש) and he die." In the priest's code, Num. xxxv. 20-21, it is: "If, in hatred (בְּשִׂנְאָה) he push him or cast anything upon him designedly (בִּצְדִיָּה) so that he has died, or if in enmity (בְּאֵיבָה) he hath smitten him with his hand so that he hath died." In these cases according to our code he is taken from the divine altar and put to death. The cases in 1 Kgs. i. 50, 11, 28, were in accordance with this code. According to the Deuteronomic and priests' codes he was delivered over from the cities of refuge into the hands of the avenger of blood.

4. וְנִמְצָא בְיָדוֹ, or he (the man stolen) be found in his hand = power = possession. Thus there are two cases, in the one, the stolen man was sold; in the other, the stolen man became the slave of the thief. In either case the man-stealer was to be put to a violent death. In Deut. xxiv. 7 it is thus expressed: "If a man be found stealing a person (נפש) from among his brethren the children of Israel, and he lay hands upon him and sell him, that thief shall die."

V. 17: "Whoso curseth his father or his mother shall be put to death."

It is doubtful whether this command really belongs in this place. It is placed by the LXX. in immediate connection with v. 15. Dillmann thinks that was the proper place, and he separates the law of the man-stealer as beginning another pentade, all the rest of which has been used by the Redactor elsewhere. But we cannot see the propriety of attaching a command against irreverence with a series of deeds of violence, whereas men-stealing belongs properly to that series. In our judgment this parental law has crept into the text from a marginal note or reference. It is more appropriate to the pentade, xxii. 27–29. It may be the remnant of a pentade, making, with xxii. 27–29, a decalogue. We find the same command in similar terms in Lev. xx. 9 (H): "Verily whosoever curseth his father or his mother shall be put to a violent death. His father and his mother he has cursed, his blood be upon him." The law of the rebellious son in Deut. xxi. 18–21, also involves the penalty of death by stoning.

V.—*Pentade of Injuries* (xxi. 18–25).

(1). And if men strive together and one smite the other with a stone or with his fist and he die not but taketh to his bed;—if he rise and walk about without his house on his staff, then the one who smote him shall be quit. Only the time of his abiding at home he shall pay and he shall cause him to be entirely healed.

(2). And if a man smite his slave or slave-woman, with his rod and he die under his hand he shall be severely punished,

(3). If he linger a day or two he shall not be punished, for he is his silver.

(4). And if men strive with one another and smite a woman with child and her children go forth from her and no hurt follow, he shall be heavily fined according as the woman's husband shall impose upon him and he shall pay in accordance with the decision of the judges.

(5). But if hurt transpire thou shalt give person for person, eye for eye, tooth for tooth, hand for hand, foot for foot, burning for burning, wound for wound, bruise for bruise.

The principle of judgment is given in connection with the special case of the injury to a woman with child. It doubtless applied also to all other injuries to persons, of a graver sort, such as we have had in the last two pentades or indeed in this decalogue of laws of injuries, xxi. 12–25. This *lex talionis* is also found in Lev. xxiv. 19 sq. in connection with laws respecting injuries in a brief form; "fracture for fracture (שבר), eye for eye, tooth for tooth. According as one puts a blemish in a man so shall it be put in him," שבר is not used in our code. In

Deut. xix. 21, the law is given in connection with false witnessing, "person for person, eye for eye, tooth for tooth, hand for hand, foot for foot." The Deuteronomic code uses בְּ = for, where our code and priest's code use תַּחַת.

VI.-VII.—*Pentades. Injuries in Connection with Property in Slaves or Cattle* (xxi. 26-37).

(1). And if a man smite the eye of his slave or the eye of his slave-woman and destroy it, to freedom he shall dismiss him for his eye's sake.

(2). And if the tooth of his slave or the tooth of his slave-woman he cause to fall out, to freedom he shall dismiss him for his tooth's sake.

(3). And if an ox gore a man or woman and he die, the ox shall be stoned to death and his flesh shall not be eaten. The owner of the ox shall be quit.

(4). But if the ox was wont to push with the horns yesterday and the day before, and it used to be made known to his owner and he used not to keep him in, and he shall kill a man or a woman, the ox shall be stoned and his owner also shall be put to death.

(5). If a ransom be imposed upon him, he shall give the redemption of himself according to all that is imposed upon him, whether he gore a son or gore a daughter, according to the law it shall be done to him.

(6). If a slave or a slave-woman, the ox gore, thirty shekels of silver shall he give to the owner and the ox shall be stoned.

(7). And if a man open a pit or if a man dig a pit and do not cover it and an ox or ass fall therein, the owner of the pit shall pay. Silver shall he render to its owner and the dead animal shall be his own.

(8). And if one man's ox smite another man's ox and it die, they shall sell the living ox and halve its silver and also the dead ox shall they halve.

(9). Or if it was known that the ox was wont to push with its horns yesterday and the day before and his owner used not to keep him in he shall pay heavily, ox for ox, and the dead ox shall belong to him.

(10). If a man steal an ox or a sheep and slaughter it or sell it, five cattle shall he pay for the ox and four sheep for the sheep.

THE GREATER BOOK OF THE COVENANT

VIII.—*Pentade. Theft and Damage to Property* (xxii. 1-5).

(1). If the thief be found while breaking in and he be smitten and die, there shall be no blood-guiltiness for him.

(2). If the sun has risen upon him there shall be blood-guiltiness for him. He shall pay heavily and if he have nothing he shall be sold for his theft.

(3). If the theft be at all found in his hand alive, from ox to ass to sheep, he shall pay double.

(4). If a man shall cause a field or vineyard to be devoured and shall send his cattle and they feed in another man's field, he shall pay, making good his field and making good his vineyard.

(5). If fire go forth and find thorns, and stacks of grain or standing grain, or a field be consumed, the one who kindled the fire shall pay.

IX. and X.—*Decalogue of Breaches of Trust* (xxii. 6-16).

(1). If a man give his neighbour silver or vessels to keep and it be stolen from the man's house, if the thief be found he shall pay double.

(2). If the thief cannot be found, the master of the house shall be brought near unto God to see whether he has not put forth his hand to the property of his neighbour. For all kinds of transgressions, for ox, for ass, for sheep, for garment, for any lost thing which any one saith that it is his, unto God shall the cause of both come. He whom God pronounces wicked shall double to his neighbour.

(3). If a man give unto his neighbour an ass or ox or sheep or any cattle to keep and it die or be hurt or captured without any one seeing it, an oath of Jehovah shall be between them that he hath not put forth his hand to the property of his neighbour and its owner shall accept it, and he shall not pay.

(4). If it was stolen away from him he shall pay its owner.

(5). If it was torn in pieces he shall bring it as a witness. That which is torn in pieces he shall not pay for.

(6). And if a man ask it of his neighbour and it be injured or die, its owner not being with it, he shall pay it all.

(7). If its owner was with it he shall not pay.

(8). If it were hired it came for its hire.

(9). And if a man entice a virgin who is not betrothed and lie with her he shall buy her altogether to himself for a wife.

(10). If her father utterly refuse to give her to him he shall weigh out silver according to the price of virgins.

The first pentade has to do with property which the owner wishes to entrust with his neighbor. The second pentade has to do with property where the request for it comes from the side of the person who would borrow or hire or buy it from the owner. The seduced damsel belongs to the latter because of her value to her father as property. The Deuteronomic code enlarges this law in Deuteronomy xxii. 28–29.

"If a man find a damsel that is a virgin, which is not betrothed, and lay hold on her, and lie with her, and they be found; then the man that lay with her shall give unto the damsel's father fifty *shekels* of silver, and she shall be his wife, because he hath humbled her; he may not put her away all his days."

D uses נער בתולה for the בתולה of E, fixes a definite sum to be paid in any case to the father, and refuses the option given to the father in E. The man must pay the price to the father, must marry the virgin, and must keep her all his life.

Fragments of several Pentades (xxii. 17–19).

(1). Whoso practiceth magic shall not live.

(2). Every one who lieth with a beast shall be put to a violent death.

(3). Whoso sacrificeth to gods except to Jehovah only shall be put under the ban.

It needs but a moment's consideration to see that the only bond of unity between these commands is in the penalty of death. This penalty is, however, expressed in a different way in each command, and there is no resemblance whatever between any of them in structure or idea such as we have found in the ten groups that have preceded and will find in the six groups to follow.

1. Looking now at the prohibition of magic and the term female magician מְכַשֵּׁפָה, we notice the peculiarity of this term and also the absence of any reference to necromancy which was the most striking feature in the magical rites of the Canaanites. In the Deuteronomic code, xviii. 10–14, there are no

THE GREATER BOOK OF THE COVENANT

less than eight distinct terms used for these rites. In the Holiness code there are five passages in which there is a reference to this subject. In three of them, Lev. xix. 31; xx. 6, 27, the same two terms are used, אוב, אבת and ידעני. In the other passage, Lev. xix. 26, the verbal forms תנחש and תעונן are employed. The emphasis upon this subject in H shows that this must have been a serious and common transgression, when this code was codified. These several commands were doubtless taken from several older codes.

This one command probably represents here an original pentade relating to this class, and it may be the other commands of this pentade have gone into the Holiness code.

2. This is the only case of sexual crimes or vices mentioned in our Covenant code. We cannot suppose that this subject could have been so neglected at this time in view of the fact that the great sins of the Canaanites and of the Patriarchal history, and of the Israelites, during their wanderings, were in this class. We have here a single command representing an entire *decalogue*. There is such a decalogue in the Holiness code, Lev. xviii. 6-16, followed by seven other commands of the same sort in vs. 17-23. Another series, mostly parallel but in a different order, is found in the same code, Lev. xx. 10-21, of twelve commands. The Holiness code there combines laws of that sort from a variety of sources. On that account the Redactor seems to have omitted them here. The Deuteronomic code has several special cases in xxii. 13-30.

(3). This law stands by itself in a peculiar manner. It is also the sole remnant of an original pentade. The Deuteronomic code, xiii., gives the fullest statement on this subject. The command, as given here, is peculiar in the expression בלתי ליהוה לבדו. This is so against the style of our Covenant code that we do not hesitate to follow the Samaritan text and strike it from our text as having crept in from a marginal note. The Samaritan text inserts אחרים after אלהים. This would then be necessary, so that the verse should read, "Whoso sacrificeth to other gods shall be put under the ban." The חֶרֶם (= ban) was a sacrifice.

The penalty is sacrifice for sacrifice, or an exact retribution. The same penalty is assigned by Deut. xiii. 16, to an idolatrous city. Possibly an original decalogue was constituted by the combination of the pentades (1) and (3).

XI.—*Pentade of Dealings with the Weak and Poor* (xxii. 20–26).

(1). A stranger thou shalt not maltreat and thou shalt not oppress him for ye were strangers in the land of Egypt.

(2). Thou shalt not afflict any widow or orphan. If thou at all afflict him, surely, if he cry unto me, I will attentively hear his cry and my anger will burn and I will slay you with the sword and your wives shall be widows and your children orphans.

(3). If thou lend my people silver, the poor man who is with thee, thou shalt not become like a money-lender to him.

(4). Ye shall not put upon him usury.

(5). If thou take the cloke of thy neighbour as a safe-pledge, ere the sun go down thou shalt return it to him, for it is his only covering. It is his cloke for his skin. In what shall he lie down? And it shall come to pass when he cry unto me I will hear, for I am gracious.

This pentade is remarkable for the reasons assigned. They are so tender. The certainty of divine interposition in behalf of the stranger, widow and orphan, and poor, is so grand.

1. The law of the stranger is fuller and richer in Deut. xxiv. 17-18.

"Thou shalt not wrest the judgment of the stranger, *nor* of the fatherless; nor take the widow's raiment to pledge: but thou shalt remember that thou wast a bondman in Egypt, and Yahweh thy God redeemed thee thence: therefore I command thee to do this thing."

It is also emphasized among the attributes of God, Deut. x. 18-19, and in the curse Dt. xxvii. 19. In the Sanctity code, Lev. xix. 33-34, it is also grandly set forth.

"And if a stranger sojourn with thee in your land, ye shall not do him wrong. The stranger that sojourneth with you shall be unto you as the homeborn among you, and thou shalt love him as thyself; for ye were strangers in the land of Egypt: I am Yahweh your God."

It is found in its second member in somewhat more fulness in connection with a pentade of justice in our code, Ex. xxiii. 19. This might seem to be a vain repetition, were it not for the propriety of the prohibition from both of these points of view.

2. The law of the widow and orphan is richer and grander here

than anywhere else. It is associated with the law of the stranger in the passage cited above from D.

3. Kindness to the poor is emphasized in the Priests' code, Lev. xxv. 35: "If thy brother wax poor and his hand becomes feeble with thee, thou shalt strengthen him whether a stranger or a sojourner, and he shall live with thee."

4. The propriety of separating this from the previous command is in the change to the second plural of the verb of command, and in the emphatic prohibition of usury. Usury is forbidden in Deut. xxiii. 19–21: "Thou shalt not lend upon usury to thy brother, usury of silver, usury of food, usury of any thing that is lent upon usury. Unto a foreigner thou mayest lend on usury, but unto thy brother thou mayest not lend on usury." In the priests' code also, Lev. xxv. 36, "Do not take from him usury or interest." תַּרְבִּית = interest is only found in the Pentateuch in this passage.

5. The law of pledges is fuller in Deut. xxiv. 6, 10–13, prohibiting the taking of the hand-mill and the going into his house to take the pledge from him, as well as our law of the cloke.

XII.—*Pentade of Reverence and Offerings* (xxii. 27–29).

(1). God thou shalt not revile.

(2). And a prince among thy people thou shalt not curse.

(3). Thy abundance and thy overflow of liquids thou shalt not delay (to offer).

(4). The first born of thy sons thou shalt give me.

(5). So shalt thou do to thy cattle, to thy sheep; seven days shall it be with its mother, on the eighth day thou shalt give it to me.

1. אלהים is God and not elders, and on this account the reverence of נשיא, the prince, constitutes a second command. These two make up a group of laws of reverence. We would expect here also a law with reference to reverence of parents such as we found in xxi. 17.

3. This command seems to concern first fruits in recognition of the מְלֵאָה = abundance, and דֶּמַע = tears = overflow of oil and wine (only found here in this sense), of the harvests.

4. The law of the first born is given in the little book of the

Covenant, Ex. xxxiv. 20, in connection with the feast of unleavened bread, where 5 is also connected with it. It is also given in the historical narratives, Ex. xiii. 2, 11 *seq.*; in the code of Holiness, Lev. xviii. 15 *seq.*; and in the Priests' code, Num. iii. 12 *seq.*, viii. 16 *seq.* We notice the absence of any provision for the redemption of unclean animals such as is in the little book of the Covenant, xxxiv. 20 (J), and of man as well as unclean animals in Lev. xviii. 15 *seq.* (H).

Laws of Purity (xxii. 30).

(1). And men of holiness shall ye be unto me.

(2). And flesh torn in the field ye shall not eat. To the dogs ye shall cast it out.

(1). These two laws seem to us to be fragments of a pentade or decalogue, the rest of which the Redactor has used elsewhere. The first command is so general that it seems to demand a series to follow. It is hard to explain the absence of the distinction between clean and unclean animals, but especially the failure to prohibit the use of blood. The prohibition of blood is in the Deuteronomic code, Deut. xii. 16, 23–27, xv. 23, and in the Holiness code, Lev. xvii. 10–14, xix. 26 *a*. The laws of the clean and unclean of animals are given in the Priests' code, Lev. xi. *seq.*, and the Deuteronomic code, Deut. xiv.

(2). The law as to animals found dead in the field unfolds in the subsequent legislation as follows:

D.—" Ye shall not eat of anything that dieth of itself: thou mayest give it unto the stranger that is within thy gates, that he may eat it; or thou mayest sell it unto a foreigner: for thou art an holy people unto Yahweh thy God." (Dt. xiv. 21.)

H.—" And every soul that eateth that which dieth of itself, or that which is torn of beasts, whether he be home-born or a stranger, he shall wash his clothes, and bathe himself in water, and be unclean until the even: then shall he be clean. But if he wash them not, nor bathe his flesh, then he shall bear his iniquity." (Lev. xvii. 15, 16.)

P.—" And if any beast, of which ye may eat, die; he that toucheth the carcass thereof shall be unclean until the even. And he that eateth of the carcass of it shall wash his clothes, and be unclean until the even: he also that beareth the carcass of it shall wash his clothes, and be unclean until the even." (Lev. xi. 39, 40.)

In E the carcass of the animal found dead in the fields was to be cast to the dogs. In D it might be given to the stranger to eat and sold to the foreigner. In H it could not be eaten by home-born or stranger. In P the distinction between stranger and home-born has passed away and the prohibition is a universal one.

XIII.—*Pentade of Testimony* (xxiii. 1-3).

(1). Thou shalt not lift up a vain report.

(2). Put not thy hand with a wicked man to be a witness of violence.

(3). Thou shalt not go after many to do evil.

(4). And thou shalt not respond to a cause to incline after many to wrest it.

(5). And a poor man thou shalt not favour in his cause.

This pentade is to be compared with a similar one in the code of Holiness, Lev. xix. 15-18, and with the law of the witness, Deut. xix. 15-20.

LEV. xix. 15-18.

"Ye shall do no unrighteousness in judgment: thou shalt not respect the person of the poor, nor honour the person of the mighty: but in righteousness shalt thou judge thy neighbor. Thou shalt not go up and down as a talebearer among thy people: neither shalt thou stand against the blood of thy neighbor: I am Yahweh. Thou shalt not hate they brother in thine heart: thou shalt surely rebuke thy neighbor, and not bear sin because of him. Thou shalt not take vengeance, nor bear any grudge against the children of thy people, but thou shalt love thy neighbor as thyself. I am Yahweh."

DEUT. xix. 15-20.

"One witness shall not rise up against a man for any iniquity, or for any sin, in any sin that he sinneth: at the mouth of two witnesses, or at the mouth of three witnesses, shall a matter be established. If an unrighteous witness rise up against any man to testify against him of wrong-doing; then both the men, between whom the controversy is, shall stand before Yahweh, before the priests and the judges which shall be in those days; and the judges shall make diligent inquisition: and, behold, if the witness be a false witness, and hath testified falsely against his brother; then shall ye do unto him as he had thought to do unto his brother: so shalt thou put away the evil from the midst of thee. And those which remain shall hear, and fear, and shall henceforth commit no more any such evil in the midst of thee."

Laws of Kindness (xxiii. 4, 5).

(1). If thou shalt meet an ox of thine enemy or his ass straying, thou shalt bring it back to him.

(2). When thou shalt see the ass of one hating thee crouching under its burden, thou shalt desist from forsaking him. Thou shalt altogether with him release it.

These two commands are certainly out of place here. They interrupt the connection between the previous and following pentades, which belong together as making up a decalogue of justice. They are the fragments of a pentade, as in other similar cases which we have considered. We find the same law in Deut. xxii. 1-4, in somewhat different language: "Thou shalt not see thy brother's ox or his sheep driven away and hide thyself from them; thou shalt bring them back to thy brother. . . . . Thou shalt not see thy brother's ass or his ox fallen in the way and hide thyself from them; thou shalt lift them up with him." Not considering the two verses of Deut. omitted as containing new matter, we note these differences: Deut. uses (a) "brother" for the "enemy" of our code, (b) נִדָּחִים = *driven away*, for תֹּעֶה = *straying*, (c) נֹפְלִים = *fallen*, for רֹבֵץ = *crouching, lying down under a burden*, (d) הָקֵים = *lift up*, for עֹזֵב = *release*. עִמּוֹ is used in common by the codes.

XIV.—*Pentade of Justice* (xxiii. 6-9).

(1). Thou shalt not wrest the judgment of thy poor in his cause.

(2). From a lying word remove far off.

(3). And an innocent and righteous man do not slay, for I will not justify a wicked man.

(4). A bribe thou shalt not take, for the bribe blinds the seeing, yea it perverts the words of the righteous.

(5). A stranger thou shalt not oppress, inasmuch as ye know the feelings of the stranger for ye were strangers in the land of Egypt.

With this pentade we must compare Deut. xvi. 18–20, which is similar in many respects. We notice, in connection with (4), that the Deuteronomic code is the same except in the use of עיני חכמים for פקחים.

The curse Deut. xxvii. 25 corresponds with No. 3, save that every word is different except נקי. "Cursed be he that taketh reward to slay an innocent person. And all the people shall say Amen." (Dt. xxvii. 25.)

XV. and XVI.—*Two Pentades of Feasts and Offerings* (xxiii. 10–19).

(1). Six years thou shalt sow thy land and gather its produce, but in the seventh thou shalt release it and when thou shalt release it, the poor of thy people shall eat it, and what they leave over, the wild beasts of the field shall eat. So shalt thou do to thy vineyard and to thine oliveyard.

(2). Six days shalt thou do thy work and on the seventh day thou shalt keep Sabbath in order that thine ox and thine ass may rest and that the son of thy slave-woman and the stranger may take breath.

(3). And in all that I have said unto you, take ye heed and the names of other gods ye shall not record. They shall not be heard in thy mouth.

(4). Three times thou shalt keep feast unto me in the year. The feast of *Mazzoth* thou shalt observe, seven days thou shalt eat *Mazzoth* according as I have commanded thee, at the season of the month *Abib*. For in it thou didst go forth from Egypt. And they shall not appear in my presence empty.

(5). And the feast of reaping the first fruits of thy work which thou shalt sow in the fields (thou shalt keep).

(6). And the feast of ingathering in the going forth of the year when thou gatherest in thy work from the field (thou shalt keep). Three times in the year shall all thy males appear in the presence of the lord Jehovah.

(7). Thou shalt not offer with leaven the blood of my peace-offering.

(8). The fat of my feast shall not abide until morning.

(9). The first of the first fruits of thy land thou shalt bring to the house of Jehovah thy God.

(10). Thou shalt not boil a kid (which is still) with the milk of its mother.

This decalogue we have compared with that of the little book of the Covenant in eight of its ten sentences of command. We shall only refer here to the remaining two. These are (1) The *Sabbath year*. The Sabbath year is here conceived as a year of the release of the land (שמט) for the advantage of the poor, who are to have the free use of all that grows of itself without tillage in that year. This year has already been mentioned in our code as the year of the release of the Hebrew slave (xxi. 2). The law of the Sabbath year is more fully given in connection with the year of Jubilee in the priests' code, Lev. xxv. The Deuteronomic code gives it, xv. 1-18, under the point of view of remission of debts שְׁמִטָּה.

3. The third command here is to be compared with the third of the first pentade of our code, xx. 24. There the place of the altar was designated by the recording הזכיר of the divine name. Here there is the prohibition of the recording of the names of other gods. This we take to be attaching them to altars or places of worship, using הזכיר in the same sense in both passages. The prohibition from speaking their names is different from recording their names, although the general idea is the same. It reminds us of the words of the Ephraimitic prophet Hosea ii. 19 (17 English), "For I will take away the names of the Baalim out of her mouth, and they shall no more be mentioned by their name."

The concluding Exhortation and Promises (xxiii. 20-33).

"Behold I am about to send a *Malakh* before thee to keep thee in the way and to bring thee unto the place which I have prepared. Take heed of his presence and hearken to his voice. Do not rebel against him, for he will not forgive your transgression, for my name is in his midst. On the contrary attentively hearken to his voice and do all that I shall speak, and I will be an enemy of thine enemies and an adversary of thy adversaries. For my *Malakh* will go before thee and bring thee unto the Amorites and the Hittites and the Perizzites and the Canaanites and the Hivvites and the Jebusites, and I will destroy them. Thou shalt not worship their gods and thou shalt not be led to serve them, and thou shalt not do according to their doings. But thou shalt altogether tear down and break in pieces their *Mazzeboth*. If ye shall serve Jehovah your God, He will bless thy bread and thy water, and I will remove sickness from thy midst. A barren and sterile one shall not be in thy land. The numbers of thy days I will fill full. My fear I will send before thee and I will discomfit all the peoples against whom thou shalt come and I will give all thine enemies unto thee as to their neck, and I will send the hornet before thee and I will expel the Hivvite, the Canaanite and the Hittite from before thee. I will not drive them out from thy presence in one year, lest the land become desolate and the wild beasts of the field multiply against thee. Little by little I will drive them from thy presence until that thou be fruitful and inherit the land and I set thy boundary from the Red sea even unto the sea of the Philistines and from the wilderness unto the river. For I will give into your hand the inhabitants of the land and thou shalt drive them from thy presence. Thou shalt not conclude a covenant with them and their gods. They shall not dwell in thy land lest they cause thee to sin against me in that thou wilt serve their gods, for it will become a snare unto thee."

These exhortations and promises at the conclusion of this book of the Covenant are to be compared with the brief ones in the introduction to the little book of the Covenant, xxxiv. 11–13, with the fuller conclusion of the code of Holiness, Lev. xxvi., and the blessings and curses of the Deuteronomic code, Deut. xxvii.–xxx. The peculiarity of our code as distinguished from these others in this section is the emphasis laid upon the *Malakh*, מַלְאָךְ, the angel of the divine presence, the *Theophanic* angel. The code of Holiness uses instead of the Theophany, "And I will give my tabernacle in your midst and I myself will not reject you, and I will walk about in your midst and become your God and ye shall become my people" (Lev. xxvi. 11 *seq*.).

Reviewing our arrangement of the laws we observe that we have found *six* complete decalogues, (1) xxi. 6-11, of Hebrew slaves; (2) xxi. 12-25, of deeds of violence; (3) xxi. 26-37, of lesser injuries; (4) xxii. 6-16, of breaches of trust; (5) xxiii. 1-3, 6-9, of justice; (6) xxiii. 10-19, of feasts and offerings. We have also found *four* separate pentades, (1) xxii. 23-26, of worship; (2) xxii. 1-5, of theft and damages; (3) xxii. 20-26, of treatment of poor and weak; (4) xxii. 27-29, of reverence and first fruits. We have also observed several remnants of pentades and decalogues. We suppose that we have fragments of *three* decalogues, (1) of Magic and Idolatry, in *two* pentades, xxii. 17 and 19; (2) of sexual laws, xxii. 18; (3) of laws of purity, xxii. 30; and *two* pentades, (1) of kindness, xxiii. 4-5, and (2) cursing of parents, xxi. 7. In all we would have nine decalogues and six pentades. If the pentades could be combined in decalogues we would have twelve decalogues. If this could be accomplished we might conclude that these were written upon the twelve מַצֵּבָה which Moses built in connection with the altar (Ex. xxiv. 4) for which we can find no use in the historical narrative. If this were so, we would have an analogy with the case of the Deuteronomic code which was written upon stones in connection with the altar erected on Ebal, after the entrance into the holy land, Deut. xxvii. 8; Josh. viii. 30 *seq*. In both cases the code would then have been written on stones as well as in books.

VII.

VARIATIONS OF D AND H.

The following specimens of variation between D and H will suffice:

(1). *Law against Mixtures.*

D.	H.
(1). "Thou shalt not sow thy vineyard with two kinds of seed: lest the whole fruit be forfeited, the seed which thou hast sown and the increase of the vineyard.	(2). "Thou shalt not let thy cattle gender with a diverse kind:
(2). Thou shalt not plow with an ox and an ass together.	(1). thou shalt not sow thy field with two kinds of seed:
(3). Thou shalt not wear a mingled stuff, wool and linen together." (Deut. xxii. 9–11.	(3). neither shall there come upon thee a garment of two kinds of stuff mingled together." (Lev. xix. 19.)

(1). D uses "vineyard," H "field." The forfeit of seed and increase is peculiar to D.

(2). D uses "plow," H "gender"; D "ox and ass," H "cattle of diverse kind."

(3). D uses "wool and linen," H "two kinds of stuff"; D "thou shalt not wear," H "neither shall there come upon thee a garment."

On the whole H generalizes the more specific commands of D, and transposes 1 and 2 of D.

(2). *Law against Gleaning*.

D.

(1). "When thou reapest thine harvest in thy field, and hast forgot a sheaf in the field, thou shalt not go again to fetch it: it shall be for the stranger, for the fatherless, and for the widow: that Yahweh thy God may bless thee in all the work of thine hands.

(2). When thou beatest thine olive tree, thou shalt not go over the boughs again: it shall be for the stranger, for the fatherless, and for the widow.

(3). When thou gatherest *the grapes of* thy vineyard, thou shalt not glean it after thee: it shall be for the stranger, for the fatherless, and for the widow. And thou shalt remember that thou wast a bondman in the land of Egypt: therefore I command thee to do this thing." (Deut. xxiv. 19–22.)

H.

(1). "And when ye reap the harvest of your land, thou shalt not wholly reap the corners of thy field, neither shalt thou gather the gleaning of thy harvest.

(3). And thou shalt not glean thy vineyard, neither shalt thou gather the fallen fruit of thy vineyard; thou shalt leave them for the poor and for the stranger: I am Yahweh your God." (Lev. xix. 9–10.)

(1). "And when ye reap the harvest of your land, thou shalt not wholly reap the corners of thy field, neither shalt thou gather the gleaning of thy harvest: thou shalt leave them for the poor and for the stranger: I am Yahweh your God." (Lev. xxiii. 22.)

In Lev. xxiii. 22 P gives a literal extract from Lev. xix. 9, 10b of H. H omits the second command of D.

(1). D prohibits going to the field for a forgotten sheaf; H forbids reaping the corners and also gleaning, and so is more comprehensive.

(3). D forbids the gleaning of the vineyard; H prohibits both gleaning and gathering the fallen fruit: and so gives an additional feature.

The motives of D are, that "Yahweh thy God may bless thee," and that the left fruit may be for "the stranger, the fatherless and the widow." The motives of H are, "I am Yahweh your God," and that the left fruit may be for "the poor and the stranger."

H here seems to indicate by his reference to "the poor," a different situation and a later conception from D.

(3). *Law of Weights and Measures.*

D.	H.
(1). "Thou shalt not have in thy bag divers stones, a great and a small. (2). Thou shalt not have in thine house divers ephahs, a great and a small. A perfect and just stone shalt thou have: a perfect and just ephah shalt thou have: that thy days may be long upon the land which Yahweh thy God giveth thee." (Deut. xxv. 13-15.)	"Ye shall do no unrighteousness in judgment, in meteyard, in weight, or in measure. Just balances, just stones, a just ephah, and a just hin, shall ye have: I am Yahweh your God, which brought you out of the land of Egypt." (Lev. xix. 35-36.)

D prohibits (1) · divers stones (אֶבֶן) in the bag "a great and a small," and prescribes "a perfect and just stone." H uses instead מִשְׁקָל *weight* and "just stones," and adds "just balances."

(2). D prohibits divers ephahs "a great and a small," and prescribes a "perfect and just ephah." But H uses the late word מְשׂוּרָה *measure* (elsewhere only Ez. iv. 11, 16; 1 C. xxiii. 29), and besides a "just ephah," a "just hin."

H only uses מִדָּה *meteyard*, a measure not contemplated in D. It seems evident that H is a later enlargement and generalization of D.

VIII.

THE SEVERAL REPRESENTATIONS OF THE THEOPHANY.

We shall simply place four accounts of theophanies to Moses, side by side, and then two accounts of theophanies to representatives of the people and to the people. The differences are evident. In E Moses sees God's face and form habitually. In J he is not permitted to see God's face, but only His back parts, and that as the greatest privilege of his life. In D the prohibition of making images is based on the fact that the people had seen no form of God in the theophany, but only heard His voice; whereas in E, the elders see God standing on a platform, and eat and drink in His presence. In P the glory of the theophanies lights up the face of Moses every time he enters into the presence of the glory. Nothing of the kind appears in any of the other narratives. These representations are sufficiently difficult to harmonize in different documents of later writers depending on different sources of information. How could Moses give such various accounts of what he himself had seen and heard?

E.	J.
"Now Moses used to take the tent and to pitch it without the camp, afar off from the camp; and call it The tent of meeting. And it used to be, that every one which sought the Lord went out unto the tent of meeting, which was without the camp. And it used to be, when Moses	"And he said, Shew me, I pray thee, thy glory: And he said, I will make all my goodness pass before thee, and proclaim the name of Yahweh before thee; and I will be gracious to whom I will be gracious, and will be compassionate to whom I will be compassionate. And

went out unto the Tent, that all the people rose up, and stood, every man at his tent door, and looked after Moses, until he was gone into the Tent. And it used to be, when Moses entered into the Tent, the pillar of cloud descended, and stood at the door of the Tent: and spake with Moses. And all the people used to see the pillar of cloud standing at the door of the Tent: and all the people rose up and worshipped, every man at his tent door. And Yahweh used to speak unto Moses face unto face, as a man speaketh unto his friend. And he used to turn again into the camp: but his minister Joshua, the son of Nun, a young man, departed not out of the Tent." (Ex. xxxiii. 7-11.)

E.

"If one is to be your prophet, I, Yahweh, in the vision make myself known to him; in a dream I speak with him. Not so my servant Moses, with all my house he is entrusted, mouth to mouth I speak with him, in an appearance without riddles; and the form of Yahweh he beholds. Why then do ye not fear to speak against my servant Moses?" (Num. xii. 6-8.)

he said, Thou canst not see my face: for mankind shall not see me and live. And Yahweh said, Behold, there is a place by me, and thou shalt stand upon the rock: and it shall come to pass, while my glory passeth by, that I will put thee in a cleft of the rock, and will cover thee with my hand until I have passed by: and I will take away mine hand, and thou shalt see my back: but my face shall not be seen." (Ex. xxxiii. 18-23.)

P.

"And when Moses had done speaking with them, he put a veil on his face. And when Moses went in before Yahweh to speak with him, he used to take the veil off, until he came out; and he used to come out, and speak unto the children of Israel that which he was commanded; and the children of Israel used to see the face of Moses, that the skin of Moses' face shone: and Moses used to put the veil upon his face again, until he went in to speak with him." (Ex. xxxiv. 33-35.)

E.

"Then went up Moses, and Aaron, Nadab, and Abihu, and seventy of the elders of Israel: and they saw the God of Israel; and there was under his feet as it were a paved work of sapphire stone, and as it were the very heaven for clearness. And upon the nobles of the children of Israel he laid not his hand: and they beheld God, and did eat and drink." (Ex. xxiv. 9–11.)

D.

"And Yahweh spake unto you out of the midst of the fire: ye heard the voice of words, but ye saw no form; only (*ye heard*) a voice. And he declared unto you his covenant, which he commanded you to perform, even the ten commandments. . . . . Take ye therefore good heed unto yourselves; for ye saw no manner of form on the day that Yahweh spake unto you in Horeb out of the midst of the fire: lest ye corrupt yourselves, and make you a graven image in the form of any figure (etc.)" (Deut. iv. 12–16.)

INDEX OF NAMES AND TOPICS.

Aben Ezra............... 36
Acts of violence, Pentade of.. 217 *seq.*
Addis, W. E................ 144
Astruc, Jean, 46, 47, 49, 52, 56, 143
Augustine 33
Authorship, special indications of.. 38

Bacon, B. W................ 75
Bartlett, E. T............... 144
Basil....................... 33
Bäthgen, F. W.............. 143
Batten, L. W............... 144
Baudissin, W. W., 130, 132-134, 143
Bauer, G. L................. 53
Baur, Ferd................. 162
Beecher, W. J.............. 130
Bellarmin................... 33
Bertheau, E................ 211
Bissell, E. C.......... 130, 137
Bleek, Ferd................ 61
Böhmer, E.................. 64
Breaches of trust, decalogue of..221 *seq.*
Bredenkamp, C............. 143
Brown, Francis....... 47, 130, 144
Brown, C. R................ 144
Bruston, C................. 143
Budde, K.............. 135, 143
Buhl, F.................... 143

Calmet................. 44, 56, 59
Calvin................. 34, 99, 209
Canus...................... 35
Carlstadt............... 36, 41
Carpenter, J. E............ 144
Carpzov, J. G.......... 42, 43, 62
Carrière, A................ 143
Castelli, David............ 144
Cheyne, T. K............... 144

Chrysostom 33
Clark, Adam................ 43
Clementine Homilies........ 33
Clement of Alexandria...... 33
Clericus................... 41
Codes; of D., 8 *seq.*, 81 *seq.*, 99 *seq.*, 110 *seq.*, 133 *seq.*, 157 *seq.*, of E., 101 *seq.*, 122, 132 *seq.*, 156 *seq.*; of H., 101 *seq.*, 127 *seq.*, 133 *seq.*, 157 *seq.*; of J., 101 *seq.*, 132 *seq.*, 156 *seq.*; of P., 99 *seq.*, 110 *seq.*, 132 *seq.*, 157 *seq.*; of Sinai, 131 *seq.*
Colenso.................... 92
Concubines, Hebrew slave, pentade of .... 216 *seq.*
Cornill, C. H......... 134, 135, 143
Covenant, Greater Book of, 7, 18 *seq.*, 100, 156, 158, 185, 189, 211 *seq.*; little Book of, 7, 100, 156, 184, 189, 211 *seq.*
Criticism, Higher, what is it, 1 *seq.*; problems of, 2 *seq.*; evidences used by, 4 *seq.*; obstacles to, 145; Lower...................... 1
Curtis, E. L............... 144
Curtiss, S. Ives....... 130, 144

D., 68; style of............ 75
Darmstetter, J............. 144
Davidson, A. B............. 129
" Samuel............. 66
Davison, W. T.............. 144
Dealings with the weak and poor, pentade of................ 224 *seq.*
Decalogues, of J., 189 *seq.*; of the Tables.................. 189 *seq.*
De La Saussaye, Chautepie....... 144

INDEX OF NAMES AND TOPICS

Delitzsch, Franz... 14, 23, 67, 130, 132
" Fred 143
Deuteronomy, date of, 81 *seq.*;
 style of .... 168 *seq.*
De Wette, 60, 62, 65, 81, 92, 100, 107, 132
Diatessaron, Tatian's .... 138 *seq.*
Dillmann, August, 63, 69, 88, 130, 131, 132, 134, 143, 153, 218
Dods, Marcus 212
Douglas, George 129, 130
Drechsler. 62
Driver, S. R., 47, 69, 70, 83, 85, 88, 135, 143, 144, 151, 157, 168
Drummond, James 144
Duff, A 144
Duhm, B 93, 143

E., 68; style of 74
Eichhorn, J. G., 49, 50, 51, 52, 53, 56, 57, 58, 60, 99, 100, 107, 142
Ewald, H...... 61, 63, 64, 132, 211, 212

FEAST of Passover, 106, 204 *seq.*;
 of unleavened bread, 106, 195 *seq.*; of weeks, 106, 199 *seq.*; of harvest, 106, 199 *seq.*; of ingathering, 106, 201 *seq.*; of booths (tabernacles).... 106, 201 *seq.*
Feasts and offerings, pentades of, 229 *seq.*
Fleury, Abbé 44
Floigl, Victor 144
Francois, Abbé L.... 44
Fulda, F. C 53

GABLER, J. G........ 52
Gast, F. A 130, 144
Gautier, Lucien 143
Geddes, Alex... 56, 57, 58, 60, 61, 107, 137
George 90, 93
Giesebrecht, F. 94, 143
Gleaning, law against 234
Gleig, Bishop 44
Gore, Charles 29
Graf, Karl H 91, 92, 127

Graves 43
Green, W. H. 74, 110, 113, 117, 130, 142
Gregory 35
Grill, J 143
Guthe, H 143

H., style of..... .... 172 *seq.*
Harper, W. R................ 130, 144
Hartmann, A. T.................. 58
Hasse, G........ 53
Haupt, Paul..................... 144
Hävernick, A. C.... 62
Heidegger 42, 62
Hengstenberg, E. W........... 62, 63
Hexateuch, term explained.. 1
Hirsch, E. G..................... 144
Hobbes, T....................... 36, 41
Hodge, A. A........ 130
Hommel, Fritz................... 143
Horne, T. H....... 54, 55, 56, 58, 118
Horst, L........................ 127
Huet, P......................... 42
Hupfeld, H................. 48, 63, 64
Hypotheses, documentary, 46 *seq.*;
 fragmentary, 57 *seq.*; supplementary, 60 *seq.*; development, 90 *seq.*, 129 *seq.*

ILGEN, C. D............... 48, 53, 63
Injuries, pentade of.......... 219 *seq.*
Irenæus. 33
Israel, religious development of, 124 *seq.*

J., 68; style of.................. 74
Jahn 53, 56
Jasher, book of 12, 13, 95
Jastrow, M...................... 144
Jerome.......................... 33
Jerusalem....................... 49, 52
Jülicher, A..................... 143
Junilius......... .... 33, 34
Justice, pentade of........... 228 *seq.*

KALISCH, M..................... 93
Kamphausen, A................. 143
Kautzsch, E.......... 69, 75, 94, 143

INDEX OF NAMES AND TOPICS

Kayser, A. 93, 127
Keil, F 62, 63
Kellner, M. L 144
Kennedy 144
Kindness, laws of 228
Kirkpatrick, A. T 144
Kittel, R 130, 132, 143
Kleinert, P 67, 143
Klostermann, A 127, 143, 152
Knappert, J 144
Knobel, A 64, 212
Köhler, A 143
König, E 94, 95, 143
Kuenen, A 92, 93, 94, 95, 115, 128, 131, 143, 162
Kurtz, J. H 62, 67

LADD, G. T 144
Lange, J. P 67
Language, argument from .... 69 seq.
Law Book of Josiah .... 15 seq.
Lemme, L 143
Lenormant, F 94, 95
Lotz, W 144
Luther 34, 209
Lyon, D. G 144

MARESIUS 42
Marsh, Bishop 54, 55, 56, 58, 118
Marti, K 143
Masius 36, 42
Merx, A 60, 143
Michaelis, J. D 52, 57
Mishna 32
Mitchell, A. F 35
Mixtures, law against 233
Montet, E 143
" F 143
Moore, G. F 130, 138, 140, 144
Mozley 54
Myer, E 143

NEANDER, A 162
Nöldeke, T 65, 91, 143
Nowack, W 143

OETTLI, S 143
Oort, H 144

Orelli, K. von 143
Osgood, H 130, 137, 138
Ottmar (Nachtigall) 53

P., 68; style of .... 74, 174 seq.
Patton, F. L 130
Paul of Nisibis 33
Pentateuch, term explained 1
Peters, J. P 130, 144
Perowne, J. J. S 66, 141
Peyrerius 36, 39
Piscator 209
Plagues, Egyptian, 78 seq., 148 seq., 188
Poems, Pentameter, 75 seq.; trimeter .... 75 seq.
Poole, Matthew 35, 54
Popper, J 91, 92
Prideaux 43, 44
Purity, laws of .... 226 seq.

RANKE, F. H 61
Renan, E 162
Reuss, E., 90, 91, 93, 94, 95, 96, 98, 100, 107, 115, 118, 125, 126, 128, 129, 130, 131, 132, 134, 143, 162
Reverence and offerings, pentade of .... 225 seq.
Reville, A 143
Riehm, E ... 81, 82, 83, 84, 91, 99, 100
Robertson, J 144
Robinson, Edward 59
Roediger 63
Rosenmüller 53, 56
Ryle, H. E 16, 144
Ryssel 143

SCHRADER, E 65, 143
Schultz, H 9, 94, 143
Schürer, E 143
Semler 41
Sharp, S 94
Siegfried, C 94, 143
Simon, R 40, 41, 42, 49, 75
Slave, Hebrew, rights of, pentade of .... 215 seq.
Smend, R 94, 143
Smith, G. A 130, 144

Smith, H. P. 130, 144
"   W. R. 94, 96, 129, 144
Socin, A. 75, 143
Spinoza, B. de 36, 39, 40, 41, 42
Spurrell, G. J 144
Stade, B. 94, 143
Stähelin, J. J 63
Stanley, A. P 66
Stanton, V. H. 144
Stickel, J. G. 143
Strack, H. L.... .... 63, 130, 143
Strauss, D. 162

Tatian. 138, 141
Ten words, genesis of .... 181 *seq.*
Tertullian 33
Testimony, pentade of .... 227 *seq.*
Theft and Damage to property, pentade of 221
Theodoret. 33
Theophany, several representations of .... 146, 236 *seq.*
Thorah, the book of 8, 14, 16, 17
Tiele, C. P. 144

Toy, C. H. 94, 96, 144
Tuch, F. 63

Valeton, J. J. P. 144
Van Dale, A 41
Vater, J. S. 57, 58, 61, 137
Vatke, W. 90, 93, 94
Vernes, M. 94, 144
Vitringa. 44
Volck, W. 143
Vuilleumier, H. 143

Wars of Yahweh, book of. 12, 95
Weights and measures 235
Wellhausen, J... 94, 95, 115, 128, 129, 137, 143, 162
Whitehouse, O. C 144
Wildeboer, G. 144
Witsius, H. 43
Worship, pentade of .... 212 *seq.*
Wright, C. H. H. 144

Yahweh, revelation of the name of .... 46 *seq.*, 165 *seq.*

INDEX OF TEXTS.*

GENESIS.

i....	52, 75
i. 1–ii. 3	50
i. 2.	151
i. 25	70
ii.	75
ii. 4–iii. 24	50
ii. 1	73
ii. 2	186
ii. 2, 3	183, 185, 195
ii. 7	73, 151
ii. 9	72
v. 1–28, 30–32	50
v. 22, 24	166
vi. 3	151
vi. 9–22	50
vi. 9, 11	166
vi. 20	70
vii. 20–23	46
vii. 22	73
viii. 1–4, 13–19	50
viii. 20	101
ix. 1–17	50, 149
ix. 13 *seq*	195
ix. 28, 29	50
xi. 10–26, 32	50
xii. 1–3	79
xii. 4, 5 *bis*	50
xii. 6	36, 44, 71
xii. 7, 8	101
xii. 10–20	78
xii. 11	72
xiii. 6, 11, 12 *bis*	50
xiii. 7	71

GENESIS.

xiii. 18	101
xiv.	46, 50, 135
xiv. 14	36, 44
xv. 2, 8	49
xv. 4, 5	79
xv. 7	166
xv. 16	71
xv. 18	149
xvi. 3, 15, 16 *bis*	50
xvii.	149, 195
xvii. 1–8	79
xvii. 1–27	50
xvii. 18	166
xix. 29	50
xix. 29–38	46
xx. 1–13	78
xx. 4, 13	49
xx. 9	72
xx. 16	217
xxi. 2–5	50
xxi. 22, 32	73
xxii. 9	101
xxii. 14	38, 42, 44
xxii. 15–18	79
xxii. 20–24	46
xxiii. 1–20	50
xxiii. 4	71, 166
xxiv. 3, 37	71
xxiv. 16	72
xxv. 6	72
xxv. 7–11, 17, 20, 26 *bis*	50
xxv. 12–18	46
xxvi. 6–11	78

---

* This Index does not include the Word Lists of Canon Driver, for which see pp. 168-180.

INDEX OF TEXTS

GENESIS.

Reference	Page
xxvi. 7	72
xxvi. 25	101
xxvi. 26	73
xxvi. 34, 35	46, 50
xxvii. 20	48
xxviii. 1-9	50
xxviii. 6-9	46
xxviii. 12-15	146
xxviii. 13, 21	166
xxix. 17	72
xxxi. 1	152
xxxi. 20	71
xxxi. 28	73
xxxi. 39	105
xxxi. 51	72
xxxiii. 18–xxxiv. 31	50
xxxiii. 14	72
xxxiii. 20	101
xxxiv	46
xxxiv. 30	71
xxxv. 28–xxxvi	46
xxxv. 7	49, 101
xxxv. 14	105
xxxvi	37, 50
xxxvi. 3	44
xxxvi. 31	37, 42, 43
xxxvii. 5-10	146
xxxix. 1, 6	72
xl. 5-8	146
xli. 1-15	146
xli. 2, 4	72
xli. 38	150
xlii. 9	146
xliii. 7, 27, 28	72
xlii. 14	166
xlv. 3, 26, 28	72
xlv. 13	152
xlvi. 2, 30	72
xlvi. 3	73
xlviii. 16	155
xlviii. 22	71
xlix	95
xlix. 1-27	50
xlix. 6	152
xlix. 25	166
l. 20	73

EXODUS.

Reference	Page
i.–ii	52
ii. 4	73
ii. 24	166
iii	48
iii. 5	152
iii. 12-15	165
iii. 19	73, 147
iii. 20	147
iv. 1-9 bis	147
iv. 14	158
iv. 18	72
iv. 20	39
iv. 21	154
vi	47, 48
vi. 2-3	47
vi. 2-7	165
vi. 4	149
vi. 6	155
vii. 3, 13, 14, 22	154
vii. 4-5, 9, 19-20	147
vii. 17	147, 166
viii. 1-3, 12-13, 17-19	147
viii. 11, 28	154
viii. 11-15, 16-28	78
viii. 15	147, 154
viii. 18	166
ix. 1-7	78, 188
ix. 3, 15, 23	147
ix. 7, 12, 34, 35	154
ix. 8-12	78, 148, 188
x. 1, 20, 27	154
x. 2	166
x. 13 bis, 19	147
xi. 10	154
xii	205
xii.–xiii	74
xii. 1-28, 43-51	91
xii. 2, 18	70
xii. 3-11, 21-27, 43-46	206
xiii. 2, 11 seq	226
xiii. 3, 9, 14	147
xiii. 4	70
xiii. 12-13	198
xiv. 4, 8, 17	154
xiv. 16, 21	147
xv	95

INDEX OF TEXTS

EXODUS.

xv. 4	72
xv. 11	152
xv. 13	152, 155
xv. 17	49
xv. 25	147
xv. 26	48, 166
xvi	185
xvi. 25-30	185
xvi. 27-30	147
xvi. 35	37, 43, 44
xvii	79
xvii. 8-13	147
xvii. 14	10
xvii. 15	101
xviii	157
xviii. 2 seq	39
xviii. 12	158
xviii. 18	73
xix. 5, 6, 22	104
xix. 6	152
xix. 13	72
xx	183, 189
xx.-xxiii	18, 19, 23, 100, 136, 158
xx.-xxiv	99
xx. 1-17 bis	189
xx. 3	49, 190
xx. 3-7, 3-17	211
xx. 4-6, 5	191
xx. 4, 23 bis	190
xx. 6	155
xx. 8	192
xx. 9, 10	73, 193
xx. 11	194
xx. 22-26	6, 211 bis
xx. 23-26	212
xx. 24	230
xx. 24-26	102, 159, 212
xxi. 28-xxii. 16, 17-30	211
xxi. 33-xxii. 5	212
xxi.-xxiii.	6
xxi.-xxiii. 19	211
xxi. 1, 2-11 bis, 12-16, 17, 12-27	211
xxi. 2	230
xxi. 2-6	215
xxi. 6-11	231
xxi. 7	232

EXODUS.

xxi. 7-11	216
xxi. 12-16	217
xxi. 12-25	219, 232
xxi. 14	102
xxi. 15	218
xxi. 17	218, 225
xxi. 18-25	219
xxi. 18-32	212
xxi. 26-37	220, 232
xxii. 1-5	221, 232
xxii. 6-16	212, 221, 232
xxii. 7, 10	72
xxii. 17-19	222
xxii. 17-30	212
xxii. 17, 19; 18, 23-26, 30	232
xxii. 20-26	224, 232
xxii. 26	217
xxii. 27-29	219, 225, 232
xxii 28	198
xxii. 28-29	197
xxii. 29	209
xxii. 29-31	159
xxii. 30	226
xxii. 31	106
xxiii. 1-3	227, 232
xxiii. 1-8, 9-13, 26-43	211
xxiii. 1-9	212
xxiii. 4-5	212, 228, 232
xxiii. 6-9	228, 232
xxiii. 10, 11	121
xxiii. 10-17	106
xxiii. 10-19	212, 215, 229, 232
xxiii. 12	186, 192, 194
xxiii. 14-19	159, 211
xxiii. 14, 17	203
xxiii. 15	19, 70, 195, 196, 198
xxiii. 16	199, 201
xxiii. 18 bis	49, 204
xxiii. 19	207, 208, 209, 224
xxiii. 20-33	211, 230
xxiii. 21	154
xxiv	105
xxiv. 1, 9	158
xxiv. 3, 4-7, 8	211
xxiv. 3-8	149
xxiv. 3, 4, 7	6

Exodus.

xxiv. 4	101, 189, 232
xxiv. 5	104
xxiv. 7	18
xxiv. 9-11	238
xxiv. 12	8
xxv.-xxxi. *bis*	91
xxvi	103
xxvii. 1-5	214
xxvii. 1-8	102
xxviii. 2, 40	153
xxix. 31	209
xxx. 1-6, 27	103
xxx. 23	72
xxx. 28	102
xxxi	91
xxxi. 3	151
xxxi. 8	103
xxxi. 9	102
xxxi. 13	192
xxxi. 13, 17	194
xxxi. 14-16	193
xxxi. 16-17	149
xxxi. 18	190
xxxii. 11	147
xxxii. 21, 30, 31	72
xxxii. 30-34	155
xxxiii. 7-11	103, 158, 237
xxxiii. 11	39
xxxiii. 18, 22	152
xxxiii. 18-23	237
xxxiii. 20-23	146
xxxiv	23, 99, 100
xxxiv. 1, 4, 14, 17	190
xxxiv. 1, 11-28	189
xxxiv. 6, 7	151, 184, 192
xxxiv. 6-9	155
xxxiv. 7	184
xxxiv. 10 *seq*	136
xxxiv. 10-27	149
xxxiv. 11-13	231
xxxiv. 14	49, 184, 191
xxxiv. 14, 16	190
xxxiv. 18	70, 195, 196
xxxiv. 19-20	197
xxxiv. 20	198, 226
xxxiv. 21	185, 192, 193

Exodus.

xxxiv. 22	199, 201
xxxiv. 23	49
xxxiv. 23, 24	203
xxxiv. 25	203, 204
xxxiv. 26	207, 208
xxxiv. 27	7, 189, 211
xxxiv. 33-35	237
xxxv.-xl. *bis*	91
xxxv. 11, 15	103
xxxv. 16	102
xxxvii. 25	103
xxxviii. 1, 1-7, 30	102
xxxix. 32, 38	103
xxxix. 39	102
xl. 2, 5, 6, 26, 29	103
xl. 2, 17	70
xl. 6, 10, 29	102

Leviticus.

i.-xvi.	91
i.	118
i. 5	118
ii. 11	204
iv. 7, 10, 25, 30, 34	102
iv. 7	103
iv. 13 *seq*	117
vii.-ix.	91
vii. 12, 13	204
xi. *seq*	226
xi. 34	70
xi. 39, 40	106, 227
xii., xiii., xiv., xv.	106
xv. 23	152
xvi	121
xvii.-xxvi.	95, 127, 133
xvii. 3-9	213
xvii. 7	192
xvii. 10-14	226
xvii. 15, 16	106, 226
xviii	217
xviii.-xxiii.	91
xviii. 6 *seq*	214
xviii. 6-16, 17-23	223
xviii. 15 *seq*	226
xix. 2	152
xix. 3, 30	192

INDEX OF TEXTS

LEVITICUS.

xix. 4	190
xix. 9–10	234
xix. 15–18	227
xix. 19	223
xix. 26	223, 226
xix. 33–34	224
xix. 35–36	235
xx. 5–6	192
xx. 6, 10–21, 27	223
xx. 7, 8, 26	152
xx. 9	219
xx. 25	70
xxi. 2	217
xxi. 6–8	152
xxii. 9, 16, 32	152
xxii. 27	209
xxiii.	106, 195, 199, 203
xxiii. 3	194
xxiii. 5	70
xxiii. 5–6	195
xxiii. 6–8	196
xxiii. 10–14	208
xxiii. 15–21	200
xxiii. 17	204
xxiii. 22	234
xxiii. 34–36, 40–44	201
xxiv. 10–23	91
xxiv. 17	217
xxiv. 19 *seq*	219
xxv.	91, 121, 230
xxv. 10	72
xxv. 35, 36	225
xxv. 37	70
xxv. 39–46	215
xxv. 49	217
xxvi.	17, 91, 231
xxvi. 2	192
xxvi. 3–45	64
xxvi. 9, 42, 45	149, 166
xxvi. 11 *seq*	231
xxvi. 34 *seq*	121
xxvii. 13, 15, 19, 20, 31	155
xxvii. 26–27	197

NUMBERS.

i. 48–x. 28	91

NUMBERS.

i. 1	39
ii. 2	39
iii. 12 *seq*	226
iii. 25	103
iv. 11	103
v. 1	39
vi	112
viii. 16 *seq*	226
ix. 1	70
ix. 12	205
ix. 15	103
xi. 18–33	147
xi. 24 *seq*	158
xi. 24, 26	103
xi. 25–29	151
xii. 3	39
xii. 4 *seq*	158
xii. 5, 10	103
xii. 6	72
xii. 6–8	237
xiv. 18–20	155
xiv. 21–22	153
xiv. 33	192
xv.–xix.	91
xv. 39	192
xvi.	79
xvi. 9	49
xvi. 30	70
xvii. 21–25	147
xvii. 22, 23	103
xviii. 2	103
xviii. 12–13	208
xviii. 15–18	198
xix.	106
xx	79
xx. 8–17	148
xx. 21	73
xxi. 8–9	147
xxi. 14	12, 38
xxi. 21, 31 *seq*	71
xxi. 30	72
xxii. 13, 16	73
xxiii.–xxiv.	95
xxiii. 7, 14, 29	102
xxiv. 11	152
xxv. 12–13	149

NUMBERS.

xxvii. 11	217
xxviii.	106, 199
xxviii.–xxix	203
xxviii.–xxxi	91
xxviii. 9–10	194
xxviii. 16	70, 205
xxviii. 16–17	195
xxviii. 17–25	196
xxviii. 26–31	200
xxix	199
xxix. 12–19, 35–38	202
xxxi. 14	39
xxxiii. 2	9
xxxiii. 3	70
xxxv	218
xxxv. 16–xxxvi. 13	91
xxxv. 20–21, 22	218

DEUTERONOMY.

i.–xxx	66
i. 1–xxii. 47	64
i. 1	37
ii. 5	38
ii. 12	37, 44, 81
ii. 30	154
iii. 11, 14	37, 44
iii. 24	49
iv. 12–16	238
iv. 13	149
iv. 15–19, 24	191
iv. 19	18, 83
iv. 20	19, 20
iv. 34	147
iv. 37	155
iv. 40	186
v.	189
v. 7	49
v. 8–10	191
v. 10	155
v. 12	192
v. 12–14	193
v. 13, 14	73
v. 14–15	194
v. 21	152
v 29	183
v 13	7

DEUTERONOMY.

vi. 2	186
vi. 5	155
vi. 18	183
vii. 2–4	192
vii. 5	84
vii. 8, 9, 13	155
vii. 22	86
viii. 3–4, 15–16	147
viii. 18	149, 166
ix. 9	189
ix. 26	49
x. 5	20
x. 6	158
x. 8	39
x. 8, 9	104
x. 12, 15	155
x. 18–19	224
xi. 1	155
xi. 6	79
xi. 9	186
xii.–xxvi	8, 23, 99
xii. 3	84
xii. 5	18, 19, 213
xii. 5–7, 12–14	212
xii. 6, 11, 13	213
xii. 9, 10	20
xii. 16, 23–27	226
xii. 25	183
xii. 26	152
xii. 27	102
xiii	223
xiii. 2	190
xiii. 2, 4, 6	146
xiii. 4, 22	155
xiii. 16	223
xiv	226
xiv. 3–21	106
xiv. 21	106, 209, 226
xv	106
xv. 1–3	121
xv. 1–18	230
xv. 12–18, 16–17	215
xv. 15	183
xv. 17	215, 217
xv. 19–22	197
xv. 23	226

INDEX OF TEXTS

DEUTERONOMY.

xvi.	106
xvi. 1	70, 195
xvi. 1–8	18
xvi. 2, 4–7	204
xvi. 3–4, 8	196
xvi. 8	73
xvi. 9–12, 17	199
xvi. 11, 12	183
xvi. 13–15	201
xvi. 16	199, 203
xvi. 18–20	229
xvi. 21, 22	84
xvii. 3	18, 83
xvii. 8 *seq.*, 14–20	82
xvii. 11	159
xvii. 14 *seq.*	20
xvii. 18–20	19
xviii. 9–14	18
xviii. 10–14	222
xviii. 15 *seq.*	88
xix.	218
xix. 4 *bis*	217
xix. 5, 11	218
xix. 9	155
xix. 14	81
xix. 15–20	227
xix. 21	220
xx. 1–15, 19	86
xx. 16	73
xxi. 10–14	86
xxi. 18–21	219
xxii. 1–4	228
xxii. 9–11	233
xxii. 12	217
xxii. 13–30	223
xxii. 28–29	222
xxiii. 6	155
xxiii. 10 *seq.*	106
xxiii. 15	152
xxiii. 19–21	225
xxiv. 5	73
xxiv. 6, 10–13	225
xxiv. 7	218
xxiv. 8	159
xxiv. 16	19
xxiv. 17–18	224
xxiv. 18, 22	183

DEUTERONOMY.

xxiv. 19–22	234
xxv. 13–15	235
xxv. 17	86
xxv. 19	20
xxvi. 2–11	207
xxvi. 13, 15	152
xxvi. 17	166
xxvii.–xxx.	231
xxvii. 2 *seq.*	38
xxvii. 6	102
xxvii. 8	232
xxvii. 15	190
xxvii. 19	224
xxvii. 25	229
xxviii.–xxxi.	17
xxviii. 36	82
xxviii. 37	17, 19
xxviii. 68	83
xxviii. 69	149
xxix. 1	19, 20
xxix. 1–4	147
xxix. 9, 14, 21, 24, 25	19
xxix. 9–14	99
xxix. 12	166
xxix. 20	149
xxix. 24	17, 19
xxx.	27
xxx. 6, 16, 20	155
xxxi. 1	39
xxxi. 9	39, 104
xxxi. 9–11, 24–26	88
xxxi. 9, 26	8
xxxi. 14 *seq.*	158
xxxi. 14, 15	103
xxxi. 16	192
xxxi. 18, 20	49
xxxi. 22	9
xxxi. 27	72
xxxii.	9, 11, 27, 95
xxxii. 3–4	151
xxxiii.	64, 95
xxxiii. 1	39
xxxiii. 8–11	104
xxxiii. 10	158
xxxiv. 10	38
xxxiv. 11–12	64

JOSHUA.

Reference	Page
i. 7, 8	9
i. 8	19, 23
iii. 3, 6	104
iii. 15-17	147
iv. 3, 9	104
iv. 7, 9, 20	79
iv. 13	73
iv. 24	147
v	120
v. 5	119
v. 10	112
v. 12	37
v. 14, 15	73
v. 15	152
vi. 4, 6	104
vi. 5	147
vi. 19	152
vii. 7, 13, 19, 20	49
vii. 19	153
viii. 30	102, 110
viii. 30 *seq*	38, 232
viii. 31	9, 102
ix. 18, 19	49
x. 12, 13	12
x. 40	73
x. 40, 42	49
xi. 11, 14	73
xi. 20	154
xiii. 14, 33	49
xiii. 33	104
xviii. 6	72
xviii. 7	104
xxii. 5	155
xxii. 10-34	102
xxii. 24	49
xxii. 34	166
xxiii. 11	155
xxiv. 2, 16	49
xxiv. 8, 12, 15, 18	71
xxiv. 19	49, 152
xxiv. 25	149
xxiv. 26	11

JUDGES.

Reference	Page
ii. 5	110
ii. 18	166
vi. 24	102, 110
xi. 11	110
xiii. 4-5	112
xiii. 19	110
xiv. 15-20	112
xvii. 13	158
xviii. 29	36
xx.	119
xxi. 4	102
xxi. 8	110
xxi. 19	112

I. SAMUEL.

Reference	Page
ii. 22	103
iii. 15	72
v.-vii	112
vii. 5	112
vii. 17	102, 112
ix. 9	150
ix. 12 *seq*	112
x.	113
x. 5, 8	112
xi. 15	112
xiv. 35	102, 112
xv. 21-33	112
xv. 25	155
xvi. 4-5	112
xvii. 42	72
xx. 6	112
xx. 14	72
xxi. 9	112

II. SAMUEL.

Reference	Page
i. 18	12
vi. 1-17	114
vi. 17	104
vii. 6	104
vii. 24	166
xi. 2	72
xii. 22	72
xiv. 27	72
xviii. 14	72
xxiii. 5	150
xxiv. 25	102

I. KINGS.

Reference	Page
i. 39	104

I. KINGS.

i. 50, 51	102
i. 50	218
ii. 3	19
ii. 28	102, 218
ii. 28–30	104
iii. 4	102
vi. 20	102
viii	19
viii. 4	104
viii. 9, 53, 56	20
viii. 12, 13	12
viii. 27 *seq*	122
viii. 51	19
viii. 64	102
ix.	19
ix. 3, 7, 8	19
xii. 32	102
xviii. 30 *bis*, 32	102
xx. 32	72

II. KINGS.

i. 31	20
xii. 16	118
xiv. 6	19
xvi. 10	71
xvii	41
xvii. 21	72
xviii. 4	83
xviii. 12	20
xxi. 3, 5	18
xxi. 8	20
xxii. 3 *seq*	81, 85
xxii. 8	20
xxii. 8, 11	15
xxii. 11–13, 16, 17, 19	17
xxiii	19
xxiii. 2, 21	15, 16, 18
xxiii. 4, 5, 11, 12, 21–23, 24	18
xxiii. 8–20, 15	102
xxiii. 25	15, 16, 20

I. CHRONICLES.

vi. 17 *bis*	103
vi. 34	22, 103
ix. 19, 21, 23	103
xv. 1	104
xv. 17	114
xvi. 1	104
xvi. 15	149, 166
xvi. 39, 40	114
xvi. 40	21, 103
xvii. 1	71
xvii. 5	104
xvii. 22	166
xviii	38
xxi. 18	102
xxi. 29	103, 114
xxii. 1	102
xxii. 12	21
xxiii. 29	114, 235
xxiii. 32	103
xxviii. 19	114

II. CHRONICLES.

i. 3, 6, 13 ; 5, 6	103
i. 4	104
iv. 3	71
v. 5	104
vii. 8–10	114
viii. 3	114
xii. 1	21
xvii. 9	22, 23
xix. 8–11	82
xxiii. 18	22
xxiv. 6	103
xxv. 4	22
xxix. 20–24	117
xxix. 22	118
xxx. 16	22
xxxi. 1	83
xxxi. 3, 4	21
xxxiv. 14	22, 55
xxxiv. 14, 15, 19, 30	15
xxxiv. 15	22
xxxiv. 30	16
xxxv. 3, 6	15, 16
xxxv. 12	22
xxxv. 26	21
xxxvi. 21	121

EZRA.

iii. 1–6	122
iii. 2	22

INDEX OF TEXTS

EZRA.

vi. 18 22
vii. 6 22
vii. 10 21

NEHEMIAH.

i. 8 22
ii. 1 70
viii. 1 .... 22, 23
viii. 3, 8, 14, 18 22
viii. 9, 13 21
viii. 13-17 122
viii. 17 120
ix. 3 22
x. 29, 30 21
x. 34, 37 22
xii. 44 21

ESTHER.

i. 11 72
ii. 2, 3, 7 72
iii. 7 70

JOB.

vii. 21 155
xviii. 19 166
xix. 23 10

PSALMS.

v. 9 141
x. 7 141
xiv 141
xiv. 2-3 141
xxxii. 1 72
xxxvi. 1 141
xl 117, 118
xl. 7 72
xl. 8 20
lv. 16 166
lviii. 5 71
lxxii 153
lxxiv 149
lxxviii 78, 148
lxxviii. 20, 27 217
lxxviii. 60, 67 103
cv 78, 148
cv. 8 .... 149, 166

PSALMS.

cvi 149
cvi. 45 .... 149, 166
cix. 7 72
cxi. 5 .... 149, 166
cxix. 54 165
cxl. 3 141

PROVERBS.

x.-xxii. 16 24

ECCLESIASTES.

vii. 20 141

ISAIAH.

ii. 9 155
iv. 3 217
x. 26 149
xi. 15-16 149
xiii. 4 71
xix. 19 .... 84, 102
xxvii. 9 102
xxxiii. 24 155
xxxvi. 7 83
xl. 18 71
xliii. 16 149
l. 2 149
li. 10 149
liii 88, 117
liii. 10 118
liii. 12 154
lix. 7-8 141
lxi. 1 72

JEREMIAH.

viii. 8 14
xxv. 11, 12 121
xxxiv. 8, 15, 17 72
xli. 5 *seq* 116

EZEKIEL.

i. 1 72
iv. 11, 16 235
viii. 3 72
xvi. 60 *bis*. 62 .... 149, 166
xvii. 22-21 127
xx. 38 166

INDEX OF TEXTS

EZEKIEL.
xxx. 24 166
xxxvi. 28 71
xxxvii. 1-14, 15-28 127
xxxviii.-xxxix 127
xl.-xlviii 115, 126
xl. 2 72
xli. 1 103
xliii. 3 72
xlv. 18-20 122
xlvi. 17 72

DANIEL.
i. 4 72
ix. 7 154
ix. 11, 13 22
x. 7-16 72
x. 11, 16 71

HOSEA.
ii. 19 230
iv. 8 118
viii. 12 13
xiv. 3 155

AMOS.
i. 9 166
v. 25 119

MICAH.
iii. 11 158
vi. 7 118
vii. 18 155

ZECHARIAH.
vii.-viii 122
viii. 8 166
x. 11 149

MALACHI.
iv. 4 21

MATTHEW.
iii. 13 138
iii. 14 *seq.*, 16, 17 139
iv. 2-7 139
xix. 7-8 26

MARK.
i. 12, 13 139
i. 44 26
vii. 10 26
xii. 26 25

LUKE.
iii. 21, 22 139
iii. 23 138
iv. 1, 2 139
iv. 5-7 140
x. 7 27
xx. 28 26
xx. 37 27
xxiv. 44 25

JOHN.
i. 29-31, 32-34 139
i. 45 27
v. 46, 47 27
vii. 19 26
vii. 23 25

ACTS.
iii. 22-24; 24 27
vii. 37 27
xv. 21 25
xxvi. 22 27

ROMANS.
iii. 9-18 141
x. 5, 19 27

I. CORINTHIANS.
ix. 14 26
xi. 23 *seq.* 27

II. CORINTHIANS.
iii. 15 25

HEBREWS.
iv. 7 26
vii. 14 26
viii. 5 27
ix. 19 27
x. 28 26
xii. 21 27

INDEX OF HEBREW WORDS AND PHRASES.[1]

אביב	(pp. 70, 195, 196, 229.)
אבן	(p. 235.)
(ה)אדמה	(pp. 70, 169, 212.)
אדני	(p. 48.)
אדני יהוה	(p. 49.)
אהב	(p. 168.)
אהל העדות	(p. 103.)
אהל מועד	(pp. 103, 158.)
אוב, אבת	(p. 223.)
אחזה, נאחז	(p. 177.)
(ב)איבה	(p. 218.)
איש איש	(p. 173.)
אכל, (ל)אכלה	(pp. 70, 175.)
אלהי אבות	(p. 166.)
אלהים	(pp. 11, 46 seq., 52, 56, 165, 175, 225.)
(ה)אלהים	(pp. 165, 166, 215.)
אלהים אחרים	(pp. 49, 169, 223.)
אלה תולדות	(p. 175.)
אלילים	(p. 174.)
אל שדי	(pp. 47, 165, 166.)
אמה	(p. 70.)
אמנה, אמנם, אמן	(p. 70.)
אמץ לבב	(p. 154.)
אני, אנכי	(pp. 71, 165, 166, 180.)
אני יהוה	(pp. 165, 166, 172.)
אסיף	(p. 202.)
ארב	(p. 218.)
(ה)ארץ (הטובה)	(pp. 70, 169, 170.)
בגד	(p. 217.)
בחר	(p. 169.)
בית אבות	(p. 178.)
בית עבדים	(p. 169.)

[1] Some of the words contained in this index are cited, in the passages referred to, in the English translation.

INDEX OF HEBREW WORDS AND PHRASES

בכל מושבותיכם (p. 178.)
בלי (p. 71.)
בעל (p. 71.)
בער, בעיר (p. 71.)
בער מקרבך (p. 170.)
ברא (p. 77.)
ברית עולם (pp. 150, 176.)
בשל (p. 209.)
בשנאה (p. 218.)
בשר (p. 71.)
בתולה (p 222.)

גאל (pp. 155, 171.)
גוע (p. 176.)
גלגלת (p. 178.)
גרש (p. 71.)

דבק (p. 170.)
דבר את (p. 71.)
דבר עם (p. 71.)
דמות (p. 71.)
דמיו בו (דמיהם בם) (p. 174.)
דמע (p. 225.)
דֵּעָה for (p. 73) דַּעַת
דרור (p. 72.)

הדף (p. 218.)
הוליד (pp. 73, 179.)
הזכיר (pp. 213, 230.)
היה (לכם) לאלהים (pp. 165, 166.)
היטיב (p. 170.)
הכהנים הלוים (p. 171.)
הֲלֹךְ for (p. 73) לֶכֶת
הלך בחקות (p. 173.)
הקים (p. 228.)
הקים ברית (pp. 149, 166.)
הקמתי את בריתי (p. 165.)
הקריב (p. 204.)
הקשה לב, רוח (p. 154.)

והיה בך חטא (p. 170.)
ויראת מאלהיך (p. 174.)

INDEX OF HEBREW WORDS AND PHRASES

זבח (pp. 106, 204, 206, 209.)
זבח (ה)פסח (p. 206.)
זבח חג הפסח (p. 206.)
זבח השלמים (p. 204.)
זכר ברית (pp. 149, 165, 166.)
זמה (p. 173.)

חנג (p. 203.)
חזה (p. 72.)
חזק, חזק (לב) (pp. 154, 179.)
חטא, חטאה (pp. 72, 105.)
חלל (p. 174.)
חמץ (p 204.)
חסד ואמת (p. 151.)
חקותי ומשפטי (p. 173.)
חרם (p. 223.)

טובת (טובי)מראה (p. 72.)

ידעתם כי אני יהוה אלהיכם (p. 165.)
ידעני (p. 223.)
יהוה (pp. 11, 46 *seq.*, 52, 56, 165, etc.)
ילד (pp. 73, 179.)
ימכר (p. 215.)
יפת (ה)מראה (p. 72.)
יצא צבא (p. 73.)
ירה (p 72.)

כבד, הכביד (לב) (pp. 154, 179.)
כבוד (p. 152.)
כבש, כשב (pp. 198, 206.)
כנם (p. 78.)
כסות (p. 217.)
כרת ברית (p. 149.)

לב, לבב (p. 72.)
לדרתם, לדרתיכם (p. 177.)
ליראה (p. 171.)
לכל (p. 176.)
למשפחותם-יהם (p. 176.)
לרשתה (p. 172.)

מאד, במאד (p. 177.)
מאה, מאת (p. 176.)

INDEX OF HEBREW WORDS AND PHRASES 257

מנור, מגורים, מגריהם (pp. 165, 166, 177.)
מדה (p. 235.)
מועדים (p. 193.)
מחצית (p. 179.)
מטה (pp. 73, 179.)
מין (p. 175.)
מכשפה (p. 222.)
מלאה (p. 225.)
מלאכה (pp. 72, 185, 186, 194.)
מלאך (pp. 230, 231.)
מנחה (pp. 105, 199, 200 *seq.*)
מעל (pp. 154, 179.)
מעשה (ידים) (pp. 171, 185.)
מצבה, מצבת (pp. 84, 101, 231, 232.)
מצות (pp. 195, 204, 229.)
מקרא קדש (p. 194)
מקרב (p. 173.)
מקנה (p. 177.)
מראה (p. 72.)
משורה (p. 235.)
משלח ידך (ידיך, ידכם) (p. 172.)
משפטים (p. 214.)
משקל (p. 235.)
מתוך (p. 173.)

נאקה (pp. 165, 166.)
נביא (pp. 88, 150.)
נדבה (p. 106.)
נדרים (p. 106.)
נחמד למראה (p 72.)
ניסן (p. 70.)
נמכר (p. 216.)
נער בתולה (p. 222)
נפלים (p. 228)
נפש (אדם) (pp. 175, 177, 217, 218.)
נשא (p. 155.)
נשא חטא, עון (p. 174.)
נשיא, נשיאי העדה (pp. 178, 179, 225.)
נשמה (p. 73.)
נָתֹן (p. 73) for תֵּנֶת
נתן ביד, לפני (p. 171.)

INDEX OF HEBREW WORDS AND PHRASES

סין (p. 79.)
סכת (p. 202.)
סלח (p. 155)
סקל (p. 180.)

ערה (p. 178.)
ערף (p. 178.)
עוד חי (p. 72.)
עולות (p. 212.)
עז (pp. 198, 206.)
על, אל פי יהוה (p. 179.)
עם סגלה, קדוש (p. 169.)
עמים (p. 177.)
עמית (p. 173.)
עמר (p. 200.)
ענה, ען (p. 217.)
עצם היום הזה (p. 176.)
עצרת (pp. 196, 203.)
ערב (p. 78.)
ערות (p 214.)
ערמה (p. 218.)
עשה, עשו, עשהו, עשות, עשתו (pp. 73, 77.)
עשה שבת (p. 194.)

פדה (pp. 155, 171.)
פעמים (p. 203.)
פרה ורבה (p. 175.)
פרך (p. 178.)

צאן (pp. 198, 206.)
צבא (p. 73.)
צבאות (p. 178.)
צרה (p. 217.)
צריה (p. 218.)
צן (p. 79.)

קדש, קדוש (p. 152, 193.)
קדוש אני יהוה (p. 173.)
קנא (p. 190.)
קנין (p. 178.)
קרב, בקרבך, מקרבך (p. 171.)
קרבן (pp. 105, 209.)

INDEX OF HEBREW WORDS AND PHRASES

ראה	(p. 150.)
ראשית	(p. 208.)
רגל, רגלים	(pp. 180, 203.)
רגם	(p. 179.)
רדָה	(p. 73) for רֶדֶת.
רכש, רכוש	(p. 177.)
רצע	(p. 215.)
שאר, שארה	(pp. 173, 217.)
שבט	(pp. 73, 179.)
שבת	(pp. 193, 194)
שבתון	(pp. 179, 194.)
שה	(pp. 198, 206.)
שכן, לשכן, שמו שם	(pp. 172, 213)
שלמים	(pp. 106, 212.)
שמט, שמטה	(p. 230.)
שמר (לעשות)	(pp. 169, 172.)
שנא	(pp. 217, 218.)
שערים	(p. 169.)
שפחה	(p. 70.)
שפטים	(p. 178.)
שרץ	(p. 175)
תודה	(p. 106.)
(לא)תוכל, יוכל	(p. 171.)
תור	(p. 180)
תורה	(pp. 8, 14, 16, 17.)
תועבה, תועבת יהוה	(p. 172.)
תושב	(p. 178.)
(לא)תחום עינך	(p. 170.)
תחשים	(p 103.)
תקופת השנה	(p. 202.)
תרבית	(p. 225.)